THE
COMPUTERIZATION
OF
WORK

THE
COMPUTERIZATION
OF
WORK

A COMMUNICATION PERSPECTIVE

JAMES R. TAYLOR
CAROLE GROLEAU
LORNA HEATON
ELIZABETH VAN EVERY

Sage Publications, Inc.
International Educational and Professional Publisher
Thousand Oaks ▪ London ▪ New Delhi

For information:

Sage Publications, Inc.
2455 Teller Road
Thousand Oaks, California 91320
E-mail: order@sagepub.com

Sage Publications Ltd.
6 Bonhill Street
London EC2A 4PU
United Kingdom

Sage Publications India Pvt. Ltd.
M-32 Market
Greater Kailash I
New Delhi 110 048 India

Printed in the United States of America

Library of Congress Cataloging-in-Publication Data

The computerization of work: A communication perspective / by James R. Taylor ... [et al.].
   p. cm.
Includes bibliographical references and index.
   ISBN 0-7619-0698-3 (alk. paper) — ISBN 0-7619-0699-1 (pbk.: alk. paper)
   1. Employees—Effect of technological innovations on—Philosophy. I. Taylor, James R., 1928- II. Title.
   HD6331 .C676 2000
   658'.05—dc2   00-009513

01 02 03 10 9 8 7 6 5 4 3 2 1

Acquiring Editor:	Margaret H. Seawell
Editorial Assistant:	Sandra Krumholz
Production Editor:	Diana E. Axelsen
Editorial Assistant:	Candice Crosetti
Typesetter:	Rebecca Evans
Indexer:	Virgil Diodato
Cover Designer:	Michelle Lee

Contents

1

Organizations Meet I/CT

◆ The computerization of the workplace confronts us with an apparent paradox. On the one hand,

◆ Everyone agrees that the fusion of new information and communication technologies (I/CT[1]) is radically transforming modes of work and the organizational contexts where work goes on. It is not just because computerization turns administrative tasks into automated data flow systems; the development of increasingly sophisticated electronic equipment has spawned new categories of workplace practice and occupations. How we work is changing. And telecommunication linkages spanning the globe now easily bypass traditional organizational hierarchies and boundaries. Organization itself is undergoing a sea change in the global economy. The economy, fueled by the new technologies, is booming.

Yet, on the other hand,

◆ The actual result of any single I/CT implementation is often disappointing when benchmarked against the usual standards of contribution to efficiency and organizational performance. The technologies, it repeatedly has been found, fail to deliver at the level that people expected, either singly or in aggregate. Although the levels of U.S. investment in I/CT during the 1980s (on the order of $1 trillion) were "spectacular" (Churchward & Bennett, 1993; Pearson, 1993), white-collar productivity actually fell in the period from 1970 to 1992. Overpromotion by systems developers ("hype") undoubtedly contributed to the disappointment and a certain measure of disillusionment, as Heygate (1994) found: "The failure of computer technology to deliver on ambitious promises of bottom-line value, together with a number of conspicuous systems disasters has led many top managers to question the notion that I/CT can be used to gain competitive advantage" (p. 137). And, although a dramatic transformation of the workplace may be under way and I/CT may be its principal contributor, individual experiences in computerization often fail to measure up to expectations.

1

This book offers an explanation for the contradiction between expectations and the often less-than-satisfactory results. Using communication theory as a basis, we show that the "paradox" has a simple explanation, once account is taken of how organizations work and how change occurs in them.

The transformation of work that was both enabled and fueled by the post-World War II revolution in computing and telecommunications is less than a half-century old. It has come upon us gradually, almost insidiously. Perhaps it was inevitable, then, that those most concerned with the human, social, and organizational consequences of technological progress—the sociologists—resorted to conventional models of society in which technology plays a minor or, in critical circles, a negative role. One of the authors we cite most frequently in this book is the British sociologist Anthony Giddens. Yet, a close examination of the three books in which he outlined the structuralist hypothesis (and on which our own work is based) uncovers very few references to technology and none that links it to the dynamics of *structuration*. Other sociologists of a more leftist bent, such as Braverman, simply demonized technology as just another instrument of worker oppression in the arsenal of capitalist weapons.

Among those who have taken seriously the role of technology in organizational transformation, the tendency has been to phrase the relation as one of cause-effect: technology as an exogenous agent of change. As we see in the course of this book, the results of such a formulation, translated into a research program, turned out to be mostly confusing. In spite of the many studies undertaken to isolate the "effect" of technology on organizations, the evidence proved to be either inconclusive or downright contradictory (Barley, 1986; Markus & Robey, 1988; Orlikowski, 1992).

The problem with framing the issue as one of cause (technology) and effect (organization) is that it catches us up in a dualism. We are led to assume that there is an essential technology, independent of its use in the ordinary circumstances of work, and that there is an essential organization, independent of its grounding in situated work. Neither assumption, we argue, is tenable. Instead, we offer what Westrup (1996) calls a *constructivist* explanation of work, technology, and organization. We argue for multiple modes of organizing work processes that are in continual evolution, out of which the realities of technology, organization, and group collaboration emerge.

The explanation that we develop in the chapters that follow takes us beyond both generalizations about cause and effect and dualistic models of organizational change. As we explain it, *technology* is no more than an assemblage of artifacts and procedures for their use that also evolve over time and from one context to another. We build on structuration theory to present an explanatory

2

model of what occurs at the interfaces of organization, collaborative groups, and work, mediated by systems. Our explanation is motivated by what we see as the tension that characterizes the interfaces of globally extended and locally situated forms of organization, a tension that is made particularly salient by the introduction of technology. It is this tension, and the contrasting communicational dynamics that underlie it, that is the source of the paradoxical results. The book argues that we are caught up in a complex cycle of learning, which transcends the capabilities of individuals or even groups and involves a transformation of our ideas of organization itself, and of its dynamic.

However, before we introduce the main outlines of our argument, let us look at several examples of contradictory or inconsistent results taken from research on I/CT implementation.

◆ Examples of Less Than Fully Successful Implementations

There is always turbulence around the implementation of technology in an organization. The introduction of I/CT into a work setting often sets off dynamics that can surprise equally both the initiators of the project and its opponents. We offer four illustrative cases.

1. Implementation of I/CT in a large telephone company. Our first example is based on Sachs's (1995) description of an I/CT implementation in a large telephone company, one of the "Baby Bells." Sachs, an ethnographer, participated in a design team composed of diverse members drawn from the host organization. In their push for reorganization to reduce costs and increase productivity, the management had targeted a service department, responsible for troubleshooting problems that arise in providing line service to customers. The object of the new system was to eliminate phone conversations between employees. Technicians' usual practice always had been to consult with each other to establish what and where the trouble was and how to deal with it, exchanging information and advice. In management's eyes, these telephone conversations were time spent "off task." They also saw the interaction as a source of bottlenecks in the process of efficient routing of work orders and delivery of service to customers. They decided to automate the service call process. A new electronic dispatcher, known as a Trouble Ticketing System (TTS), was introduced.

The system consisted of a central database and a set of procedures for scheduling work requests, routing problems to repair and technical staff, and monitor-

3

ing workers' hours and number of tickets handled. There were no more consultations: If a question arose relating to a problem that the technician had trouble solving, he or she was now expected to send a trouble ticket back to the central TTS dispatcher for rerouting to someone else. The technician then picked up the next ticket in the queue.

From the workers' perspective, Sachs (1995) reported, the TTS failed to perform the task it had been set up to do, that is, speed up the workflow. On the contrary, ironically enough, a principal effect of substituting an electronic dispatcher for employee communications was, instead, "that it got in the way of being able to work out the kinks in a job" (Sachs, 1995, p. 39). Because they were no longer permitted to compare notes on a problem, a coherent network of coworkers was turned into "an aggregate of dissociated workers" (p. 40), each handling only a small portion of a service order—a kind of relay race. In the end, in frustration, employees began to develop what Sachs called "workarounds." To make the service call process function as well as it had before TTS, they found covert ways to check with each other and to fool the record-keeping function so that it did not quite match what they were actually doing.

2. Implementation of I/CT in a police department. A second example of implementation was reported by Akzam (1991; Taylor & Van Every, 1993). Dissatisfied with the low quality of its 25-year-old 911 emergency radio dispatching equipment and service, the police department management in a large city decided to replace it with a more advanced I/CT technology, one that already was being used in several other cities of similar size. The new system offered an integrated technology mix, including a computerized database containing vital information for dispatchers (the layout of the city, one-way streets, dangerous neighborhoods, criminal histories, etc.); it combined digital and voice communication for the cars, an information terminal in each car offering access to components of the data source, and mobile hand phones linked into the system to provide continuous connection with the dispatching office. Management saw the new system as capable of accomplishing three tasks:

1. At the level of actual police work, it would provide an improved information backup for the dispatchers, a more secure voice channel, and a communication system that would allow officers in cars to perform rapid checks on vital data like car registration.

2. It was a way of cutting costs, because with all the necessary information now transferred to the database and available to dispatchers on a computer screen, they

could replace the higher-paid dispatcher-officers (men with years of service) with less expensive clerks (young women with no experience in police work).

3. The more centralized communication channel would increase district managers' control over the cars on patrol.

After a frustrating period of initial debugging, the system proved to be, technically speaking, a marked improvement over the old equipment, and the patrol officers' reaction was generally favorable.

Things came adrift, however, in the way the system meshed with the police culture. As they put the new technology to use, the officers complained that it was not "police minded." Managers had elected to replace the veteran 911 dispatchers—officers with a long experience in police work—by inexperienced operators who relied on a centralized database for their knowledge of the city. But the database had serious limitations. The image of the city's streets it furnished had little connection with the more immediate experience of those in the cars. At the same time, the old pattern of intercar radio communication was cut off, eliminating much of the back-and-forth exchange of information at the level of street work. The officers now found themselves dependent on the central dispatcher system precisely when they had lost confidence in the reliability of that office. They had doubts about the judgment of the new greenhorn dispatchers in the rapid-fire communication of daily 911 operations and identified them as creatures of management, not as colleagues. Police discipline suffered, as well. Because the new dispatchers had little authority in their dealings with the cars, and because management left coordination to the system, it often turned out that the cars were on their own.

3. Implementation of I/CT in a metropolitan university hospital. In a third example, Raymond and Giroux (1998) described how a developer of an innovative communication technology for monitoring patient signs approached the administration of a large metropolitan university hospital with a proposal for a pilot project with inpatients recovering from heart surgery. The developers were hopeful that a successful experience in the cardiology department would result in a sale and, even better, an eventual request to develop the technology further. Their system consisted of a small Walkman™-size unit of electrodes that an ambulatory patient could strap around the waist. Its signal would be picked up by antennae implanted in the ceiling at strategic locations in wards and corridors and relayed to a central mainframe, where it could be fed to terminals accessible to the nursing staff in the patient's ward. It also would record data on patient recovery progress.

Although the developers' contacts in the hospital management and the bio-medical research division initially encouraged the project as a way of recording patient data as well as increasing the efficiency of patient care, it turned out that establishing even the parameters of the implementation became a 3-year effort. Complex questions about funding, evaluation, technical implementation and re-liability, clinical and research benefits, and the nature of the participation by medical and nursing staff as well as patients had to be settled before any testing could proceed. When, after much debate, the system was finally introduced in two units, no support structure in the form of a training program or involvement by the medical staff was forthcoming. Although they gave the technology a fa-vorable response overall, the few nurses who agreed to try it out reported techni-cal problems and delays. They used it very little. They saw it as having little rele-vance to their daily work. Finally, the project was dropped. A before-after evaluation had been foreseen, but this also was canceled when the project ended.

4. Implementation of I/CT in a telecommunications network. As was the case in the previous example, this fourth project was initiated in the system design group of another large telecommunications organization. Hovey (1992; Taylor & Van Every, 1993) was a member of the team who developed an administrative system that was built around the concept of an electronic form. They called it a Generic Forms Tool (GFT). They sold the system to management in their orga-nization as a way of consolidating and increasing the efficiency of the many ad-ministrative jobs of transmitting and storing data that go into running a telecom-munications network. They thought they had designed the GFT to be so flexible that it could take account of all the forms (orders, invoices, accounts, bills requi-sitions, invoices, permissions, bids and offers, etc.) currently in use. They saw it as centralizing the workflow procedures to the point that, in principle, they could be run from a single workstation. The technology, as conceived, fitted in very well with management's intention to implement an eventual reduction in clerical staff.

With management's approval, the developers began to tailor the generic tool to the company's procedures. This involved drawing up a plan, in the form of a representation of the work of the company. In systems design, this is referred to as a *requirements analysis.* It assumes that the designers have understood the na-ture of the work they are modeling. To this end, they enlisted the methods depart-ment in the host organization to assist them in completing the required set of reports—including an operations plan, technical proposal, user needs require-ments, and project management. Once these documents had been approved, they assembled the programmers who would build the system and established a liaison committee to work with the representatives of the departments in which the system would be used.

When this planning group began to work through the detailed design necessary to make the system operational, the rational design process found itself derailed. Two crucial contradictions emerged. One was jurisdictional rivalry between divisions of the company. If productivity was to be increased, some functions would have to be eliminated. Of course, this meant that longstanding lines of authority and access to information would be transgressed. The second contradiction appeared as a result of the organization's structural diversity. Despite the fact that it was one company, the designers' attempt to rationalize and centralize administrative procedures failed to take account of the many regional and divisional differences in procedure and terminology. The result of these contradictions was that agreement on these issues took more than 1 year to negotiate, and then only partially. More and more adaptations had to be written into the original system. Although the implementation of the GFT finally went ahead, it was far from the technology that had been envisioned at the beginning.

Successes or Failures?

So what do we make of these examples? One reader of this chapter remarked to us that it would give a more balanced picture if we were to include some success stories. For him, at least, we had been reporting on failures. But, in fact, these are not failures at all, but examples of successful implementations. The team that designed the system described by Sachs won an award from its organization for outstanding design (once the results of their study had been incorporated in design), the police department's 911 system works reasonably well (after a period of readjustment), and Hovey's (1992) design group produced a system that is now operational. Even Raymond and Giroux's (1998) aborted implementation is not so much a failure as an example of a new technology that was launched prematurely for reasons that had more to do with financing and hospital politics than technology. We could quite reasonably mark it down to experience—a bit of road kill on the information highway; it may well lead to what will eventually turn out to be a useful monitoring system for hospital patients.

Our reader's reaction was not wrong, however. On the contrary, it speaks to a rather different phenomenon: the overblown expectations that have surrounded the drive to computerization, and the relative disappointments that have marked its progress when benchmarked against the promised transformation of the work environment. Indeed, each of the cases would have to be rated a failure if what was accomplished (a much less automated system than anticipated)

7

is measured against the original aspirations. They succeeded, but less majestically than predicted.

Manteiro and Hanseth (1995) argued that the phenomenon of disappointing results presents an opportunity both to rethink our understanding of I/CT and what they are for and to reexamine our ideas about organization. They agreed with the general conclusion that information technology is a—if not the—critical element in the restructuring of organizations, but they remarked that "this belief does not carry us very far: it is close to becoming a cliché" (p. 326). It is time, they urged us, to look behind the generalizations and the failures for new explanations of what is occurring. We need "a satisfactory account of the interwoven relationship between IT and organizational transformations. More specifically, . . . we need to learn more about how this interplay works, not only that it exists" (Manteiro & Hanseth, 1995, p. 326).

Manteiro and Hanseth (1995) are, of course, not the only ones to feel the need for a better explanation of the disappointing results. Analysts have developed four different types of explanation for such apparent "failures" that we consider in turn. In the conclusion to the chapter, we then consider how our approach differs from theirs and outline the path we follow in this book.

◆ Some Explanations of the Technology-Organization Link

On the face of it, when we look at examples of I/CT implementation that failed to meet expectations, it may seem plausible to argue in one of two ways: either that the system was at fault or that the organization was not ready for computerization. Although they differ considerably in their treatment of technology and organizational change, most of the commonly offered explanations for the disappointing results of I/CT take the concepts of work and technology as a given and frame questions in terms of the causal relation that links them. This, for us, is *dualistic thinking*. It has generated four kinds of explanation that can be classified according to the hypotheses to which they lead:

1. That much of work is so "situated" that it is simply not amenable to systemization.
2. That traditional organizational structures of management impede the revolutionary changes that I/CT offer.
3. That I/CT promoters choose to ignore or fail to take account of the inevitable play of organizational "interests."
4. That the properties of I/CT systems are self-limiting.

Now let us consider each these explanations in turn.

The "Situatedness" of Work:
Its Inevitable Circumstantiality

This is the ethnographic explanation for the failures of I/CT to meet expectations. Underlying it is the notion that there is a limit to how far work lends itself to being formalized in a system, especially if the formal representation obscures the communicative practices and human relationships that are crucial to effective collaborative work. It is a line of investigation that can be traced back to influential books that appeared in the 1980s (Lave, 1988; Suchman, 1987; Winograd & Flores, 1986). Those scholars urged researchers to move away from the traditional scientific generalizations about work organization and examine what really goes on in the workplace.

The approach also can be attributed to a practical dilemma faced by a manufacturer. One of the truly innovative research laboratories in the high-tech world has continued to be the Palo Alto Research Center of the Xerox Corporation (known as PARC). At one point, Xerox found itself faced with a puzzle: why the buyers of some of its most sophisticated and powerful copying machines were reporting equipment breakdowns when its own engineers could find no technical fault with their performance. Because the complaints of the clients continued, Xerox's response was to engage the services of anthropologists to delve into the sources of the dissatisfaction by undertaking field studies in the context of use of the technology: the client's organization.

The PARC investigators found that different organizations develop radically divergent practices in the way they use photocopy machines—so divergent, in fact, that it would be hard to say that it was exactly the "same" technology from one site to another. In some sites, copying was a tightly regulated bureaucratic function; in others, it was a machine left available for individual workers to use at their convenience. Suchman (1987) drew a more general lesson from these and similar findings: namely, that the work world is situated, circumstantial, and grounded in local practices and culture in a way that escapes the more rational modes of thought of system designers and planners generally.[2]

Although Suchman's point is well taken, it complicates the work-technology equation. Because they are working in a formalistic medium, designers and planners aim to capture those features of work that are typical of every environment, not just one. Only by ignoring local variations in work patterns and the contingencies that characterize them can they develop equipment to be produced for very large markets. To accomplish that goal, they have to strip away most of what is specific to a particular context. Seen through what Sachs (1995) called an "organizational/explicit" lens, the workplace has to be conceived as a rational entity. It must be viewed as a set of defined tasks and operations and predictable procedures that can be described, and it must be mimicked by software programs that imitate the steps of work successfully enough that the outcome is indistinguishable from the "real" thing, that is, the same sequence but as it would have been carried out by humans. The trick in design is to get the description right and then to inscribe it in computer code.[3]

The problem with such thinking, as Sachs (1995) also pointed out, is that work is never merely procedural. There is another side to it that is "activity-oriented/tacit," that takes account of what people actually do to get work done. It is this aspect of work that is responsive to unforeseen crises and vexing contingencies—what Winograd and Flores (1986) called "breakdowns"—that cannot be represented as routine or as a logical task flow. Handling breakdowns requires experience and shared knowledge, and there is no system that can conceive in advance of all the possible "information needs" (Kuutti, 1996) that people in the usual circumstances of work encounter. In the TTS example cited previously, what was ignored by the new system was "the whole activity of work in which a worker engages—in this case, following a trouble from beginning to end" (Sachs, 1995, p. 40). It is the side of work that involved communicating and forging alliances, "making sense of problems, conditions, kinds of orders, the routing of the circuit and learning as a way of getting work done reveals the importance of *knowing* in doing a job" (Sachs, 1995, p. 40, italics added).

Sachs puts special emphasis on the question of how knowledge is accumulated and shared in the accomplishment of work. People's knowledge, she maintained, encompasses not only their understanding of past experiences and problems solved but also their recognition of patterns and anomalies. It is this that constitutes the basis on which they can resolve situations successfully. Knowing on the job is not routine. It is built up collaboratively in the course of shared tasks and workplace communication and sociability. Sachs called these contexts of joint activities "work communities" in which "knowledge about how to get work done is stored and replenished. Work communities can provide 'natural' arenas and systems for this collaborative learning to take place" (Sachs, 1995, p. 42).

A work community had been established around the old dispatching system for police cars, in a previous example. When that system was replaced and the police in the cars no longer had available the veteran dispatchers' know-how and "feel" for the job, they felt bereft of both vital information and moral support.

Randall, Bentley, and Twidale (1994) made the same point as did Sachs regarding work communities. They drew a distinction between *workflow* (the systems view of linked routines) and *the flow of work* (the ethnographer's view), that is, "describing work with all its contingencies: interruptions, good and bad practices, seeking help, making mistakes, and so on" (pp. 57-58). They also argued

> Very little work in an organizational context is ever done in isolation. That is, even when the person doing the work is physically isolated, doing the work will normally involve an awareness of the work other people are doing or might do. To oversimplify the point, "who's doing what" is an important organizing principle of working life. (p. 62)

In summary, for the analysts who adopt an ethnographic perspective, the mixed success of I/CT implementation is easy to explain: They claim that designers and their managerial clients are tone-deaf when it comes to evaluating the symphony of natural work. Any of the examples we raised earlier in the chapter could serve to illustrate their injunction, "Please just go out and look!"

The Dead Weight of Tradition as an Impediment to Organizational Change

A quite different line of explanation for the mixed success of I/CT implementation targets the organization rather than the technology developers and implementers. Some analysts emphasize the inertia that derives from the historical configuration of practices of work. They see our inherited organizational patterns of administration and division of labor as the important causal variable explaining the relation between technology and organizational change. In their view, the technological capacity to transform work for the better is certainly there, but old organizational forms hold back an innovative application of the new technology to the problems of today.

The rationale underlying this line of thinking has been developed in considerable depth by Zuboff (1988, 1996). She argued that the form of organization known as a *functional hierarchy*, until recently so effective in managing large enterprises, has now become an impediment to change. In the early decades of the 20th century, the functional hierarchy became the most efficient way of managing the very large enterprises responding to the growth of the mass market. For these great corporations, maximizing throughput and minimizing unit costs were of prime importance. Functional organization eventually was to become a commonplace, the "modern" way of doing things.

But the newer information and communication technologies, Zuboff argued, operate on a different logic, and, when they are implemented in an organizational frame that is still fixed in the structures and habits of organizing that were engendered by the earlier ideology, the result is a stalemate:

> The brilliant inventions of the early twentieth-century workplace are now the barriers that inhibit the next great leap forward. . . . Unlocking the promise of an information economy now depends on dismantling the very same functionalized hierarchy—with its moral vision, social system, entrenched interests, and vertical focus—that once spelled greatness. (Zuboff, 1996, p. 14)

In the 1970s, when computerization first became seen as a transformative agent leading to new organizational levels of productivity, people interpreted it in the old industrial guise of automation—enabling workers to perform well-defined operations repetitively, with greater efficiency, to multiply the scale of industrial processes. It was this automating model—termed the *Fordist principle*—that had made American manufacturing operations the envy of the entire world. But now, claimed Zuboff, it is this same model that holds back progress. We should forget computer technology as an instrumentality by which to automate the established organization, she argued, and look at its unique property: how it allows us to "informate." Let us now see what she means by *informate*.

The principal characteristic of computer technology, according to Zuboff, is that it turns *embodied knowledge* (a kind of innate talent like judging height or distance) into *abstract knowledge,* no longer part of some individual's skill set but a mediated (i.e., now represented in the technology) idealization of it. This transformation can occur because information technologies have the capacity to "symbolically render processes, objects, behaviors, and events so that they can be seen, known, and shared in a new way" (Zuboff, 1988, p. 15). The mill foreman who could inspect a rough log and, on the basis of long experience, size up its potential to yield the optimum quantity of manufactured timber (and therefore figure out how to cut it into boards) now finds himself replaced by software that accomplishes the same task by measurement and analysis. As a result of such abstraction, the foreman (if he successfully adapts to the change of perspective that has occurred) has at his command a different, more abstract, much longer-range vision of the process of manufacturing. It is one that encourages initiatives of a new kind, including reconceiving and reorganizing the whole chain of production, not just one part of it.

As long as computerization continues to be seen by management as automating current practice, Zuboff thinks, the potential advantage for radical organizational restructuring through I/CT will be lost, and there will be few significant gains in productivity. It is the implications of this transformation for management that she wishes to highlight, however. The essence of informating is that knowledge no longer enters "at the top" but that the whole organization becomes "imbued" with an electronic text that can be read by anyone with the skills to access and understand the relevant information. This kind of new information infrastructure opens up the possibility for firms to deal with complexity at whatever point it enters the organization—at the customer interface, in production processes, or during service delivery—and to do so with speed and informed problem-solving skills leading to immediate action. It is a new kind of value that has been added by the technology.

The catch is that to take advantage of this technological possibility, organizations must be prepared to revamp their whole structure. As Zuboff (1996) put it, "For firms to avail themselves of such opportunities, they must be prepared to drive a stake into the heart of the old division of labor and the division of love from which it continues to draw sustenance" (p. 16). (By "division of love" she means something like executive privilege, manifesting itself in an unequal distribution of the spoils of enterprise, monetary and otherwise.) But many firms (even most) are unprepared to "drive a stake" into the body of the corporation they have known for so long (and, of course, their own privileged status within it). Instead of liberating the virtual informated organization incubating within, just waiting to be born and to grow into adulthood, they abort it. It is easier is to implement a system that reinforces the lines of authority than it is to obliterate them (as we saw in the police example). The result of this managerial inertia, however, is that computerization regularly disappoints.

I/CT-Based Approaches That Ignore the Inevitability of Organizational Politics

Of course, Zuboff's voice is hardly the only one pleading for a radical revision of our concept of how work should be organized. The rage of management theory in the early 1990s was "business process reengineering" (BPR) (Hammer & Champy, 1993; Johansson, McHugh, Pendlebury, & Wheeler, 1993). The proponents of BPR, not without a smidgen of immodesty (Jones, 1994), see themselves as heralding nothing less than a reversal of the Industrial Revolution, "starting all over, starting from scratch" (Hammer & Champy, 1993, p. 2). They advocate a veritable deracination, or rooting out, of the past (Grint, Case, & Willcocks, 1996). The classic industrial pattern of organization of work, they think, was (and still largely is) inspired by a concept of breaking down industrial processes into their separate parts and then specializing by function—a model associated with the name of an 18th-century Scottish philosopher and entrepreneur, Adam Smith.

BPR proposes a total break from emphasis on the division of labor and its analysis into component parts in favor of a refocalization onto the customer and his or her needs—seeing the whole activity of serving the customer as an integral process. The previous preoccupation with task, BPR's proponents argue, translated into turf wars, inflexibility, sectarian thinking, a confusion about employee accountability—and, as a result, poor service to the client. All of this is a recipe for disaster, they think, in the intensely competitive, high-energy world of global market-driven business. What is needed is a more holistic approach to business in which its processes are made visible to every employee from management down. Everyone can then see how what they are doing contributes to the whole and how their efforts affect the relationship with the customer. This is where I/CT enter the BPR scheme of things.

I/CT are the "critical enabler" of the BPR "revolution" (the subtitle of Hammer and Champy's 1993 book is "A Manifesto for Business Revolution"). They render the process of work more transparent than has ever before been possible (Zuboff's point). Accountability to one's boss can be replaced by accountability to the customer. Hierarchy then melts into collegiality, as a much flatter (and downsized) organizational structure takes shape. The old pre-I/CT hierarchical control mechanisms, such as the restrictive channeling and hoarding of information and localization of decision making and control in a few privileged hands, will be replaced by control from the marketplace. Discriminating customer demand weeds out the weak, inefficient performers on the way to superior performance and greater productivity of those who have adapted successfully.

Because BPR is a "revolution," the whole philosophy of managing and working must change. We can cite Willmott and Wray-Bliss (1995, p. 73), who base their observations on Miller and O'Leary (1993):

> It is claimed that the reengineered corporation frees workers from the outdated, constraining practices of traditional organizations. Employees are co-equal rather than coerced. Employees control their own work and support their teams of co-equal colleagues. Few managers exist, and those that do act as coaches, helping teams and individuals to achieve the best results they can. Workers are not accountable to managers, but instead have a responsibility to the team. (Willmott & Wray-Bliss, 1995, p. 73)

And all, of course, are primarily responsible to the client.

But some analysts are less sanguine and view the limited success of techno-logical innovations as rooted in the omnipresence in any human society of the play of interests and the political negotiation of outcomes. The telemedicine technology in our earlier example was hampered in its tryout more by conflict-ing hospital interests than by its capacity to track ambulatory cardiac patients. And even BPR, despite its brave face, has not had a string of unqualified suc-cesses to its credit. Hammer and Champy (1993) themselves estimated a 70% failure rate for experiments in radical change they had observed. Further studies have continued to show results that hardly matched up with the more optimistic expectations. Grint et al. (1996) reported that in their study of British firms "high risk, radical BPR approaches were generally not being taken" (p. 41). Instances of dramatic improvement in performance, these same authors reported, seem to be "few and far between" (p. 41). The reason they give for this reluctance is that, somewhat paradoxically given its pretensions, "BPR is an essentially political intervention" (p. 45). Let us see why they might think so.

BPR's appeal lies in its simplistic rationalist approach to the reconfiguring of the organization. It focuses on the logically structured processes of work (that is why it is called "engineering") and the role of technology in facilitating them. It treats the contextual nature of work, if not as an irrelevancy, at least as a manipu-lable variable of no great importance. The single-minded power of senior man-agement is taken as a given, with nary a mention of politics. In this respect, BPR is not atypical of much of the technological literature, which regularly wishes away the contaminating influences of ambition and intrigue.

Willmott and Wray-Bliss (1995) have made a careful analysis of the social logic that permeates technology-supported management theories such as BPR. They question the heart of the BPR proposal that claims to alter the ways in which people at work are held to account. In Hammer and Champy's (1993) words, "People who once did as they were instructed now make choices and de-cisions on their own instead. . . . Workers focus more on the customers' needs and less on their bosses'. Attitudes and values change in response to new incen-tives" (p. 65).

But can such a change really work the way they describe? Willmott and Wray-Bliss think not. For one thing, BPR is a strategy imposed from the top of the hierarchy, without a scintilla of a chance for negotiation at any other level. Hammer and Champy (1993) are clear that it "never, ever happens from the bot-tom up" (p. 207, cited by Willmott & Wray-Bliss, 1995, p. 75). Moreover, pro-cess teams, once established, are not free from interference. As Willmott and Wray-Bliss put it, "Managers are encouraged to allow no disagreement and to 'break eggs' where necessary" (p. 76). Third, the vaunted I/CT-enabled trans-

15

parency of process, celebrated by the BPR theorists as well as by Zuboff, is a two-edged sword. Transparency, it is evident to Willmott and Wray-Bliss, also can mean that "instantaneous and simultaneous information on workers' performance" is rendered available, not just to the workers, but to those at the top of the enterprise, and, as a result, "the principle of 'unsurveilled communication between workers' is most unlikely to be met in the reengineered organization" (p. 76).

Politics are never far from the surface, in other words, despite the fact that "BPR is adopted and deployed as if office politics either do not, should not or will not exist in the reengineered corporation" (Grint et al., 1996, p. 44). From the workers' perspective, for example, the political dimension is clear. BPR is typically a precursor to the firing, retirement, or relocation of a large number of employees ("a 75% reduction in head count" at Ford is mentioned by both Hammer, 1990, p. 106, and Willmott & Wray-Bliss, 1995, p. 70). Furthermore, according to Grint et al., management "is as much a political process as a rational one. . . . There is nothing inherent in BPR as a process or outcome that depoliticizes organizational life; if anything, politics breed in times of major, I/CT-enabled change" (p. 44). In fact, it is clear that an implementation of BPR, like any other managerial intervention that aims to reconfigure the work world of its employees as radically as BPR claims to do, is an instance of the operation of power.

For Grint et al. (1996), the idea of "operation of power" offers an explanation of why I/CT-based efforts to change the organization often fail. Their analysis took up Latour's (1986) argument that our usual way of thinking about power as a force exerted by someone on someone may be deceptive. On the contrary, it turns out that "in practice, if subordinates themselves do not act, then a leader has little power; only as a consequence of subordinate actions can leaders be deemed to have power" (Grint et al., 1996, p. 46). It is naive to imagine that the people who work in an organization have no control over their own actions or that they are merely the helpless pawns of their superiors. In fact, if they were such passive instruments, this would be an outright contradiction of the principles of BPR, which insists on the autonomy of the individual in responding to customer needs. So there is a profound anomaly at the heart of the BPR proposal (and perhaps of all such technology-driven proposals) with the result that "even assuming senior management support for BPR, it inevitably runs into political problems" (Grint et al., 1996, p. 46).

One final irony that these authors note is that organizational prescriptions such as BPR are being sold as an I/CT solution to earlier I/CT problems. BPR's overriding justification for reorganizational change, they think, derives "from the construed failure of past I/CT investment to deliver promised productivity improvements" (Grint et al., 1996, p. 52).

Is the Technology Its Own Worst Enemy?
The Self-Limiting Properties of Systems Design

The fourth type of explanation that has been given for why I/CT results disappoint is, in some sense, a mirror image of the second. Rather than claim that management, by clinging to old patterns, is failing to live up to the promise of the technology, as Zuboff and Hammer argued, this alternative line of reasoning suggests that technology has been unable to bootstrap itself up to deal with the complex problems of organization.

According to Lea and Giordano (1997), systems designers who are modeling organizational activities are caught in a loop of their own creation. When they analyze and model organizational processes, they tend to represent them, according to these authors, "in ways most appropriate to the tools and techniques they have in mind" (p. 5). Designers' models of a task are not neutral and objective descriptions of work but have "embedded within them elements of the technologies used in creating them" (p. 5).

It follows, of course, that if a model is, in fact, not sufficiently descriptive of the work organization, then its implementation is hampered, and it would not be surprising if the performance of the technology turned out to be a disappointment. Either the workers will perform at less than their capability because the technology channels them in unproductive ways (the problem with the 911 system and the police), or they will find workarounds of the kind described by Sachs (1995), or the technology will suffer from neglect, as Raymond and Giroux (1998) reported.

Lea and Giordano (1997) described the conceptualization of computer architecture in the design community as having passed through two phases. Initially, there were the block-structured computer languages of the 1960s—PL/1 and ALGOL—that evolved into the design tool known as "structured analysis" (DeMarco, 1979; Martin, 1990; Yourdon, 1989). In a block-structured language, the process to be modeled is broken down into its components or tasks that are treated as *modules*. Once programmed, the modules become invariant functions to be called up when needed within the larger program to perform a specialized operation (i.e., to act on data in a certain way by the application of defined operations). The architecture of a block-structured language is thus a hierarchy in which there is a main program or routine that in turn is composed of subroutines, each of which is responsible for one, and only one, task. To this

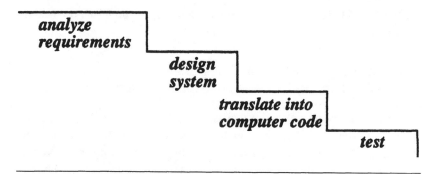

Figure 1.1. System Design Conceived on the Model of a Waterfall

methodology, structured systems analysis added the principle of analysis of the work situation, in which analysis precedes design, a sequence known in the design community as the *waterfall life cycle* (see Figure 1.1). The analysis and design sequence followed by the GFT design team in Hovey's (1992) earlier example was a typical waterfall operation.

In this type of planning cycle, processes are conceptualized as information processing problems in which there are data to be analyzed and operations that act on them. Note that the logic of this design paradigm is task-oriented, a model that, according to Lea and Giordano (1997) "has . . . dominated systems development since the late 1970s, and is still the most widely used formal methodology in large organizations today" (p. 10).

Structured analysis, of course, is evolving into new directions. One such trend is the flexible methodology known as *object-oriented design,* in which operations are no longer locked into a hierarchical structure but treated as objects that have certain attributes and relationships to other objects. The "print" icon on your computer screen is an example of an object: It performs a function that may be called up in different contexts, the sum of such contexts forming its environment.

The shift of perspective from block language architecture may seem minor, in one respect, because it is still a description of tasks, but there is a considerable advantage from an analysis and design perspective. The designer is led toward a more incremental strategy for building models by being able to carry out analysis and design concurrently. Business processes, for example, can be conceived as a set of interrelated entities rather than as a hierarchy of routines.

Nonetheless, Lea and Giordano (1997) argued, object-oriented programming, like all structured systems analysis, remains a method of representing the world that is "at root deterministic, mechanistic, rational. . . . That which gets modeled, in turn, depends on whatever is perceived to be systematic in what is going on" (pp. 10, 11). Their point is that the approach must necessarily retain "a classical vision of organizations, where goal-directed, rational routines and their interactions are fundamental building blocks" (p. 13). There is little place for worker initiative, for responding to the specifics of customer demand, or for adapting operations to take account of contingencies as they arise.

As a result of this logic, organizational change is not seen by the systems developer as an intrinsic property of the work he or she is modeling. The designer stands outside the work process, and, when the model is finished, the problem domain, objects, and interactions between them become relatively fixed. Change in the system only can originate and be responded to from outside, that is, by building yet one more system to deal with new complexity.

The Pros and Cons of Dualistic Explanations

There is undoubtedly a measure of truth in each of the four types of explanation we have briefly outlined. Certainly, there is a tendency to underestimate the complexity of the most ordinary of work environments and the ingenuity people bring to dealing with the contingencies of daily life at work. Work quickly becomes "invisible," as Suchman (1995) has put it, to everyone but those who do it—and often even they cannot easily explain what they do and how they do it. The successful enterprise depends, more than we usually are inclined to admit, on these little-noticed problem-solving, very *un*-high-tech activities that keep processes flowing smoothly.

Similarly, it is unquestionably the case that habits of work and organizational structures become encrusted with tradition and resistant to change. It is all too easy to fall into a rut—managers as much as anyone else. And politics are a part of organizational life, and even the central preoccupation of many people, from the CEO down. Finally, there is certainly a tendency to idealize technology and to lose from view its very considerable limitations, compared to the expectations that are loaded onto it by its impatient promoters and prospective clients.

But it is equally true that none of these explanations (and each has its critics) furnishes a complete answer to our question of why I/CT has disappointed. If computerization of the work world often fails to live up to expectations, it is not just because we gave insufficient attention to the local circumstances in which it takes place. Some work has to be procedural if the organization is ever to grow beyond the dimensions of a mom-and-pop enterprise (Winograd, 1994; we come back to his argument in Chapter 4). Similarly, it is hard not to suspect that Zuboff, Hammer, and others might be romanticizing the technology somewhat, or that, as Grint et al. (1996) think, "solutions" such as BPR might not be a bit like the patient who, when suffering from an allergic reaction to a medicine, decides to double the dosage. "Driving a stake into the heart" of the old kind of enterprise, as Zuboff proposed, is also likely to encounter some of the problems Sachs reported in her work.

It may be true that politics is forever rearing its ugly head, but that has not seemed to prevent previous generations of management from effectively putting technology to work. Finally, although it is true that we can easily fall into the habit of overrating the technology and the pace of its development, the risk of underrating it is equally great. It has visibly been transforming work and organization over the past generation, and that is a fact we need to address and understand.

◆ Toward a Structurational Explanation of the Technology-Organization Link

We have been sampling—selectively—some of the ways the technology-organization link has been conceptualized in the literature. Different though they may be in other respects, they all share one assumption: that there is something called *technology* and that it is changing (or risks changing) *organization*.

Not everyone buys into this technology-organization dichotomy. Westrup (1996, p. 158), for example, argued that we have been looking at the technology-organization relation in the wrong way: "Neither technology nor organization have an essential quality so that we can talk about social and technical factors. Rather, what becomes social and what becomes technical is an outcome of a systems development process" (p. 158; with equal plausibility, he could have said "an outcome of a social development process."). He argued for a "constructivist" approach, one that "does not take either the organization or technology for granted but proposes that they are constituted and reconstituted through the activities of various agents" (p. 167). King and George (1991, p. 70) expressed a similar skepticism:

> As with many aspects of computing in organization, the most interesting "impacts" of the technology have been to alter our views of what we are studying. . . .
> In the process, we have learned that the real mysteries lie in the nature of organizations themselves. (p. 70)

This book was written in the conviction that we need to move toward a radical reframing of the question of the "impact" of "technology" on "organization."

20

With this in mind, let us reconsider the four lines of explanation we have been reviewing.

Reevaluating the Four Hypotheses

There is first the issue of the centrality of situated work. Hypothesis 1 presents us with an image of people at work doing skilled tasks and confronted with an alien presence: a "technology" that has been imposed on them by their "organization." But the principle of situated work is not limited to the "users" of technology. Managers of the "organization" also turn up at their offices and do work. "Technology" developers, as we describe in Chapter 5, are involved in highly situated settings of work.

The difference between the communities of work described in the ethnographic literature is not between some people who do skilled tasks in ordinary circumstances of work and others who do not, but between different communities of people, all of whom are working. If there is an "organization," then it is an interrelated network of communities of workers. We should be paying attention to the pattern of relationships and how it is mediated in practice. It does not help to reify *organization*—to lend it an essentiality independent of its realization in the everyday practices of people.

Similarly, Hypothesis 2 confronts us with the dramatic image of a new "technology." It is one, it is said, that has radically different properties from those of the past. But using technology is, and always has been, a normal part of the human experience. There is no way to go far enough back in history, nor far enough into the remote areas of the non-Westernized world, to find people without technology. Managers, technology developers, and ordinary workers all depend on technology. Technology is so integrated into our usual modes of living that it becomes a fundamental part of ourselves and our own identity. It evolves endlessly. It adapts to us and we to it. As the dictionary says, technology is just the applied science of craftsmanship, the science of the art of working.

The advocates of informating and reengineering would have us see it differently, as possessing innate properties—of having an essentiality. But this amounts to another form of reification. None of the "technologies" described in our earlier examples turned out to be what their designers thought they were once they had been implemented in real circumstances of work.

So how should we be thinking about the relation of technology and organization? Hypothesis 3 presents us with an answer: politics. But using the term *politics* introduces a negative connotation. It suggests a derogation from a concern for excellence or respect for democratic values. An alternative conception is one that we already have mentioned: organization as a network of interrelated communities of work. What we would now have to begin to do, if we accept this view, is to consider what the object of each of these communities was and how they relate to each other with respect to their objects.

Some communities (management), we would find, take other communities (workers) as their object and relate to them by assuming they are a resource to be mobilized and instructed, using as a tool the products of a third community (systems design). Some communities (systems design) take the technologies of other communities (collaborative work) as their object and depend on the recruitment of a third community (management) to effect the implementation of their products into the work world. Some communities (collaborative work) find themselves confronted by new systems designed by other communities (systems design) and imposed on them by a third community (management). It is the interface dynamics of these communities that we need to understand if we are going to comprehend the computerization phenomenon.

There is involved here what we refer to in Chapter 2 as a *dialectic of control* (the expression is borrowed from Giddens, as we shall see). As Grint et al. (1996) observed, the power of management to mobilize communities of work and of systems design to implement its products is conditional on a degree of compliance on the part of the worker community. In each of our illustration cases cited earlier, it was the responses of the people doing the work that effectively sidelined efforts at implementation. In not one case did the implementation match the expectations of management or the designers. If this is politics, it is the *realpolitik* of practice, not the rhetoric of speech. But it is nonetheless effective, for all that.

Finally, there is Hypothesis 4: the limits of formalization as a means of representing work. It is undeniably true that systems design uses as its inscription device an abstract code—an artificial language constructed on the principles of formal logic. But, as we see in Chapter 5, this is hardly all that goes into systems design. On the contrary, the products that come out of the designer's lab incorporate assumptions about what work is, what culture is, and what organization is. The representations of work that support the design enterprise are anything but neutral. In fact, they are better thought of as a manifestation of contemporary rhetoric—skillfully crafted discursive devices designed to persuade as well as to function as machines. They carry with them an ideology.

When we combine these images, we arrive at a complex process of collective learning in which each of the communities is involved. Those at work in the circumstances of the multiple tasks of the enterprise are constantly adjusting to the changing circumstances imposed on them, in part, by their "organization" and by "technology." Those who produce the technology struggle to fit their products to the circumstances of work, in search of the "correct" definition, which never quite comes. And management migrates from one image of how to organize to another: "just-in-time," "total quality," "reengineering," "the learning organization," and so on. It is the complex self-organizing loop this interaction generates that we need to understand.

More than a decade ago, Markus and Robey (1988) observed, "It is no secret that research on information technology and organizational change has produced conflicting results and few reliable generalizations" (p. 596). They argued, as we have, that explanations that emphasize a causal connection—either technology or organization as an "imperative"—fail to explain the phenomenon of computerization. Instead of one-way causality, they argue for what they call an "emergent perspective" that focuses on process. But they concede that emergent/process models of change "require detailed understanding of dynamic organizational processes," and this added complexity makes them "difficult to construct" (p. 589).

In this book, we offer one possible line of investigation that might begin to respond to the criterion Markus and Robey (1998) established. Our approach draws on the theory of structuration. Structuration theory was first proposed by Anthony Giddens in a series of books and articles (Giddens, 1976, 1979, 1984). It has been adapted to the study of computerization by a number of researchers, including Barley, Poole and DeSanctis, and Orlikowski (we review their work in Chapter 7). However, our interpretation of the theory has elements that are distinctive because it incorporates understandings that originate in communication theory that are not to be found in the original texts or in subsequent revisions of structuration theory.

A Brief Overview of Where We Are Heading in the Book

Briefly (because we consider Giddens's theory in greater depth in Chapter 2), the theory of structuration is built around a dominant concept, that of *duality of structure*. Giddens assumes that all societies are composed of situated communities, involved in purposive action and sharing a discourse for talking about their concerns. Such communities are marked by regularities in how they deal with their world; they are *systemic* (note that Giddens's use of the term *system* is sociologically, not technologically, grounded). But the regularities that appear in locally situated communities of practice also reflect commonalities of systemic patterning that persist in time (sometimes very long stretches of time) and characterize many geographically dispersed worlds of local adaptation. To understand how widely separated communities of practice can come to share so many common patterns of dealing with their world, Giddens introduces the idea of *structure*. Structure is that which is shared by many communities. It has no expression other than in the patterning of their activities. Thus, structure is *virtual*. It is what shapes activities and creates the foundation for the emergence of communities that transcend the strictly local (a potentiality that human beings are unique in possessing among animal populations).

Although we share Giddens's concept of duality, we differ from him in how we conceptualize structure. His presentation of the idea leaves an impression of structure as systemically coherent; we see structure differently, as potentially inherently *contradictory*—and a source of double binds. Our analysis emphasizes the importance of levels of structure: individual, group, and organization (a dimension that figures much less in Giddens's writings). We see structuring dynamics as specific to a level, as well as to the society as a whole. Each level is characterized by its own organizing processes and differing communicative modalities. Individual structures are mediated by thought; group structures are mediated, principally, by conversation; organizational structures depend to a significantly greater extent on text as its medium of exchange. The consequence of this bifurcation of organizing process is to generate inconsistencies at the interfaces: individual/group and group/organization. The implementation of technology poses a learning problem for all three levels: individual, group, and organization. The interfaces between levels then become a key explanatory factor in the success of an implementation of technology, either facilitating or inhibiting adaptation at the immediately adjacent level. Explaining the outcomes of computerization thus requires us to take account not only of the processes of learning at one level but also of understanding as well the organizational context in which they take place, with its embedded levels of structuring.

It is this framework on which we build in this book. The framework assumes both the centrality of process that Markus and Robey (1998) argue for and the possibility of emergence—system and structure existing in a dynamic (and interdependent) duality. Computer-based machines, we argue, are carriers of structure, but they also trigger organizing processes and make salient interface contradictions. They aim to shape the systemic world of local practice but, when they are implemented in the context of contradictory structural constraints, they do not always succeed. When the technical "structures" of the machine fail to incorporate in their design the systemic constraints of practice, they also fail to be realized as social "structures." There is a dialectic of control, mediated by organization. To map that dialectic must be the goal of research.

24

Organization of the Chapters

In Chapter 2, we outline the general theory of structuration as proposed by Giddens. However, there are important gaps in the theory as it applies to the subject of this book—the computerization of work. For one thing, as we have noted already, there is little attention given to technology. Nor are the sections on organization fully enlightening: Giddens's theory is focused on society-in-the-large and modernity. Finally, although the concept of duality of structure is potentially rich, the modalities by which structure informs practice and system becomes structure remain underdeveloped. Giddens's treatment of communication is particularly restrictive. Perhaps as a result, he does not develop a theory of organizational dynamics in much depth and underplays an aspect of the computerization of work that we develop in the book: the role of levels of organization and the contradictions that may characterize them.

Chapter 3 incorporates insights from other research that serve to enrich the structurational perspective (even though none of them is explicitly structurational, as Giddens defines the term). The chapter draws principally on the work of five schools of thought: situated action theory, distributed cognition theory, activity theory, translation theory, and interactionist theory. The situated action approach (Suchman) emphasizes the local groundedness of work but does so in a way that brings out, as Giddens does not, the role of the physical environment in structuring work. Giddens's theory of action is centered on the individual; the concept of distributed cognition (Hutchins) enlarges the idea of action to take account of collaborative construction of events and response. Activity theory (Engeström) reinforces these ideas but adds a concept of community as an integral component in action. Translation theory (Latour) brings to our attention the importance of artifacts as nonhuman agents and carriers of structure. Interactionism (Star) introduces additional concepts of boundary object, infrastructure, and categorization as key elements in any constructivist theory of collective action. Each of these approaches, in other words, constitutes a significant addition to the basic ideas of structuration.

Chapter 4 presents a revised theory of structuration that assumes communication to be the essential mechanism by which structure is integrated into practice. We develop a model of communication that assumes a continuing two-way translation of (a) the circumstances and interaction of conversation into text to produce interpretation and coordinated action and (b) text into conversation to support interaction. The core of the theory is the concept of agency, which we conceptualize quite differently from Giddens because we see it as acting-*for* rather than merely acting, a communicational as opposed to individual interpretation. The chapter then addresses implications of the model at two levels—that of the situated world of work and that of the extended networks of the organization.

The enactment of a situated world is conceptualized as an ongoing "dance of agency" or "dialectic of resistance and accommodation" (Pickering, 1995). Out of this dance or dialectic, stable relationships of agency emerge, resulting in a division of labor and accepted rules of relationship. Patterns of agency (acting-for) emerge from the necessity of co-orientation in response to a complex environment. *Co-orientation,* it is argued, is the building block of all organizational processes and structures. *Imbrication* is the process by means of which co-orientational systems become translated into infrastructure.

The chapter then elaborates on the model to deal with the dynamics of organization as an extended system of enactment. It develops an explanation of the critical interface between local and global and explores the differing communication dynamics characteristic of each. It introduces the argumentative dimension of communication and the role of rhetoric in the constitution of the organization and the role of ideology in the construction of organizational identity.

Chapters 5 to 7 are reports on field studies we have carried out, within the framework of the structurational principles of analysis outlined in Chapter 4. Chapter 5 is a comparative study of design practices in Scandinavia and Japan. In both contexts, assumptions of culture prove to be of central importance in designing systems to support group interaction. Chapter 6 reports on the implementation of a new system in the purchasing department of a commercial operation. It explores a particular dimension of co-orientation: the relation of function to process. It then documents the elements of a dialectic of control in the context of a single department. Chapter 7 reviews some of the previous literature on structuration and uses this work as a jumping-off point for an investigation of the comparative strategies of learning of two organizations with a similar vocation but very different cultures of management.

Chapter 8 concludes with a reflection on learning and its place in computerization. Using Bateson's characterization of "orders of learning," the chapter explores sources of contradictory pressures in organization, particularly as they arise at the group/organization interface. Computerization acts as a mediator in that its representations of work become the agency that intervenes in both triggering learning at the level of the collaborative group but also in rethinking the nature of organization. The missing variable in much previous work on computerization is communication. The book concludes with a reflection on the role of learning as the key process in facilitating the integration of information/

communication technology and the place communication research might play in reconciling the interface paradoxes.

◆ Notes

1. Common abbreviations for the new technologies are IT ("Information Technology") and IS ("Information Systems"). More recently, ICT ("Information Communication Technologies") has been used, in recognition of the fusion of computing and telecommunications that has been taking place over the past quarter century (culminating in the Internet). The term CT is commonly reserved for telecommunication technologies. Each of these expressions is a way of suggesting that the new technologies are merely innocuous tools for information transmission. We see them quite differently, as media of communication, in which the latter term is understood to mean the complex experience of human interaction in all of its dimensions. Thus, we have chosen to introduce a different term—I/CT—to emphasize that the technologies are indeed *employed,* in contexts of work and social interaction, as both information and communication supports. The slash ("/") of I/CT should thus be read to mean the interface between information and communication uses. One of the points of this book is that this "interface" is frequently a source of tension during the implementation of new technologies, and it explains some of the ambivalent results that we report in this chapter.

2. Her finding is in accordance with the dictionary definition of technology: that *technology* is not the machinery that people use but how they use it and for what purposes, a distinction that sometimes tends to get lost in general usage.

3. Management as well as systems designers, according to Randall, Bentley, and Twidale (1994), all too often adopt the organization/explicit view and, by so doing, fail to examine the work of their employees closely. Because the skills and knowledge that go into work only become apparent on close acquaintance, they agree with Suchman (1995) and Barley (1996a) that "management often has only the most glossed understanding of the skills necessary to the completion of work tasks" (Randall et al., 1994, p. 63). They observed, "All organizations experience a gap between managerial pictures of situations and those of individuals in more specific organizational positions" (p. 56).

2

Structuration Theory:
Basic Concepts

◆ The four types of explanation for the ambiguous results of computerization in organizations that we described in our introductory chapter are based on what have been termed (Markus & Robey, 1988) *deterministic* models—models that attribute a direct cause-effect relation linking technology and organization. One version of the determinist model (the most prevalent in the literature) views technology as the cause or determining factor in organizational change—as having an "impact." The other version of determinism sees the organization as acting like a filter that influences—even determines—the course of technological implementation, use, and consequences. Both views treat technology and organization as nonproblematic entities, as existing essentially. Neither has produced a clear understanding of why mixed results of computerization are the rule rather than the exception.

Markus and Robey (1988) cited two reasons for this mixture of results. On the one hand, they think the deterministic model is inappropriate for studying computerization because (a) it is too macro (it tends to analyze information flows, delegation of authority, etc.), and, in assuming an invariant relation between antecedents and outcomes, (b) its cause-effect attributions are "too stringent for social phenomena" (p. 592). Microlevel dynamic or "emergent" models that attempt to understand process are, on the other hand, difficult to construct (Markus & Robey, 1988, p. 589). Because they aim to capture subtle internal feedback processes rather than clear-cut relations between independent and dependent variables, they are more complex than models that depend strictly on analysis of variance.

As we saw in Chapter 1, a rather different reason given for the ambiguity of research findings echoes Westrup's (1996) observation that neither technology nor organization has yet been properly theorized. Although there is by now a solid body of empirical work on computerization, few theoretical constructs have been developed to explain the empirical findings (Jackson, 1996). Markus and Robey (1988) agree that research on computerization has been hampered by conflicting definitions and unclear measures of information technology and organizational structure.

In this chapter and the next, we address the issue of how to theorize the relation between technology and organization in a way that takes us beyond the determinist cause-effect model and research strategy. How is it possible, we ask, to bridge theoretically the gap between local practices and knowledge and the structural constraints within which these activities occur? We turn away from concepts of cause and effect, or "impact," and move toward the development of the kind of perspective that Markus and Robey described as "emergent"—one that focuses instead on process and activity.

The explanatory framework we construct is based on an important body of social theory known as structuration. It has significant strengths. Notably, *structuration theory*, as it was conceived by its original proponent, Anthony Giddens, is a process-based theory that reconciles both macro and micro levels of analysis. It centers its attention on human activity and treats concepts such as organization and technology as derived from the focused world of practical action. It thus de-essentializes technology and organization and, in doing so, frees us to frame questions of research differently—as process and emergence rather than as cause and effect. It thus constitutes a step in the direction Markus and Robey (1988) saw as desirable: computerization as emergence. And because it already figures in the literature on computerization (notably Barley, Orlikowski, and Poole and DeSanctis), it provides us with a link to some of the more creative work in the field (work that we review in Chapter 7).

Of course, structuration theory does not provide all the answers to the questions we have raised. It is a starting point, not a conclusive step. In this chapter, we describe central theoretical precepts in structuration. In Chapter 3, we consider some alternative perspectives that enlarge the range of the theory. In Chapter 4, we present a revised theory of structuration, centered on communication as the central mechanism of emergence of structure.

◆ Structuration Theory as an Emergent/Process Model

Historical Origins of the Theory

Structuration theory is the brainchild of an extraordinarily prolific British sociologist, Anthony Giddens. Giddens is one of the postfunctionalist generation of social scientists whose work came into growing prominence during the 1960s and 1970s, including such luminaries as Pierre Bourdieu and Alain Touraine in France, Jürgen Habermas and Niklas Luhmann in Germany, Roy Bhaskar in Great Britain, and Randall Collins in the United States. All were inheritors—and critics—of the dominant figure in American sociology of an earlier generation, Talcott Parsons.

Sociology in the United States first took root at the University of Chicago where, inspired by the teachings of a German theorist, Georg Simmel, the emphasis was placed on the empirical study of group processes, in real-life contexts, using mainly qualitative methods. But Chicago's central role was gradually to be supplanted during the 1940s by the emergence of stars in other universities, of which Harvard (Parsons, Homans, Bales) and Columbia (Merton) were among the most salient. The Chicago school's preoccupation had been with the practical realities of lived experience of marginal groups during a rapidly urbanizing and tempestuous period of growth in American society, documented by ethnographic studies (of the homeless, of immigrants, of taxi dancers, etc.). Parsons represented a very different tendency, influenced by European theorists such as Durkheim and Weber, in that he was preoccupied with the development of an all-encompassing general theory of society, relatively little based on empirical field research.

Parsons was attempting to reconcile ideas of society that were, on the one hand, based on what he thought of as a "voluntaristic" model of individual or micro action with, on the other hand, the necessity to account for the existence of overarching institutions, characteristic of the macro social worlds of contemporary life. Giddens and his peers also take up the theme of reconciliation of macro and micro but distance themselves from their predecessor in the kind of answer they give. Giddens's thought not only incorporates the themes of classic sociology—Marx, Weber, Durkheim—but also weaves in radical ideas advanced by two exceptional individuals, Erving Goffman (of the interactionist Chicago school) and Herbert Garfinkel (who, although he was Parsons's doctoral student, was to introduce to American sociology phenomenology, a philosophically quite different tendency of thought from that of Parsons).[1] All of the newer sociological approaches could be called, broadly speaking, structurational in their orientation, but it was Giddens who generated the most systematic attack on the macro-micro problem from the new perspective. In any case, it is Giddens who has most influenced the work of communication scholars exploring the computerization of work.

A Theory Still in Construction

Although our approach is also structurational, we, like many others, have ended up constructing an interpretation of the theory that is no longer pure, undiluted Giddens. Such a revision is inevitable because, although it is filled with remarkable insights, the writing of Giddens is, as Stinchcombe (1990) tartly observed, abstract and relatively unembellished by concrete illustrations. As a result, the researchers who have been inspired by structuration theory have been stimulated to generate a quite remarkable diversity of interpretations of what it is about. At times, it has functioned as a Rorschach test for different people to project onto it assumptions deriving from rather different epistemological—and not necessarily compatible—backgrounds. As a consequence, there is not much consistency in the methodologies that have been elaborated to try to put some empirical flesh on the conceptual bones of the theory. We are thus no exception to the rule that, although everyone pretty much agrees on the general thrust of structuration theory, nobody can escape giving it their own reading, certainly if they mean to use it for actual research.

◆ Giddens's Concept of Structuration[2]

The first step in grasping what Giddens is attempting to accomplish is to see what it is that he formulated as his object or overall purpose. On that score, fortunately, he is perfectly clear, from the very first sentence of his 1984 book. He is out not so much to reconcile as to supercede what were the two previously dominant approaches in social thought—*functionalism/structuralism* and *hermeneutics/interpretivism.* Functionalism is Parsons and Merton: society as system, people as its parts. Structuralism is a branch of anthropology and sociology that focuses on social patterns. Hermeneutics is the science of interpretation. Interpretivism emphasizes individual sense-making activities. Giddens thinks functionalism/structuralism is too macro, hermeneutics/interpretivism too micro: "One of my principal ambitions in the formulation of structuration theory is to put an end to each of these empire-building endeavours" (Giddens, 1984, p. 2). So his task is to make present to us certain features of reality that, he thinks, typically have escaped notice (at least among his professional colleagues in philosophy and sociology). Let us consider what those features are.

A Recursively and Reflexively Organized World

Giddens emphasizes two important concepts—*recursivity* and *reflexivity*—in his conceptualization of human social action. We deal with recursivity first.

All human social activities, he asserts, are recursive. By recursive, he means something like the following. Social practices acquire their shape across space and time. This shaping not only requires an arena—a space in which to take place—and a *durée*—his term for the time it takes for any activity to unfold—but a consistent order or coherence that transcends the immediacy of experience to produce regularity and predictability of practice, from time to time and place to place (what he calls "continuity of practices"). It is not just that local activities are organized but that their organization reflects patterns that transcend the strictly local. A recursive pattern is one that repeats itself in a variety of contexts. Society is recursive in just this sense: repetition of pattern.

To explain why this patterning occurs, he has to put activities first. He has to make them present for us in a new way—not merely as an external projection of many social actors' individually based choices (that would be to revert to microlevel thinking) but rather as the "theater" in which actors discover their particular purposes in the first place. Students, for example, study, and, by so doing, they confirm themselves as students. They would not be students unless they studied, and they would not be able to study without a context in which to study. Conditions, as he said, make activities possible, and yet conditions are reproduced by the very activities they enable. The theater, for example, precedes the actors, and yet the actors are why there are theaters. Activities—what is occurring on the stage of the theater—are then endlessly recreated by actors "via the very means whereby they express themselves as actors. In and through their activities agents reproduce the conditions that make these activities possible" (Giddens, 1984, p. 2).

There is no starting point. There would be no actors without a stage for them to act on, but their acting on the stage is what makes it a theater in the first place. It is not the building that makes it a theater (macro thinking), but the fact that it houses plays. Otherwise, it is an empty shell. The logic is perfectly circular—chicken-and-egg thinking.

To be a human, he goes on, is to be a purposeful agent. This is not a radical idea as such, but he immediately draws a line between two views of purpose, only one of which he subscribes to (and the other of which he rejects). You could

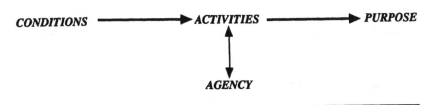

Figure 2.1. Activities as the Core of Structuration Theory

think of purposive action in the way that the term is commonly used, that is, as composed of an aggregate of individual decisions, each identified by its particular intention, reason, or motive. (This is a view not infrequently adopted by mathematically oriented decision theorists in management and political science courses.) This is not his idea at all. Instead, he sees purpose as emerging out of activity as a result of its "reflexive monitoring" by those who participate—a kind of ongoing, after-the-fact rationalization of action that was already under way or is even past (a view reiterated, incidentally, by Karl Weick in his 1995 book on sense-making). Action, Giddens (1984) specifies, "is not a combination of 'acts': 'Acts' are constituted only by a discursive moment of attention to the *durée* of lived-through experience" (p. 3; by "discursive," he means that the action is accounted for or interpreted by someone).

Note again the insistence on a recursive logic of no identifiable starting point of activity, no single operative cause or external source. Activity occurs as an unbroken flow of experience that preceded the individual's involvement and will continue afterward. One can never step out of the flowing river of experience that constitutes one's life. It is not the flow that explains its punctuation into acts but how we interpret the flow ("monitor" it) by overlaying it with categories of meaning ("rationalizing" it), to produce "a discursive moment of attention."

We warned you that Giddens takes close reading because he has no hesitancy in cloaking his thought in abstractions, such as "discursive moment of attention" and "*durée* of lived-through experience." Basically, however, the idea is not so complicated, although it is revolutionary in its implications. Let us take activities, as he does, as the starting point. Activities suppose, for them to take place, "conditions" (Giddens, 1984, p. 2). They also imply, as he says, "purposes": an envisaged future state (p. 3). Finally, there is an inseparable—and two-way—link between the action that goes into making it an activity and the actor or actors who act and the means by which they act (p. 5)—a link that he calls "agency." If we put these components all together, the result is something like Figure 2.1.

It is by putting activity at the center and explaining every other phenomenon as a function of activity, including the emergence of both individuals (the micro world) and institutions (the macro world), that the radical shift of perspective is accomplished. It allows him to reject so-called dualist (separating the macro from the micro) views of social life and to replace them with a *duality,* in which what have traditionally been thought of as "micro" and "macro" realities are no more than the outward projections of activities—and a derivative consequence of "rationalization." The constitution of agents and structures are not two independent processes (that would be a dualism). Duality of structure (p. 19) implies that structures are not external to individuals: "Structural properties of social systems are both medium and outcome of the practices they (those systems) recursively organize" (Giddens, 1984, p. 25).

As a strategy of argumentation, his reasoning allows him to take an accepted view of how things are—a dualist or essentialist ontology of the unquestioned reality of the social (functionalism/structuralism) and the unquestioned reality of the individual (hermeneutics/interpretivism)—and show what happens when we reverse the angle of view. What had previously been no more than an interstitial space (the interactive order of daily life) in the no-man's land between the psychological and the social—a mere secondary intersection linking orders of reality—can now be thought of as primary, as reality itself. It is thus hardly surprising that communication scholars were among the first to adopt the structurational perspective because that "in-between" territory is where communication is to be found (McPhee, 1989; McPhee & Poole, 1980; Poole & McPhee, 1983; Poole, Seibold & McPhee, 1985; Riley, 1983). Structuration highlighted in a new way what communication studies—interaction.

Reflexivity and Knowledge

Giddens's understanding of the term *reflexive* is grounded in how he perceives knowledge. There are, he says, two kinds of knowledge. One kind is *practical,* and, he adds, it "is not directly accessible to the consciousness of actors" (Giddens, 1984, p. 4). He specifies further that this constitutes the "vast bulk" of the "mutual" knowledge of people involved in interaction: "It is inherent in the capability to 'go on' within the routines of social life" (p. 4). It is the kind of thing you know without being able to say what you know, or how you know it, like walking and talking (and it is this that makes it singularly hard to capture in systems of artificial intelligence).

As opposed to this practical knowledge, he identifies what he calls *discursive* knowledge: that which we consciously know. Discursive knowledge is represented by the reasons actors offer for what they do (there are echoes here of Garfinkel's idea of "accounting" as how people make sense to themselves and others of what is going on).[3] Of course, there is no assurance (and it is a point he insists on) that what people say they are doing is what they are really doing, and there are often many reasons to mask the latter, especially if there is an issue of conforming to known social norms (and particularly those to which sanctions or penalties are attached). It is a recognized legal principle that one does not have to incriminate oneself. In fact, as both Giddens and, before him, Goffman, observe: the kind of performance people put on in public when they know they are being observed may not reflect how they behave or how they feel, backstage, out of range of others' scrutiny.[4]

Reflexivity enters on two grounds: (a) not only because people do not know what they do until they do it and then reflexively rationalize it (an idea that Karl Weick, 1979, also incorporated in his theory of enactment), (b) but also because the rationalization is itself what gives action its purpose and its appearance of intentionality. It is a way for human actors to know where they are: "By the rationalization of action, I mean that actors—also routinely and for the most part without fuss—maintain a continuing 'theoretical understanding' of the grounds of their activity" (Giddens, 1984, p. 5). (This includes, by the way, the social and physical contexts in which they move.)

What makes human activity an interactive order is that people routinely monitor their own and others' actions (and expect others to do the same), and they judge others on the basis of the competence they display in their performances. Mostly, there is little that is problematical about practical activity, precisely because, in ongoing situations, there is not much to explain: Everything works on the basis of tacit, implied, understood knowledge. It is only when there are "relatively unusual circumstances, situations which in some way break with the routine" (Giddens, 1984, p. 6) that people may be questioned about what they are doing and be obliged, by the ordinary rules of conversation, to proffer a motivation as explanation or justification. Most action, he thinks, is not motivated, in the usual sense of that term. Motives are called on principally to "supply overall plans or programmes" (p. 6) and thus are part of a discursively based rationalization of action that may or may not necessarily correspond very well to the practical realities of action.

Action and Power

If, reading this account of structuration, you have been tempted to see action as neutral in its effects—just cooperating with others to get the job done—it is time to revise that impression. All action, intentional or not, according to Giddens (1984), involves power. To be an agent is to have the capability of doing something (p. 9), to have a "transformative capacity" (p. 15). Again, we see the centrality of the concept of recursion in his theory: Power inheres in the activity itself. How people come to label its exercise—what they call "powerful"—is another issue: "Power is logically prior to subjectivity, to the constitution of the reflexive monitoring of conduct" (p. 15). Action constitutes power as it occurs, even in the most banal of interactions. As Giddens (1979) also writes, "Even the most casual social encounter instances elements of the totality as a structure of domination. . . . I have argued elsewhere that the concept of action is *logically tied* to that of power" (p. 88).

Giddens is once again argumentatively distinguishing his position from the mainstream of sociological thought of the time when he says, "Conceptions of power in the social sciences tend faithfully to reflect the dualism of subject and object referred to previously" (Giddens, 1984, p. 15). *Power* usually had been defined either as the capacity of an individual to realize an intended outcome or as a property of society. Instead, structuration theory sees it as a characteristic of the natural interactive order. To act is to mobilize some kind of resource: "structured properties of social systems, drawn upon and reproduced by knowledgeable agents in the course of interaction" (p. 15; remember that "knowledgeable" does not necessarily mean consciously aware). The use of power, he says, "characterizes not specific types of conduct but all action, and power is not itself a resource. Resources are media through which all power is exercised, as a routine element of the instantiation of conduct in social reproduction" (p. 16).

A Dialectic of Control

Giddens has now laid the basis for his next step, which is to extend his theory beyond the range of the face-to-face to include the whole gamut of human institutions, from the most micro to the most macro. If all activity "instantiates" power as "a routine element of conduct," then all activity will produce a structured world, both physically and socially. But, because everyone can act, the actual outcome may be unpredictable:

> Power within social systems which enjoy some continuity over time and space presumes regularized relations of autonomy and dependence between actors or collectivities in contexts of social interaction. But all forms of dependence offer some resources whereby those who are subordinate can influence the activities of their superiors. This is what I call the *dialectic of control* in social systems. (Giddens, 1984, p. 16)

36

In brief, by putting activity in the driver's seat, and as constitutive of power, Giddens has established a platform on which to build a more elaborate construction that would explain, not just the interactive order of working groups, but of society itself, including its most august and powerful institutions. What used to be a dualism of subjects (individuals who exist ontologically independent of society) and objects (societies that exist ontologically independent of the particular individuals comprising them) has been replaced by a duality of structure in which both subjects and objects are rationalized constructions realized retrospectively as an outcome of the ongoing monitoring of the stream of activity.

Now let us see how he attempts to make the bridge to systems of activity that are not bound to one single time and place but that somehow transcend the limits of time/space to take on greater permanence and scope—in a word, global society.

Structure Versus System: The Essence of "Duality"

A key step in the argument of Giddens is to make a distinction between *structure* and *system*. It is structure that will explain why there are global societies, system that will account for locally situated contexts of human interaction.

He defines structure as "the structuring properties allowing the 'binding' of time-space in social systems, the properties which make it possible for discernibly similar social practices to exist across varying spans of time and space and which lend them 'systemic' form" (Giddens, 1984, p. 17).

That seems clear enough; it certainly fits what we know about the modern world. There would be no large organizations, no powerful states, if there were not "discernibly similar social practices" that characterized their multiple operations and made it possible to think of them as in some sense "systemic." There would be no banks, or airlines, or fast food chains, without "similar social practices" that can be "discerned" in widely varying contexts. But there is no structure per se, no tangible "thing" to which we can point. How a Wal-Mart store works is an issue of system; that the Wal-Mart system is pretty much invariant from one branch to another is a manifestation of structure. Structure is what he calls "a virtual order of transformative relations," existing "only in its instantiations in such practices and as memory traces orienting the conduct of knowledgeable human agents" (Giddens, 1984, p. 17).

When such "structural properties" of the interactive order attain a sufficient level of generality (when they are "most deeply embedded," "have the greatest time-space extension") like the "law," "education," or the "family," then they will be referred to as *institutions*. But note the implication: Institutions are also virtual, not actual (until they are actualized in a situation). And he thinks it is precisely their virtuality that gives them the capacity to hold societies together.

Structure is sort of like what Koestler (1967) called, in another context, "the ghost in the machine"—that which gives a machine its "machine-ness." Only now we are talking about what gives society its society-ness or organization its organization-ness (or, indeed, technology its technology-ness).

To differentiate structure from system, Giddens borrows an analogy from linguistics. System-ness he takes to be a *syntagmatic* dimension of spoken language: "the patterning of social relations in time-space involving the reproduction of situated practices" (Giddens, 1984, p. 17). Structure corresponds to a *paradigmatic* dimension, involving, like the grammar or the parts of speech of a language, "a virtual order of 'modes of structuring recursively implicated in such reproduction'" (p. 17). Roughly speaking, then, system is what we live; structure is what we must know, and be, and reproduce, to live.

Rules and Resources

Structure for Giddens has two components: rules and resources. Let us consider rules first.

The problem with words like *rules* and *resources* is that everyone knows what a rule and a resource is. Thus, when we read that Giddens sees structure as incarnated in rules and resources, and because we are all speed readers these days, we have a tendency to race on to the next paragraph. But when he uses the term rules, Giddens should raise a big red flag to catch our attention (and he kind of does so on pages 17 and 18 of his 1984 book), because what he means by rules is not quite what we usually take that to mean (for one thing, he rejects the idea of *a* rule, in the singular). When we think of rules, we tend to think of something explicit, like the rules of a game, such as jai alai or Monopoly. That is precisely (he is quite clear on this) what he does not mean.

His argument recalls his distinction between practical and discursive knowledge. If, as he argues, most activities exhibit the presence of practical knowledge, and if rule-following enters into all activities, then it follows that most rules are practically, not discursively, grounded, and thus they are not even part of what we consciously know, but of what we naturally do. We do not have to talk about it; we just do it. They "exemplify," he said, the "routines of social life." They are how "practices are sustained," more like the way children play than a court of law.

Rules, of course, can be verbalized. Again, taking his cue from the ethnomethodologist Garfinkel, Giddens sees every "competent actor" as a "methodological specialist" because he or she has mastered the rules of action, that is, the "'methodical procedures' of social interaction." To the extent that rules are a component of discursive knowledge, then the same actor is ipso facto (his phrase) a "social theorist." But the theory—rules made discursively explicit—is not necessarily the real rules.

At some point, it seems as if Giddens (1979, pp. 217-218) was tempted to adopt Bourdieu's concept of *habitus* to explain rules. If he did not, it is probably because the word *habit* connotes too strongly individual skills rather than a collectively shared basis of behavior.[5] His point, we should continually bear in mind, is to show how rules, in the quite special way he is using that term, are what explain both the local and the global.

It may help to give an example. Over several centuries, the British empire maintained itself through the presence of administrators scattered across the four corners of the globe (of course, with the army and the navy hovering in the background, but it was the administrators—the "Colonial Office"—that kept things going in the day-to-day). These administrative offices often were staffed by very few people, almost totally cut off from the homeland in a time of painfully slow ocean travel and before electronic communication, and surrounded by vital cultures, often with ancient and well-established traditions of their own (e.g., India or Hong Kong). The temptation to "go native" must often have been very strong (and it was not always resisted), but what is extraordinary is how persistent the patterns of British life, exported from afar, remained in such environments. Of course, this was partly an effect of the imposition of a bureaucratic and legal system on the locals, supported by military conquest. But in the day-to-day, what seems to have made life tenable for the administrators was their stubborn adherence to such classically British practices and habits as tea at 5:00, a gin and orange at 7:00, and dressing for dinner—and, of course, cricket on Sunday afternoon. And now, many, many years after the empire went home licking its wounds, the best cricket players in the world are often found in India, in the West Indies, and in Africa.

Such is the power of rules, as Giddens understands the term, that they can sustain an empire over centuries. Parliament was one of the institutions that got exported. But even Parliament, looked at closely, often owes more to its unspoken practices than to its official "rules and regulations." The patterns of daily parliamentary life—and even the fact of periodic general elections—have become what Giddens (1984) calls "institutionalized practices, that is, practices most deeply sedimented in time-space" (p. 22).[6]

So that is one of the points about rules by Giddens: They are more a part of practical than of discursive consciousness. His second point to do with resources is at least as important: "Rules cannot be conceptualized apart from resources, which refer to the modes whereby transformative relations are actually incorporated into the production and reproduction of social practices" (Giddens, 1984, p. 18). One's first reaction, probably, is to ask what on earth he could possibly mean by "modes whereby transformative relations are actually incorporated into the production and reproduction of social practices"? As we said earlier, reading Giddens is sometimes a practical lesson in hermeneutics—you have to interpret. To get the drift of his meaning, we have to understand a bit better how he uses the term *resources.*

Resources, Giddens thinks, are of two kinds: *allocative* and *authoritative.* Allocative resources are capabilities ("forms of transformative capacity") to generate command over objects, goods, or material phenomena. Authoritative resources are capabilities ("forms of transformative capacity") to generate command over persons or actors.

Now, let us go back to rules. Rules, if they are inseparable from the exploitation of resources, are then always about acting on or transforming something, either material or human. They could be given discursive recognition ("rationalized") and then become rules in the usual connotation of that term, as explicitly setting out the parameters of a game or some other practice (what Searle, 1969, called "constitutive rules"). Or they could be rules constraining individual behavior within certain admitted bounds (what Searle called "regulative rules"). In the latter case, as rationalized (conscious) interpretations of practical (unconsciously followed) rules, they have become what Giddens thinks of as one of the dimensions of his duality of structure construct. Rationalized interpretations of the practical rules that we follow unconsciously become those that have to do with the institutionalized legitimating and sanctioning of activities—like law or science.

But mostly, as we have reiterated, rules remain part of practical knowledge— just how people usually organize their activities. The implication of this practicality is clear: How "command" is generated over both material and human resources, in any society, is an effect of unspoken and in a sense unknown (discursively, that is) routines of social life (i.e., rules).

This kind of control, implicit in routine, is the basis of domination or power as it is expressed in the cut and thrust of human interaction.

Dimensions of Structure

Giddens identifies three "dimensions" of structure, of which *domination* is one (the others are *legitimation* and *signification*). To understand his notion of

40

Dimensions of Structure	Modality	Dimensions of Interaction
Legitimation	*(Norm)*	Sanction
Domination	*(Facility)*	Power
Signification	*(Intrepretive Scheme)*	"Communication"

Figure 2.2. Giddens's Conception of the Duality of Structure

the dimensions of structure, we have to consider what he is trying to accomplish by introducing this idea.

As we have said, the challenge of structuration theory is to encompass within the bounds of a single explanatory framework both the dynamics of ordinary life, at the level of everyday activities, and the institutions of a society. By *institutions,* he means such things as the political system, the economic system, the legal system, and the ideological formations of a society (although he calls the latter "symbolic orders" or "modes of discourse"). Economics, he thinks, get realized in situated interaction by how people carve up *allocative* resources: who owns what, how exchange occurs, and so on. Politics, on the same principle, is expressed in the patterning of *authoritative* resources: who is entitled to exercise authority over whom. Economics and politics combined constitute the exercise of *power* in the usual sense. Law is about *sanctioning*: who gets to pass judgment on whom and on what areas of behavior. Finally, he thinks of people engaged in *communication* as expressing a symbolic order that is characteristic of a given society. The principal elements of his framework are outlined in Figure 2.2.

Giddens insists that there is a sense in which it is artificial to distinguish "dimensions" of structure. Action always incorporates all three dimensions. In practice, as we have seen, the exercise of power is an intrinsic property of action. Action, however, being reflexively grounded in sense-making, also expresses modes of belief or, to use his term for the equivalent structural dimension, *signification.* As we have already observed (see Note 3), accounting for behavior implies not only making sense of it (dimension: signification) but also its justification (dimension: legitimation).

The link between signification and legitimation, as he develops it, is particularly interesting. If most of our knowledge is practical, and if it is the case that not all practical knowledge rises to the surface of our explicit, discursively based consciousness, then it matters what does get discursively recognized. It is the discursively recognized part of knowledge that will go into the formalized structures of legitimation and sanction.[7] But neither signification nor legitimation are independent of domination. If command over both human and material resources is a function of the distribution of resources and, thus, of power, then what gets admitted discursively can hardly be independent of how power is exercised: "Domination . . . is the very condition of existence of codes of signification" (Giddens, 1984, p. 31).

Obviously, the distinction between structure and system is essential if Giddens is to retain the thesis of duality. But it leaves open the question of how structure is translated into system, and vice versa. It is here that he develops the utility of dimensionality, because it addresses the "how" question.

His answer to the translation problem is to introduce a concept that he calls *modality*. There are, he says, three kinds of modality. The structural dimension of legitimation is translated into systemic patterns of sanctioning by the modality of *norms*. The structural dimension of signification is translated into systemic patterns of sense-making (that he calls *communication*) by the modality of *interpretive schemes*. The structural dimension of domination is translated into systemic patterns of power by the modality of *facilities*. (By "facilities," Giddens [1976] means how "participants are able to generate outcomes through affecting the conduct of others; the facilities are both drawn from an order of domination and at the same time, reproduce that order of domination"; p. 122).

Modalities, considered in the abstract as linking system to structure, "represent rules and resources considered as institutional features of systems of social interaction" (Giddens, 1979, p. 81). In other words, as people act, they call on resources to do so, and because the use of resources implies following rules, those resources/rules become in combination the modality by which structure is realized in activity.

Giddens (1984) provides his theory in a nutshell: "The rules and resources drawn upon in the production and reproduction of social action are at the same time the means of system reproduction (the duality of structure)" (p. 19).

◆ Structuration as an Explanation of Computerization

To develop a nondeterministic explanation of the relation between organization and technology, Giddens's theory of structuration provides an ideal scaffolding. By placing purposeful activity at the core, it opens up a means by which to take account of both organizational structure and group interaction within a single conceptual compass. A structurational approach creates the possibility of being able to connect action that is local, time-bound, and situated, with global trends in organizational evolution enduring over time and space, and it also reminds us that structure and the local system of interaction—macro and micro—are inseparably intertwined. It thus potentially explains the computerization of work both in terms of what happens in some particular implementation and what is occurring globally.

Nevertheless, as a theory, it leaves a number of questions unexplored. Although he emphasizes the recursivity and reflexivity of human action, Giddens never provides a clear explanation of the actual dynamic processes by which structure is manifested in systemic interaction and also "reproduced" by it. In the remainder of the chapter, we undertake two tasks: (a) to consider briefly how structuration theory might reinterpret the illustrative cases described in Chapter 1 and (b) to examine some of the features of computerization it does not deal with very well.

How Structuration Might Conceptualize an Instance of Computerization

There is first the matter of recursivity. Here, structuration theory and principles of systems design seem to be in accord. Although Giddens uses the term "system" in a sociological sense, and designers use it in a technical sense, both recognize its basis in the principle of recursivity. Interestingly enough, the use of the term by both Giddens and by the systems designers can be traced back to a similar source. Giddens justifies his use of the concept by a reference to the structuralist theory of language, from which he borrows the notion of *rules of transformation* (1984, p. 17). The most famous natural language linguist of the 20th century, Noam Chomsky, is also the person who, in the early 1950s, wrote the definitive grammar of artificial languages, including those still used in software programming. The grammar of natural language he proposed, like that of artificial languages, was constructed around the mechanism of a recursive function. It was Chomsky who made the term *rules of transformation* a byword in linguistic circles.

So at this level of abstraction, systems and structuration theory are compatible. Both would agree that it is in the recursive reconstruction of action that structures are enabled to transcend the strictly local.

Where they differ is in their conception of action. We already have observed that for Giddens, action is "a continuous flow of 'lived-through experience'; its categorization into discrete sectors or 'pieces' depends upon a reflexive process of attention of the actor, or the regard of another" (1976, p. 74). He also explains it this way:

One's life activity does not consist in a strung-out series of discrete purposes and projects, but in a continuing stream of purposive activity in interaction with others and with the world of nature: a "purposive act," like act-identifications more generally, is only grasped reflexively by the actor, or isolated conceptually by another agent. (Giddens, 1976, p. 82)

And he is also insistent that the context is an "integral part" of interaction, conceived as a communicative encounter (1979, p. 83).

Recall Sachs's (1995) account of the implementation of the new TTS system in the telecommunications firm. Indeed, the work was conceived by the designers of the system as "sectors or pieces," or as "a strung-out series of discrete purposes and projects." The technology, as originally conceived, ignored the principle of "interaction with others" and made no provision for "a reflexive process of attention of the actor" or context as an "integral part" of action. In fact, it deliberately set out to block processes of reflexive sense-making, because communication was seen as time "off-task."

Much the same remark would apply to the other illustrative cases referred to in Chapter 1. If the new 911 system was rejected by active police officers as not "police minded," it was precisely because it short-circuited the usual reflexive monitoring of their own and others' actions and their continual reading of the meaning of a given context. If the nurses boycotted the new patient monitoring system, it was not because they were anti-technology (on the contrary, the technology was the feature that intrigued them) but because the system did not easily fit into their reflexive sense-making activity. In Hovey's case, if the sophisticated GFT encountered so many difficulties that it almost had to be scrapped, it was because it so seriously misread the nature of accounting work in a telecommunications enterprise.

From a structurational perspective, the problems encountered by the implementations were entirely predictable, once we understand that the designers (or the managers who bought the system) went ahead on the assumption that context does not enter into action and thus that intentions can be directly translated into actions. A structurational approach would take it for granted that an ongoing reflexive monitoring of action and context and an interactive application of interpretive procedures are an integral component of action and should figure in the design of a system (an issue to which we return in Chapter 5 when we consider one Scandinavian design group for whom this is indeed a guiding principle).

The difference of perspective is presumably in how Figure 2.1 is read. A system designer typically would read it from left to right: Computer software begins by specifying initial conditions, then performs a sequence of operations ("activities"), and finally conducts a set of tests to determine if the purpose has been realized. Agency is assumed to be built into the program—an intrinsic instrumentality resulting from the activity of the programmer. A structurational approach might well read Figure 2.1 from right to left, in that it would assume that purpose emerges out of activity through reflexive monitoring. Understanding of purpose figures in trying to understand what the "conditions" are. Agency would enter into the process interactively as interpretive schemes come into play and are accepted or rejected. Structuration theory sees the actors as themselves part of what is being constructed reflexively. And, unlike the assumption of knowledge as explicitly discursive (written in computer code), a structurational approach would admit the relevance of tacit, or "practical," knowledge. The "rules" of the system designer resemble very little those that Giddens describes; they are too cut-and-dried.

There are other differences. Perhaps the most important is that the systems approach denies duality. Duality assumes that structure and system are mutually interdependent. It is their ability to affect each other, reciprocally, that explains social dynamics. In systems logic, structure informs system, in that recursive procedures are assumed to inform local practices. But there is no provision for the local system that develops around such procedures to be reflected in structure. Structure has been "written into" the program. Thus, structures of domination, legitimation, and signification (to use Giddens's terms) are produced, but not *re*-produced. Implied is a rigidity that Giddens was endeavoring to circumvent.

Giddens reasons that the institutions of a society exist only in their actualization in the interactive arena of practical action. This implies that telecommunications technicians and clerks, police officers and nurses (to use our examples) live in a world informed by structures of signification, domination, and legitimation. It is a moral universe, and the people in it are those who reproduce its structures every day in their own intelligent self-monitoring activities. A technology that makes no sense in that moral, structured universe is going to be judged as illegitimate, as incompatible with the appropriate role of hierarchy, and ultimately as sense-less. Any design that assumes the structuring of an organization as what management does is guilty of dualism and is likely to be rejected.

What Structuration Theory Does Not Address

In Chapter 3, we consider some of the ways structurational theory could be strengthened. These include the following additions.

The structuring of time and space. Giddens emphasizes the role of time and space in mediating action but he is less than explicit on how this occurs. Suchman's (1996) work assumes that much of what Giddens thinks of as tacit or practical knowledge is embedded in the physical settings of work. Space, she argues, enters purposive action in a positive way. Structure, in other words, may be embedded in artifacts to produce a comprehensible world of meaning. Similarly, time becomes structured by the narrative reconstruction of events. Giddens tends to think of structure as "instantiated" in "memory traces," a psychological notion. Suchman sees it as instantiated in physical and temporal settings.

Knowledge is a collective achievement. Hutchins (1995) argues for a quite different view. He sees cognition not as what occurs within someone's head but as an ongoing transformation of representations of the environment that occurs in large part publicly, through people interacting, and using artifacts designed to aid in the conduct of computational tasks (of which there are many in our society). For Hutchins, as for Suchman (1996), artifacts reflect the history of their making in their construction and thus become the instruments of constructive action. Technology is seen as itself an agency. Giddens is limited in his conceptualization by treating "agent" as a synonym of "actor." He thus refers to collaborative action but never really theorizes it. His concept of communication is thus unduly restricted to exchanging the products of cognition. He fails to see communication as itself a form of cognition.

Agency as a complex of actors. Even though his theory hinges on the role of rules and resources in realizing action, Giddens, as we already remarked, skirts the issue of technology. Engeström (1990) builds his conceptualization of action around a triadic linking of subject, object, and tool. Thus, he makes technology an integral component of agency: actors and tools as mutually defining. Engeström also introduces a fourth component, *community.* In this manner, he fills in a further missing element in structuration theory as defined by Giddens. Society for Giddens is abstract—a virtuality present in the activity of people. He has notably little to say about the intermediate agency of organization. By introducing a concept of community, Engeström thus enlarges the scope of theory to include collective actors. Engeström's other major contribution is to have observed that the structures of society are inherently contradictory, that people live at the intersection of such contradictions (and are often aware that they do), and that contradiction is the motor of change. This latter theme, contradiction, becomes the cornerstone of our own explanation of the computerization phenomenon.

The symmetry of human and nonhuman. Giddens's portrayal of the relation between action and intentionality is sometimes ambiguous. On the one hand, he sees all action as imbued with human intentionality. Intentionality even figures in the definition of action. On the other hand, he recognizes that action has consequences, even when it is not motivated by intention. Latour (1994) has no such doubts. For him, whatever acts is entitled to be attributed agency, and in our world many nonhuman constructions act, in the sense of having effects. Latour then broadens the concept of agency to take account of the enrollment of others as a means to create collaborative action—and actors. The resulting pattern of enrollment offers a clarification of the concept of recursivity. Using Latour as our point of departure, we then introduce a concept of the relation of head and complement, as the indispensable agencies in the realization of action. In Chapter 4, this becomes the basis of our own theory of co-orientation.

The embedding of technology in infrastructure. Star and her collaborators contributed four additional insights. First, she observes that organizations are made up of communities of discourse that link to each other through a shared preoccupation with some "boundary object." (This is a topic we discuss in depth in Chapters 6 and 8.) She then observes that the standardization that both management and systems design aims at is achieved through classification of people and their activities, and that classification becomes a potent resource in the exercise of power. (The concept of classification becomes yet another key element in the system of explanation we develop in Chapter 4.) She introduces the concept of infrastructure as technology that is already embedded in spheres of activity, against which the applicability of new technology is judged. Finally, with Ruhleder, she proposes a complex model of learning that we use as the basis of our own evaluation of the computerization experience (Chapter 8).

In addition to these revisions of structuration theory, there is one other limitation of Giddens's original elaboration that needs to be mentioned, because it is in this respect that we hope to make our own contribution.

Communication as the essential modality of structuration. Although, as we have seen, modality is identified as the central mechanism whereby structure is linked to interaction, the concept is left curiously undeveloped by Giddens. Its presentation takes up no more that a page or two in any of his books, and, in each case, the notion of "modality" is defined in a cursory fashion. In his 1984 book, for example, he writes, "Modalities of structuration serve to clarify the main dimensions of the duality of structure in interaction" (p. 28). He explains that this is how "the knowledgeable capacities of agents" are related to "structural features" (p. 28). He speaks of actors "drawing on" the modalities of structuration. In his 1979 book, he writes that the modalities "are the media of the reproduction of the structural components of systems of interaction" (p. 81). Yet, how the reproduction takes place is left unclear.

The problem, in our view, is his restricted conception of communication. For Giddens, communication is treated only as the modality of interpretation of the circumstances of activity—the dimension of signification. From our perspective, communication is also the modality of domination and legitimation: how authority is exercised and discipline enforced. Communication, in other words, is the modality that explains the ongoing restructuring of society. When we have understood how communication works, we will have a handle on the organizing (or structuring) processes of organization.

In the two next chapters, we undertake a considerable revision of Giddens's version of structuration theory. Our version involves a reinterpretation of the concept of interaction as what we call *conversation. Interaction,* for Giddens, is an exchange among agents—interpersonal communication. Conversation, in our theory, is where agency is constructed: where circumstances are interpreted, structures of authority expressed and developed, and behavior sanctioned both positively and negatively. All these things take place in and through interactive speech. Two features of this enlargement of the conception of structuration should be flagged here.

First, Giddens is concerned to relate structure (in the singular) and system. As we discover in Chapter 3, Engeström argues for structures (in the plural). If society is characterized by structures in the plural, then they may well prove to be contradictory. They may even impose paradoxical conditions on people's activities: *double binds* (Star & Ruhleder, 1996). One of the questions we explore is whether computerization has not in fact been a source of organizational double binds and whether this may not furnish an explanation for some of the results on which we have reported.

We add a further dimension, that of *text.* This represents an extension of an idea developed by Bowker and Star (1999). Text, we argue, is an instantiation of structure and how the diverse communities of discourse of an organization are stitched together to form an organization. If, as we believe, text is an essential modality for the transmission of structure, and if computer-based systems are carriers of such a text, then we need to understand the different contexts of integration of the systems into the organizing processes of organization. A critical element in this is the quite different role text plays in local and global processes of organizing. We argue that this difference, which we explore in several chapters, is a fertile source of contradictions and makes learning a complex inter-related process, with multiple possibilities of confusion.

Technology is largely ignored by Giddens, but in our theory I/CT are a medium of communication and a carrier of structure. Where contradictions already exist, the implementation of a new I/CT system may aggravate existing tensions and reveal fault lines that were not previously visible.

Finally, our reconstruction of the theory of structuration is built around a concept of co-orientation. Although Giddens distinguishes clearly between allocative and authoritative resources and develops the notion of a dialectic of control, he does not pursue the linking of allocative and authoritative as a potential source of contradictions and power plays. This becomes a very important component in our own version of the theory.

◆ Notes

1. Giddens's tendencies are even more eclectic than this would suggest. His intellectual packrat proclivities have been analyzed by Craib (1992) under the heading of making a "theoretical omelette." Other influences on Giddens's thought include the linguistic philosophy of Wittgenstein and Winch, the phenomenology of Heidegger, Erikson on psychoanalysis, the hermeneutics of Gadamer, the structuralism of de Saussure and Lévi-Strauss, the poststructuralism of Derrida and Kristeva, Marxism, and time-geography as interpreted by Hagerstrand. These are what Craib called the "good eggs"; the "bad eggs" are positivism and functionalism.

2. There are a number of excellent summaries of Giddens's theory. One of the most readable is that of Banks and Riley (1993). Also recommended are McPhee (1989) and Orlikowski (1992). For more extensive treatment, see Clegg (1989), Cohen (1989), Held and Thompson (1989), Clark, Modgil, and Modgil (1990), Bryant and Jary (1991), and Craib (1992), the latter being possibly the most readable of this group of books. A four-volume collection of articles of published commentaries on Giddens's work appeared under the editorship of Bryant and Jary (1996). Mestrovic (1998) published a highly critical analysis of his work from the perspective of his views on modernity. Barley's 1986 study is perhaps the first ethnographically oriented interpretation of structuration theory (see also Barley, 1990), and the work of Poole, DeSanctis, McPhee, Seibold and their associates is the most prolonged effort to give it new meaning by translating it into an experimental paradigm for research. Orlikowski's work is perhaps the most directly relevant to readers of this book (Orlikowski, 1991; Orlikowski, 1992; Orlikowski & Baroudi, 1991; Orlikowski & Robey, 1991; Orlikowski, Yates, Okamura, & Fujimoto, 1994). The main sources we draw on are three texts in which Giddens develops the essential of his theory: his 1976 *New Rules of Sociological Method,* his 1979 *Central Problems in Social Theory,* and his 1984 *The Constitution of Society.*

3. As Giddens (1984) puts it, "To be 'accountable' for one's activities is both to explicate the reasons for them and to supply the normative grounds whereby they may be 'justified'" (p. 30).

4. In part, Giddens's reflections on this subject are his response to Parsons, who had argued that what makes individual behavior socially conforming is the "internalization" of norms. Giddens sees norms as boundary conditions, in that people may be aware of norms and yet not behave according to them, without exhibiting delinquent behavior. Norms, of course, are easily transformed into laws, regulations, and rules, all of which people generally treat as an external source of constraint. They are not part of practical knowledge. Giddens, reflecting the influence of Wittgenstein, thus sees society as more diverse in its rule-following than does Parsons.

5. Barley (1986) prefers the term *script* to that of rules. The concept of script was developed by Schank and Abelson (1977) to explain how people are capable of behaving in, and making sense of, a restaurant—how they know how to order, when to pay, how much to tip, and so forth.

6. For analysis of the role of ritual in parliamentary procedure, see Cooren and Taylor (1999).

7. As Giddens (1984) wrote, "Most of the rules implicated in the production and reproduction of social practices are only tacitly grasped by actors: They know how to 'go on.' *The discursive formulation of a rule is already an interpretation of it*" (p. 22).

3

Expanding the
Structurational Perspective

◆   The theory of Giddens is like a scaffolding of a new building. The evidence of structure is there, but one is left to imagine how the building will eventually look, once the walls, the roof, the rooms, and all the other parts have been put into place. In this chapter, we begin to add some specifics to the theory, drawing on work of a number of researchers, all of whom think in what might broadly be called "structurational" terms, even though none of them is counted (or think of themselves) as one of the disciples of Giddens. We address the concerns we expressed at the end of Chapter 2 to fill in some of the empty spaces in the theory. In particular, we consider, in turn, the importance of locally situated action as a locus of structure, the enlargement of the concept of agency to include collective actors, and the role of text in organizational communication.

◆ The Structuring of Situated Action

The theory of structuration, as enunciated by Giddens, emphasizes the degree to which structure informs the dynamics of locally situated activity, but it is less than obvious from his presentation how this occurs. Recent ethnographic research (Goodwin & Goodwin, 1996; Heath & Luff, 1996; Hutchins & Klausen, 1996; Suchman, 1996) provides a much more convincing picture of the embedded structure of purposeful work. It reinforces the concept of duality of structure and gives it a new dimension. The work of Suchman in documenting the responsive dynamics of work in an airport operations center provides an excellent illustration, well adapted to our purposes. Giddens insists on the role of time and space in structuration; Suchman's study strongly supports this perspective and clarifies its application to real-life contexts of work.

51

The study in question (Suchman, 1996; see also Suchman & Trigg, 1991) is based on observations of work in the operations room of an airline at a midsized metropolitan airport in the United States—responsible for getting passengers on and off planes, loading and unloading baggage and meals, running the coordination of ticket operations with flights, and so on. The analysis focuses on one incident in the life of the room, taking up no more than about 5 minutes of time, but on its basis Suchman made a number of observations that illustrate very well the situated action perspective she and her collaborators have been developing.

Briefly summarized, the episode in question goes as follows. A scheduled flight pulls into one of the airline's airport gates and the set of stairs that is supposed to provide for passenger unloading breaks down. Personnel in the operations room now have to mobilize a variety of resources to deal with the emergency. Maintenance has to be contacted, the pilot has to be kept advised, other airlines have to be solicited for the loan of a compatible unit of mobile stairs. Maintenance eventually succeeds in replacing a defective pump, and the crisis dissolves back into routine work.

The Role of Time and Space in Embedding Structure

On the surface, this is a banal story of a minor foul-up that was dealt with as expeditiously as could be expected—a small delay in getting the passengers off a plane. But Suchman finds in it matter to support her principal thesis, which is that work activity is inevitably situated. It always occurs in some place, at some time. The "place" is a structured physical world that is adapted to the purposes of the activity. The "time" is also structured in that it is punctuated into a sequence consisting of a beginning, a middle, and an end. So what Suchman means by "situated" incorporates assumptions of built-in structure.

Her analysis develops along these two dimensions of time and space. Neither dimension, she argues, is a preestablished given; each has to be constructed from within the flow of activity (in Giddens's terms, through "reflexive monitoring"). Consider first the question of time. The central point is that it is an incident, and so it is characterized by a beginning, a middle, and an end. First, "the trouble [must] be noticed, formulated and brought to the attention of relevant others" (Suchman, 1996, p. 37). Once collective attention has been focused on the "trouble," then "whatever human and technological resources might contribute to its resolution [must] be mobilized" (p. 37). (Note here the linking of human and technological; this is not just interpersonal communication, but an interactive sequence in which the resources of the physical world are as much active agents as the people who use them.) Finally, "the consequences of those mobilizations

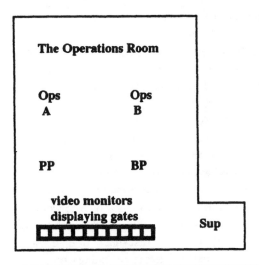

Figure 3.1. The Physical Disposition of the Operations Room of "Atlantic" Airlines
Adapted from Suchman (1996); used by permission of Cambridge University Press.

[must] be monitored and assessed for the resolution that could occur at any time, rendering further mobilization and coordination unnecessary" (p. 37). They have to know when the crisis is over, which means being able to distinguish how things are supposed to run, and when they are not doing so.

Similarly, the dimension of space is conceived as a constructed environment of work. Figure 3.1 is a simplified picture of the arrangement of people in the operations room.

In Figure 3.1, there are five workers sharing a common space without partitions. Each has his or her own workspace with its equipment, but in another sense the room is co-owned because it gets periodically rearranged depending on circumstances (e.g., the absence of someone from the room). Those stationed there are the passenger service planner (PP), responsible for monitoring booking and rebooking of passengers and connections between flights; Operations A (Ops A), responsible for monitoring incoming flights and communicating with pilots via radio and computerized telecommunications; baggage planner (BP), responsible for loading, unloading, and transfer of bags and, thus, for communications with the ramp crew; Operations B (Ops B), who coordinates servicing of an affiliated airline; and the supervisor (Sup) for ramp services, who has overall responsibility for the work of the operations room. Figure 3.1 shows their respective locations and also indicates the bank of television monitors, which is the only direct visual contact all have with what is occurring on the loading and unloading surface of the tarmac.

Suchman (1996) observes that these different stations of work are both autonomous and linked. Furthermore, they are "doubly articulated" (Silverstone, Hirsch, & Morley, 1992), in that there is an ecology of the room itself, but it is also media-linked to other airport operations, of which it forms, in the logic of work, an integral part. What is significant in the analyzed episode is how these intersecting worlds of work flow into each other in response to a "trouble" such as the breakdown at the ramp and then branch back out into separate streams of work when the crisis has been resolved. The structuredness of situated work is both local and contextual: both the internal systemic dynamics of the collaborative work team and how they relate to their outside world.

Suchman (1996) uses voice recordings of the work conversation aimed at resolving the crisis to illustrate. The first sign of trouble is a call from the pilot of the arriving flight to signal that there is something wrong with the stairs ("Would you send somebody out here the, ah, agent working the *jet*way here is running around with their *hands* up in the air"; Suchman, 1996, pp. 38-39). Although it is received on a radio channel by Ops A, and although the other members of the team seem to be according it no particular attention, they can all hear it, and their subsequent responses indicate they have been paying at least peripheral attention.

It is this bifocality of collective work contexts that Suchman means to address. As the conversation between the pilot and Ops A is going on, for example, Ops B (who otherwise has no role to play in the ensuing drama) nevertheless remarks "Must be Sarducci" (his way of speculating as to which gate is involved, because that is still not clear at this point). Immediately afterward, PP is drawn in, and it is he who radios the "lead" of the ramp crew. Then the supervisor enters the interaction, involving an actual physical change of location to place himself closer to the action, better positioned to view the monitors and interact verbally with the others. At this point, the interaction broadens to link by phone and radio with maintenance, with a second airline, and with the pilot. Eventually, everyone except Ops B is involved, as Sup brings BP into the circle of concern, accompanied by a light hand on the shoulder to get her attention. It all occurs in an instant, and then, 5 minutes later, everyone is back at their stations as if nothing had happened. Just another routine crisis!

From her analysis of the sequence, Suchman draws two lessons. First, there is a distinction between the usual and the exceptional. When everything is going as it should, that whole background of available resources that was needed to meet the crisis simply fades from view. It becomes transparent—for the moment, out of sight, out of mind.

Second—and this is an insistent theme in Suchman's account—"the physical space of a worksite comprises a complex of equipment and action or spatial orders produced in and informed by the knowledgeable practices of setting members" (p. 35). Citing Lynch (1991, 1993), she uses phrases such as "siting of knowledge production" (p. 35), "topical contextures associated with indigenous orders of equipment and practice" (p. 35), and "locally meaningful forms of lived activity" (p. 35). She cites Lave (1988) who, she noted, argued that "the classical notion of problem solving misconceives and mislocates processes of practical reasoning, being blind to their social and material grounds and assigning to them a primarily mental locus within the heads of individuals" (p. 56). As opposed to that tradition, Suchman (1996) focuses on what she calls "structuring resources, that is, culturally constituted relations of persons, settings, and activity" (p. 56). Problem solving becomes "'part of an articulatory phenomenon constituted between persons-acting and the settings of activity' (Lave, 1988, p. 159). Dilemmas are not so much solved as they are 'dissolved' through structuring resources inventively employed" (Suchman, 1996, p. 56).

This is a radical move in that it decenters our attention away from the individual task, not onto the group, as we have over the years read about in the group problem-solving literature, but onto something with a more hybrid character: part human, part technology, part acquired culture, part configuring of the physical space in which work goes on, part how action is framed semantically to give it a shape and meaning. The focus shifts away from the individual workers to the interactive processes of which they are a part, but no more than a part. The defective set of stairs was as much an actor in the microdrama Suchman described as any of the humans involved. But so was the ecology of the operations center, because it functioned not just as a room with certain "objective" geometric properties but an active participant in the subsequent structuring of the essential interaction. And, of course, this was no accident, because everyone and everything in the work context was a carrier of well-established practice. As she puts it, "The systematic organization of work is a systematic organization of space as well" (Suchman, 1996, p. 42):

> The workspace afforded by the operations room is not simply given by the room's interior design, but is a collaborative achievement involving the continuous production and transformation of personal space, of spaces jointly held, and of the boundaries between them. As a center of coordination for activities distributed in space and time, the operations room displays in its design the competing requirements of joint work and of a division of labor; of a single, common focus and a discontinuous ordering of differentiated workspaces. (Suchman, 1996, p. 57)

Attention shifts away from the individual in another respect. Throughout her analysis, Suchman emphasizes the subtle interplay of individual and collective attention or the importance of *co-orientation* in the accomplishment of work (a "single, common focus"). Depending on the context, although the orientation may sometimes be individual, it is always potentially joint, always "incipiently shared" (p. 43). This is what she is getting at when she describes the situation that initiated the response to the emergency. The pilot's call may have been received by one person, Ops A, but everyone was potentially aware of its consequences. They have what she calls "a common state of readiness." Like the rest of the background (maintenance crews, other airlines), it is not something that would be instantly evident to the casual observer, but it is this common state of readiness of all these elements that explains the flexibility of work being performed by experienced hands, as well as its efficiency. Teamwork is like an orchestra in its capacity to shift register from unaccompanied solo to a thundering crescendo in the space of an auditor's breath.

Suchman's work and that of her coresearchers gives new meaning to Giddens's (1984) concept of practical knowledge, by which he means the inherent "capability to 'go on' within the routines of social life" (p. 4). But in thus enriching the theoretical insights of the original formulation by the addition of an empirical perspective, it also throws a light on the problem of the systems designer (such as we described in Chapter 1 for Hovey's study of an administration tool for a telecommunications company). If the "needs and requirements analysis" of traditional systems design (the kind of thing the systems designers did in Hovey's example) is based on an assessment of individual tasks, then it inevitably will misconstrue the circumstantiality of work. It will have left unrecorded the potential of systems of situated interaction that have the capability to develop responses to both the routine and the nonroutine in the flow of events.

Collaborating Groups as Systems of Distributed Cognition

One of the emphases of the explication of structuration theory by Giddens (1984) that we do not share is his siting of the "instantiations" of structure in the "memory traces" of individuals (p. 25). The focus on the individual seems in part to stem from his desire to link his treatment with considerations of depth psychology and individual motivation and in part from his impoverished vision of communication. Whatever the reason, the result is to correlate knowledge with individual cognitive processes, reducing communication to the exchange of already formulated thoughts. The vision of knowledge development we turn to now leads us to a very different and more situated concept of cognition. The work we look at also has a strong ethnographic component, but it is also part of the growing literature on the relation of human to artificial cognition. The leading exponent of this view is Edwin Hutchins (1995; Hutchins & Klausen, 1996).

The choice of the term *cognition* is no accident. Distributed cognition is a theory of how teams of skilled workers transform a differentiated knowledge of a situation into a unified response to it. Unlike Suchman, Hutchins (1995) has no hesitancy in using terms such as *computation* to describe such a transformative process. But his view of both cognition and computation is unconventional. Cognition, as the term has typically been employed in the psychological literature, is usually taken to refer to mental processes, occurring in the head of some individual. Cognition for Hutchins is not head-bound but located in the communicational patterns of the working group. Similarly, computation typically has been taken to be what computers do as they run through their programmed routines. Once again, this is a view Hutchins seeks to transcend.

A key reference point in understanding the argument of Hutchins is the work of a distinguished psychologist of perception, David Marr. Marr (1982) laid out general principles of vision, grounded in his understanding of the basic pattern of processing information, as a cognitive phenomenon.[1] What is common to all the activities of seeing is what Hutchins and Klausen (1996), citing Marr, call "the propagation of a representational state across a series of representational media" (p. 19). Cognition thus involves turning a source of data into an interpretation, through successive representations of the data. Each new "representation" results in the foregrounding of "a different sort of information."

In vision research, this is equivalent to tracking how the stimuli that impinge on the retina are recoded in the neural networks of the perceiver until they are mapped onto a recognition of the object.[2] But although Marr's (1982) model may have been inspired by his psychological preoccupations, the principle that underlies it is generalizable to other forms of cognition.

In his book, Hutchins (1995) traces the "propagation of representational states" that is characteristic of the navigational location "fix" cycle of a naval vessel as it enters San Diego harbor. Observations of different landmarks are made by seamen stationed on deck using specialized sighting equipment. They are then verbally transmitted to a navigation room, where they are manually transcribed using special equipment onto a nautical chart, which furnishes a map of the harbor. Positions and angles are transformed trigonometrically by the map to locate the exact position of the ship. In the process, a number of media come into play, including the sighting equipment (in effect, specialized lenses with coordinates of location printed on the surface), the human voice, and the chart itself. The chart is a miracle of ingenuity, patiently perfected over centuries of seafaring so that when the sighting information has been inscribed on it by the navigators, the location of the ship will be self-evident (this is why it is a "fix").

Presented in this way, it is apparent that navigation is a form of cognition that involves seeing, but it is not limited to recognizing the positions of external landmarks (that would be individual cognition). Such "positions," once recorded, have to be combined or triangulated so as to make sense of them as a position, not of the observer on the deck, but of the ship with respect to the harbor. Although individuals are involved, and they undoubtedly use their inborn cognitive apparatus, the cognitive process of which they form a part is not "in the head." On the contrary, the whole point of navigational technology is to take it out of the head, with the result that, other than in situations of emergency, none of the navigators, as individuals, is at any point called on to do heavy-duty computational thinking (even though navigation implies complicated mathematical computations). They are, for the most part, themselves serving as media, like their equipment. It is this hybrid character of representational media that leads Hutchins and his collaborators to speak of cognition as "distributed."

Two other facets of Hutchins's theory need to be flagged here. The first is that it is a cycle that he is describing. The propagation of representational states is not, in other words, random. It is highly patterned—a characteristic of most work and an explanation of how it turns into routine. It is the well-learned routineness of work that forms the background against which to recognize a situation when it arises and to alert those involved that it is time to deal with an instance of nonroutine (as Suchman's study illustrates).

The second point Hutchins makes is in some ways merely an expansion of the first, namely, that activity is goal-oriented. The facts of the situation are grist for the mill, but the conclusion they lead to is always an action to be taken. This being said, however, the goal is a system goal, not that of any single individual. In a separate study of the operations of an airline crew in flight, Hutchins and Klausen (1996) observe,

> The question of interest to you as a passenger should not be whether a particular pilot is performing well, but whether or not the system that is composed of the pilots and the technology of the cockpit environment is performing well. [3] (p. 16)

Because it is a system of distributed cognition, involving both individual and collective task performance ("autonomously in parallel") as well as technology, and because it is all based on the "propagation of representational states across a series of representational media," the critical issue of design is, Does the propagation work? For it to work, there has to be, Hutchins thinks (and Suchman would agree), a good deal of built-in redundancy or duplication of information. Any datum—a voice message on a radio channel, for example—may be monitored by more than one person and needs to be understood by each of them in terms of what they know about their own task and of the performance of the system as a whole. The result of the parallel processing of the same information by several people is a more robust system of cognition, better able to detect error and offering more efficient coordination of interlocked tasks.

In a theory of distributed cognition, technology is one component in the transformative chain. For Hutchins, a nautical chart is not just an instrument, passively lending itself to the navigator's needs, but a powerful actor in its own right, in that the whole cycle is built around it to take advantage of its special properties—its capacity to transform one set of representations, a collection of sightings, into another kind of representation, in which the location of the ship is portrayed on a map, longitudinally and latitudinally fixed:

> We may attempt to put temporal bounds on the computation that we observe now, today, in any way we like, but we will not understand that computation until we follow its history back and see how structure has been accumulated over centuries in the organization of the material and ideational means in which the computation is actually implemented. This is a truly cultural effect. This collection through time of partial solutions to frequently encountered problems is what culture does for us. (Hutchins, 1995, p. 168)

For Hutchins, the concept of computation can only be understood properly when the machinery is seen in the situated context of its use, as part of a system in which the data of the situation are turned into a solution to a problem of work—to get things done. It is not computers that compute, he argues, but computers-in-a-context, linked to users who are themselves part of the computational activity.

There is one last observation to be made on the theory of distributed cognition. It is a theory of cognition and of computation, but what may be less self-evident is that it is also a theory of communication: "The communicative acts of the members of the navigation team are not just about the computation; they *are* the computation" (Hutchins, 1995, p. 283). This is to portray communication in a very special light, not as interpersonal exchange but as stages in the transformation of one kind of representation of states (data or facts) into another (a conclusion or a solution). (This is a concept we develop in depth in Chapter 4.) We are obliged to see communication in relation to the doing of work and to be more sensitive to the mediating properties of both the human and nonhuman media that are involved. It is a decentering away from individual motive to systemic purpose and a recognition of the role of culture, not just as a background to communicational practices but as an active participant in them.

In the descriptions of situated work by both Suchman and Hutchins, structure is not only to be found in the learned responses of individuals to situations ("instantiated as memory traces"), nor even in the interaction patterns of members of the collaborative group. It is inscribed in the physical accoutrements of work, both as a working environment and as its accustomed technology. How deeply embedded such structure may be is part of what Hutchins aims to show. The naval chart that is at the heart of navigation has taken centuries to perfect. Structures so deeply engrained in practice, one might suspect, do not lend themselves to rapid and dramatic transformation without a considerable upheaval. If work is a seamless interface of individual effort, collective interaction and mediation by resources deeply embedded in time and space, then change does not occur in the absence of learning.

The researchers we now consider have made this order of change, and its explanation, their object of investigation. What we have been calling "structures deeply embedded in practice" they call infrastructure. The question they ask is, how and when does an infrastructure change?

The "When" of Infrastructure

For Star and Ruhleder (1996), infrastructure is the key concept in explaining the adoption or nonadoption of a new technology. Technology is not a collection of inert artifacts, whose use is defined or fixed at the moment of their making: their meaning as tools has to be validated in the context of an activity. Infrastructure is not merely a composite of physical equipment and networks. It is "something that emerges for people in practice, connected to activities and structures" (Star & Ruhleder, 1996, p. 112). Tools that are not used do not count as infrastructure, even when it might seem to the outsider observer that they should, or could, be. If we are asking how technology affects organization and organizational transformation, then the issue is not how the introduction of a predefined system of machinery (independent variable) affects a predefined organization (dependent variable), but how and when technology becomes infrastructure in the actual contexts of constructive work.

To put the idea in the simplest possible terms: Star and Ruhleder (1996) maintain that tools become infrastructure at the moment they have become transparent, or "invisible." To understand what they mean by invisible, however, it is not sufficient to think of infrastructure merely as "something that is built and maintained, and which then sinks into the invisible background . . . something that is just there, ready-to-hand, completely transparent" (Star & Ruhleder, 1996, p. 112). That idea is fine as far as it goes, but it tends to obscure a second vital principle, which is that tools become infrastructure "in relation to organized practices" (Star & Ruhleder, 1996, p. 113). A technology that is easy to integrate in one context may present a major problem of adoption in another.

Another important insight Star and Ruhleder's (1996) work contributes is to emphasize the interdependency of the locally situated work scene with larger technological configurations and extended networks of interconnection. *Infrastructure,* as they describe it, "is 'sunk' into, inside of, other structures, social arrangements and other technologies" (p. 113). It is part of an environment larger than the strictly local work site (i.e., it is more like an air traffic system than a local network). When you become a member of an extended community of practice, familiarity with its workings is part of what you have to learn. Because it is shaped and activated by conventions of practice that extend beyond the local, infrastructure thus becomes a prime target for standardization—systems design, new technology.

Nevertheless, however elegant the design for the extended network of technology may be, it still has to work locally. One must take account of the situatedness of work. It is for this reason that Star and Ruhleder (1996) maintain that a technology is a candidate to become so much part of our work environment that we take it for granted at exactly that moment when the tension between local and global is resolved. By this, they mean that infrastructure becomes transparent when local practices are "afforded," or enabled, by a larger-scale technology, which can then be used in a natural, ready-to-hand fashion.[4] The technology becomes transparent as local variations are folded into organizational changes and become an "unambiguous home"—for somebody to occupy.

Transparency is not a permanent physical location, however, but a working relationship, "since no home is universal" (Star & Ruhleder, 1996, p. 114). The tension between local and global will be felt differently from one community of practice to another, and thus its resolution point can vary greatly from one environment to another. It is on the basis of this principle that Star and Ruhleder draw a lesson about workplace technology development—as a gradual enfolding of local variations within more encompassing processes of organizational change. They hypothesize, on the basis of their findings, "that highly structured applications for collaboration will fail to become integrated into local work practices" (p. 132). Instead, they think successful technology will emerge out of "a complex constellation of locally-tailored applications and repositories, combined with pockets of local knowledge and expertise" (p. 132).

How is a new technology transformed into infrastructure? This can be phrased as a question of learning. Star and Ruhleder (1996) borrow Bateson's (1972) classification of different "orders" of learning, according to their level of abstraction and complexity.

First-order learning issues are those that have to do with responding to problems within an established routine and in an already defined context. Second-order learning issues are those that have to do with adopting new routines, and reframing context to meet the challenge of a changed environment. Third-order issues of learning are more abstract, in that they raise questions about the nature of learning and thus lead to an interrogation of the fundamental bases of one's adaptation to the world.

To apply this concept of orders of learning to organization, we have to think of organizational learning as a multilevel problem of synchronization of the different levels of local and global adaptation to its environment. For learning to occur at one level—let us say the individual—there must be equivalent transformations taking place at other levels—the group, for example. For the individual, first-order learning involves no more than dealing with contingencies as they arise within an established context of collaborative group work. Second-order learning at the individual level implies, on Bateson's (1972) definition, changing the context, and that will be difficult to achieve if the group is not simultaneously adopting new routines and ways of interacting. Similarly, group learning implies a changed organizational context. Unless the organization's structures, procedures, hierarchies, and rules are transformed, the creativity of the group is stifled. On the other hand, radical organizational change of the kind advocated by Zuboff, Hammer, and others (see Chapter 1) will be frustrated unless it is correlated with an equivalent transformation at the level of working groups.

Star and Ruhleder's (1996) point is that we will not have understood the dynamics of implementation of new technologies unless we take account of this interdependence of orders of learning and levels of the organization. To an important degree, this interdependence is the theme of this book. The empirical studies we present later are all focused on this theme.

Structure (Singular)—or Structures (Plural)?

The presentation of the duality of structure by Giddens tends to leave the impression that structure is a property of society-in-the-large. He is impelled in this direction by his preoccupation with all-encompassing institutional realities of modernity, including its economic and political system, and its ideological grounding in a set of beliefs typical of the industrial world. But if structure is so strongly embedded in the everyday practices of people at work, and if there are so many different kinds of work, and if each is interdependent on more global systems of activity, then it would be astonishing to find only one "structure." The author we are about to consider, Yrjø Engeström, sees the issue of structure differently, as a moving target. Engeström is a leading advocate of "activity theory."

According to Engeström, all systems of activity have embedded in them inherent contradictions that reflect underlying conflicting structural realities: "An activity system is not a homogeneous entity. To the contrary, it is comprised of a multitude of often disparate elements, voices and viewpoints" (Engeström, 1990, p. 94).

As an instance, Engeström analyzes the protocols of a medical practitioner in a state system of health care (Finland). As he listens attentively to the words of the doctor, he hears more than one voice. One of those voices is that of the professional caregiver. But another voice can also sometimes be heard, that of an employee of a large modern bureaucracy under pressure to maximize the number of interviews and minimize costs spent on the patient. How does one reconcile being simultaneously a caregiver and a profit center?[5]

One way to understand the source of these contradictions, Engeström (1990) asserts, is to see them in a historical perspective as "sediments of earlier historical modes, as well as buds or shoots of its possible future" (p. 94).

The concept of systemic contradiction can equally well be illustrated by an example drawn from computerization. Both Zuboff (1996) and Hammer (1996), as we saw in Chapter 1, perceive the instrumentality of the new information and communication technologies as being in outright contradiction with the established principles of division of labor of 20th-century administrative practice and its rules of procedure. As these authors interpret the present situation, a hierarchical division of labor impedes the ability of workers to carry out their tasks professionally. Administrative rules contradict the principle of putting the customer first and thus lead to less-than-optimal outcomes. The form into which the community has evolved as a result of previous patterns of organizing is now contradicted by the technology, which favors horizontal over vertical modes of information exchange and control. The proposed new culture of management is a contradiction of the previous. This is a theme to which we return, especially in our final chapter, where we interpret computerization as a source of contradiction in a way quite different from that of Zuboff and BPR.

By his introduction of a historical perspective in which successive cultural modes of work practice come to cohabit the domain of activity, and as they do so create contradictions that are reflected in the day-to-day of ordinary work, Engeström provides himself with a way of explaining the persistence of patterns of work performance over time, but also with a mechanism of change. It might appear, he says (again using recorded transcripts as confirming evidence), that people are just going through the routine once again. But this is to miss the point, not only that there are contradictions, but also that practitioners feel them:

> These . . . contradictions of the activity are the moving force behind disturbances and innovations, and eventually behind the change and development of the system. They cannot be eliminated or fixed with separate remedies. They get aggravated over time and eventually tend to lead to an overall crisis of the activity system. In this process, practitioners may experience them as overwhelming "double binds," dilemmas where all available alternatives are equally unacceptable. (Engeström, 1990, p. 84)

As a result,

> Between the components of an activity system, continuous construction is going on. The human beings not only use instruments, they also continuously renew and develop them, whether consciously or not. They not only obey rules, they also mold and reformulate them—and so on. . . . An activity system is not only a persistent formation; it is also a creative, novelty-producing formation. (Engeström, 1990, p. 80)

In their own way, each of these authors has emphasized, in a manner different from that of Giddens, the centrality of communication in the structuring of activity. This constitutes a very important shift of perspective away from the individual and onto the group. The effect is to remind us that, once embedded, structures that are inscribed in group practice are likely to be resistant to change in a way that individual behavior is not. If learning at one level of the organization is contingent on complementary changes in philosophy and practice at others, it would not be surprising to discover that change does not always come easily in a multilevel system.

◆ The Issue of Agency

A second major problem we have with the formulation of the theory by Giddens is his characterization of the concepts of *agent* and *agency*. It will be recalled

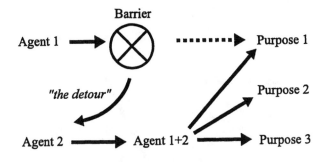

Figure 3.2. Translation as a Mediation of Action
Adapted from Latour (1994); used by permission of Oxford University Press.

that Giddens treats agent as a synonym of *actor.* Intentionality, in this interpretation, is associated with individual choice, even when it is treated as an effect of reflexive after-the-fact rationalization of the flow of events. But if structure is lodged in the "memory traces" of groups, as well as in those of individuals, we need to reconsider agency and its embodiments. We must address the possibility that it is not just the individual who acts.

This is a theme that is addressed by Bruno Latour (1994). He has advanced a notion he calls "translation theory" (sometimes referred to as "actor-network theory").

To introduce the actor-network concept, imagine that someone—let us call them $Agent_1$—whose activity is oriented to some purpose or goal finds himself or herself obliged to turn to someone or something else for help; otherwise, they are blocked. Let us call this helper (human or nonhuman) $Agent_2$. In combination, the two achieve the purpose that $Agent_1$ had in mind (and maybe $Agent_2$ as well). Let us call this coupled agent A_{1+2}. Obviously, the effective agency in achieving the purpose of $Agent_1$ is neither A_1 nor A_2, because, considered alone, neither acted. In the conjoining of the two to form A_{1+2}, a "translation" has been realized: from $A_1 + A_2$ to A_{1+2} (Figure 3.2). One link in a network—an actor-network—has been forged.

We can illustrate the idea of the actor-network using Suchman's (1996) example. The supervisor of the operations room, Sup, is confronted with a situation in which, as part of his responsibility, he must find a way to deplane the passengers in one way or another. From within the operations room, however, he has no way of achieving his objective other than by calling in the assistance of others, first among his own crew, then ground crew, then other airlines. What

65

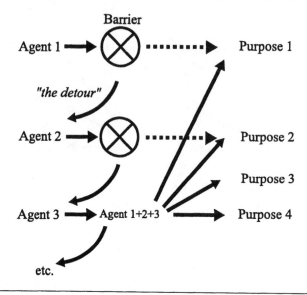

Figure 3.3. Action as Multiply Mediated by Agents of Various Kinds, Each Adding Their Own Purpose

Adapted from Latour (1994); used by permission of Oxford University Press.

finally solves the problem is a technician who replaces a defective pump and thus gets the set of stairs operational again. For Sup to mobilize the stairs, other agents had to be brought into play, both material and human, including a pump, the equipment needed to repair it, the technician who did the work, the crew lead, the telephone and radio needed to contact him, the operators in operations who worked the communications links, and, behind all of them, stretching back in an imaginary time line, the people who installed the operational and communications equipment, the company that manufactured it, the people who designed it, the people and institutions who trained them, and so on, potentially ad infinitum (Figure 3.3). The "network" is becoming larger and longer.

How, in such a densely interconnected system of agencies, are we to attribute intentionality? The issue is one of how to define the concept of agent and agency.

The word *agent* is an instance of a troublesome class of nouns that incorporates more than one meaning and thus are ambiguous. An agent, for example, is often taken in the literature to be a synonym for *actor* (as we have seen, Giddens adopted this interpretation). Read this way, it typically refers to a human being—think of a road agent in an old-fashioned Western movie. But agent can

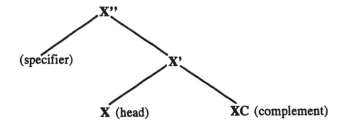

Figure 3.4. The X-Bar Construction

also mean anything that has an identifiable effect, sometimes devastating, as in Agent Orange, and in this usage it is typically thought of as nonhuman, a common way of talking in biological research, for example. It can also mean acting for someone, or for some corporation, as in the expression *insurance agent* or among Hollywood actors or professional athletes, *my agent.* Rather than opt for one of these interpretations, Latour assumes they are all intrinsic dimensions of the idea that he is pursuing.

The Head-Complement Relation

We can explore what Latour (1994) is getting at by rephrasing the formulation of Figure 3.3 in more diagrammatic terms. Suppose that we assume that the conjoining of $Agent_1$ and $Agent_2$ to form a hybrid agent $Agent_{1+2}$ is the essential structure of all activity. We make no initial assumptions as to the character of either agent; we assume for the moment that either might be human or nonhuman (and, if human, groups as well as individuals). Nevertheless, the two agents are not completely symmetrical, because one, $Agent_1$, has enlisted the aid of the other, $Agent_2$. Let us therefore designate $Agent_1$ as "Head" and $Agent_2$ as "Complement."

Because this is an instance of a general pattern, we use variable notation. We refer to the head as X and the complement as XC (i.e., the complement of X). The hybrid combination thus formed, $Agent_{1+2}$, we refer to as X' (X-bar). When the identity of this agent is specified or made clear, the result is called an X-bar construction (Chomsky, 1995; see Figure 3.4).

It is evident that for X' (or in other words $Agent_{1+2}$) to be an agent, he, she, or it must have a purpose and an identity (that is part of the definition of agent-as-actor). Presumably, because it was $Agent_1$'s purpose that led to the recruitment of Agent$_2$, it is X's purpose and identity that X' (i.e., X single bar) inherits. This is implicit in the definition of agent as someone who represents the interests of another: The identity and purposes of the head take precedence over those of the complement.

We can now make this idea less abstract with an illustration. Suchman's (1996) case furnishes more than one. For example, consider the following sequence. The Sup has just tapped the BP on the shoulder to get her attention:

Sup: Call ground maintenance at Gate 15 real quick, as fast as they can, on the radio. I got them on the phone.

BP: Call them on the radio?

Sup: Yeah, I got them on the phone.

In this sequence, the Sup has assumed the role of head and has enlisted the aid of the BP, who thus becomes, within the context of the overall activity of restoring normalcy, a complement. BP's call to "Gate 15" will be performed by her, but everyone will be clear as to the provenance of the agency that is thus communicated to ground crew (she will be acting as a translator of the supervisor's command). It is the Sup speaking through his agent (but also note that BP is speaking through the radio, which also thus functions as an agent).

In identifying the term X with supervisor and XC with baggage planner, we have simply, as in mathematics, instantiated or provided an instance of two variables, X and XC, by substituting for them constants, namely *supervisor* and *baggage planner*. But the underlying structure is the same, and it is this structure that we understand to be operative in the hierarchical relations holding within the Operations room, where, as Suchman (1996) puts it, "The Supervisor of Ramp Operations has overall responsibility for the work of operations" (p. 38). We are, in other words, in the domain of the usual understandings we have of how work is conducted—hierarchically (and these are made explicit in Suchman's text at several points).

We can now complete the picture by specifying which supervisor (and thus which operations room) is involved: "The setting for this case is the operations room of an airline (hereinafter called Atlantic) at a mid-sized metropolitan airport in the United States" (Suchman, 1996, p. 36). We term this additional information, intended to nail down the specific identity of supervisor and baggage handler, the *specifier*. When it is clear which supervisor we are reading about (i.e., the one in the Ops room of Atlantic airline) and which baggage planner

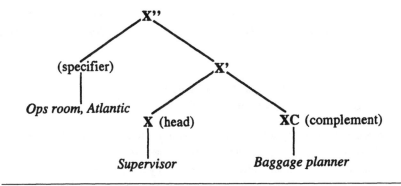

Figure 3.5. The Interaction Between Supervisor and Baggage Planner as Illustrating Its Structural Embedding

(the one who works with the supervisor), the logical unit of activity is complete. We have no difficulty understanding the small exchange we have just been citing. The resulting system (X double bar) is shown in Figure 3.5.

The Origin of Head-Complement Relations in Communication

This manner of presenting Latour's theory offers two central insights. First, to communicate is to conform to—has literally the form of—a head-complement relation (Taylor & Van Every, 2000). Repeated conformity to the same head-complement communication couple is how social roles and statuses come to be (what Giddens would think of as the institutional correlate of domination). Second, such units, once constituted, may function as heads and/or complements within other such constructions to form multiply layered systems of activity that may be treated as objective multipart realities, and thus, as Latour puts it, be "black-boxed." Agency is not a property unique to individuals. Furthermore, the pattern is found in nonhuman couplings. The relation between the wrench that turns the bolt to install the pump in the passenger stairs is yet another instance of head-complement linking, as is the relation of the set of stairs to the airplane.

It is not because there is a social hierarchy that there are head-complement relations; it is the other way around. The nature of purposeful activity—including communication—itself inevitably leads to the formation of head-complement relations, whether we term the mediator *tools* (Engeström) or *Agent$_2$* (Latour,

1994). The social hierarchy is derived from the structure of work activity, not the reverse. Language merely records (stores) the outcome (Taylor & Van Every, 2000).

Organization as an Embedded System of Head-Complement Relations

When one *X*-bar structure is embedded within another to form a multilayered linking of agencies to produce an articulated system of action, this is an instance of *recursivity*. Latour sometimes uses the analogy of a river to convey this idea. Typically, rivers begin from some modest source, a spring or a mountain lake, for example. They only become large because other streams link up with them. Each time the feeding in of some other source occurs, the river becomes wider and more powerful. We call these secondary streams "tributaries." The Missouri and the Ohio are tributaries of the Mississippi, for instance. They exemplify, in other words, a case corresponding to head-complement node formation, one that takes place many, many times before the Mississippi reaches New Orleans. Once the secondary river is merged into the greater, it gradually loses its identity. The further downstream you go, the less evident is the influence of the tributaries; the further you track back upstream, the better you comprehend the original composition of the river and how it was formed.

Latour perceives this to be the pattern of activity generally (we explore some of the organizational consequences in Chapter 6). He thinks that not just rivers, but Nature (mediated by science and technology and by society) and Society (mediated by politics and economics and by nature) are also produced on the same model (Latour, 1993). We see Latour's explanation as a model of how the infrastructure of organization is produced.

Consider again Suchman's (1996) airport. To the passenger, all that complexity of ramp operations remains invisible until something goes wrong (and even then all that is apparent to the traveling public is the inconvenience). The embedded system of head-complement relations has become *transparent*—part of something that is taken for granted. Yet if we were to break it down—"go upstream," in Latour's metaphor (*en amont*, in French)—the multiple head-complement relations that went to produce the smoothly functioning system would gradually begin to appear, like a message that, having been written in invisible ink, becomes visible when it has been subjected to the right treatment. Some of those head-complement couplings would be human-to-human (Sup-BP, for example), some would be mixed (BP-radio), some would be entirely composed of nonhumans (the parts of the set of stairs). Latour's way of imagining this "invisibilization" of systems, as we suggested previously, is to say that it is a case of black-boxing (we call it "imbrication"). Once the box is closed, what goes on inside is no longer available for viewing.

Latour, like Hutchins, perceives the instruments of action as already informed by purposes, independent of those of their users. Consider the nautical chart of Hutchins. It is an instrumentality that was progressively perfected over many generations of seafarers who made of it not just a tool (although, of course, it does function as a tool) but an integral component in a cycle of computation (or cognition), so much so that its users do not even need to comprehend totally how it does what it does to employ it effectively. The purposes of those long-dead navigators and cartographers are now inscribed in the technology to give it its capacity to function effectively in a multiplicity of contexts. The navigators who depend on it must conform themselves to its purposes before it will satisfy theirs. They have to be trained in its use. It is a powerful agent in its own right— not just a tool but a carrier of a cultural tradition and an inscription of the purposes of generations of seafarers.

The privileging of any single situation or episode as a focus of attention is always arbitrary, in that every activity is fully as much an outcome of mediations as a source of them (this is the structurational thesis in a different guise). There is no single point of origin of an activity. Human motive and purpose do not arise de novo in the psyche of some individual but in the multiple mediations, involving both humans and nonhumans, society and nature, that go into the constitution of the person as a social actor.

It is not that $Agent_1$ (some human) has purposes and $Agent_2$ (tool) does not (they both incorporate purposes, and both have a history that is grounded in previous mediations), but that we generally attribute head status to the human agent and complement status to the tool. In this way, human subjectivity is given recognition even as the subject's agency (the capability of acting) is constituted objectively, as an actor in mediated communication with others. In this sense, Giddens is right: Intentionality is a product of reflexive interpretation. However, he fails to see the implications of his own principle. That to which we accord intentionality becomes, ipso facto, an agent—individual or not.

Latour's concept of translation would explain how individuals come, through their networking, to form themselves into collective actors, with a purpose that is lodged in a network—themselves, as a collaborating unit—even though it is expressed in the voice of a spokesperson. Star extends this idea, conceiving of the organization as itself an actor-network composed of actor-networks.

71

An Actor-Network of Actor-Networks

Star focuses on the junction points of the multiple worlds of work of organization—each a semienclosed community of discourse that reflects different situated practices. She studies, in other words, "boundaries."

Like Latour, she sees the interleaving of the multiple discourse-worlds of an organization as a dynamic of construction of networks of cooperating actors held together by their joint orientation to some object, even though they may represent it very differently to themselves and to others. The word *represent,* however, has a double connotation (as we saw was the case of "agent"). In one of the meanings, *to represent* is a synonym of *to describe* or *to stand for* something symbolically; in another, it refers to the actions of *someone who speaks for someone else* (as in "service representative"). Star exploits both these conceptions of representation in accounting for the ability of "diverse intersecting social worlds" to produce a coherent and institutionally sanctioned world. She borrows the actor-network conceptualization of Latour (1987) and Michel Callon (1986), but she gives it a twist.

Actor-network or translation theory, as we have already seen in our discussion of Latour's work, focuses on the mobilizing processes by means of which many actors come to be associated with a single project, purpose, or goal. Suppose you are a baseball owner and you want to persuade your city or region to support you—and invest in—a spanking new stadium, with state-of-the-art facilities, including some very profitable executive boxes. What you have to do is get a variety of actors to buy into the idea, because it is in their interest to do so. The city has to see it as a way of attracting industrial investment and a source of revenue; local amateur clubs have to see it as making their task of building community recreation activities easier; the local press and television have to see the potential for interesting their audience; the downtown merchants have to see it as attracting tourist dollars; the state governor has to see it as enhancing his or her image with the voting public; the banker has to see it as a viable investment; and so on. When all these varied interests have been mobilized, then the building of the stadium is on its way to becoming what actor-network theorists call "an obligatory point of passage." It is only by building a ballpark, you hope to have convinced them, that all their *other* objectives will be realized.

Now, the network has come into existence as a virtual object—a symbolic representation of something that to which people can relate. But as it goes from its virtual to its actual state—as the sod is turned and the scaffolding goes up—actors emerge to give voice to ("represent") the new network. Roles appear, and ultimately a hierarchy does also. The network itself becomes an actor: an "actor-network" represented—given a voice—by one or more "macro-actors" (Callon & Latour, 1981).

What Star does with this visualization of how singular enterprises mobilize diverse actors to form a network is to see organization not as the emergence of a single actor-network but as an intersection of different actor-networks, each of which joins in the enterprise and simultaneously retains its own identity. As Star and Griesemer (1989) write, there is no consensus, nor any need for one: "Consensus is not necessary for cooperation nor for the successful conduct of work" (p. 388). What the actors have to do as they come from their different social worlds is to "establish a mutual modus operandi" (p. 388).

Thus, there will be multiple passage points or "boundary objects" in an organization and multiple interlinkages of interest within the framework furnished by them. Organization is a complex "many-to-many mapping" (Star & Griesemer, 1989, p. 390). A single concrete object may nevertheless be invested with multiple and distinct purposes, or objects.[6] The plurivalent objects thus provide the glue that holds the organizational network together, but there is no single actor-network or macro-actor because the network has more the character of a confederacy than a unitary state. Normally, pilots of airplanes and operations supervisors of airports occupy nonintersecting universes of work. For a moment, a defective passenger unloading device becomes their boundary object. This is how the organization works. For technology to be effective, it has to take account of the role of such linkages.

It is this concept of boundary objects as the linking points of the multiple conversations of an organization that we develop as a central element in the communication approach to structuration. It is a theme we develop in its different dimensions in Chapters 5, 6, and 7.

The Dimension of Community

Engeström develops a further dimension of agency we discuss in later sections of the book. Like Latour, Engeström conceives of the subject-object relationship as mediated: Whatever "subject" is chosen as a focus (what he calls the "agency chosen as the point of view of the analysis"), that subject (individual or collective), in dealing with the object, will call into play an instrumentality, which he thinks of as a *tool*. The effect is to reiterate the head-complement coupling of agencies that we described previously. In addition, however, unlike Latour, he sees the subject as intrinsically linked into a larger social community.

By including community, mediations other than technological are made salient. Engeström signals two of these that he sees as having particular impor-

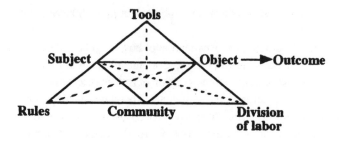

Figure 3.6. An Activity System as Conceived by Engeström (1990)

tance: rules and division of labor. Subjects, he thinks, are linked to their communities by the rules and conventions of society, which both constrain them and allow them to express their identities in interaction (in Giddens's formulation also, rules and resources are each tied to the other). And objects (the purposes to which society is oriented) are linked to community by the division of labor. Engeström's full system is shown in Figure 3.6.

The concept of community and its role in linking groups to a larger world of meaning are developed in Chapter 5.

◆ The Role of Text in Communication

A very important dimension of the theory of communication that forms the basis of our own research is the role of text. As we have noted already, communication receives cursory consideration in the work of Giddens, and the role of text almost none at all. For a study of organizational communication, this is a very serious omission, given the quite central role of text in stitching together the various communities of discourse that form the body of the organization. Often, of course, differing collaborating groups relate to each other by the ordinary modality of spoken language—the pilot of the incoming airplane and the operations crew in Suchman's (1996) case study, for example. But in many other instances of organizational interaction, there is no direct channel. Groups figure in other groups' conversations by being recreated as objects described by a text. The management of an organization with some quarter of a million employees (the subject of our Chapter 8) could hardly function in the absence of a textual translation by means of which the multiple microuniverses of activity composing the organization are translated into descriptions (sometimes no more than statistics). Among those who have been concerned to understand the implications of such a transformation are Bowker and Star (1999).

Consider the double meaning of the word *represent*. For management to have meaning, there must be something—some *thing*—to manage (an "object"). Here, the double meaning of represent comes into play. First, the organization and its parts have to be represented in the sense of being given the symbolic status of something to be talked about. They thus become an object in the first of Star's sense of a boundary object: something of common concern to management and the managed. Second, once the organization has been transformed conceptually into an object, then management can assume subject status, capable of behaving purposefully with respect to it ("managing" it). Now management is able to represent organization in the second sense of the word, by speaking for it and to it—acting purposefully to achieve some outcome. The organization is attributed an intention, vocalized by its spokespersons. Management becomes "head" when the organization is constituted as its "complement."

How is this objectifying to be accomplished? Bowker and Star's answer lies in *systems of classification*. Bowker, Timmermans, and Star (1995) see classification systems "as a kind of crucible for organizations and occupations" (p. 345). By classifying, names are given to things, and the existence of the name becomes a guarantor for the existence of the "thing."

Classification systems have both positive and negative consequences. On the positive side, they provide for comparability across sites. Classification systems make work visible—something that can be taught, for example—and this is a necessary step in the direction of standardization, the basis of complex operations such as airlines. In principle, classification systems should leave space for local initiative and discretion when it is needed. A "perfect" classification system, Bowker et al. (1996) think, "preserves common sense control, enhances comparability in the right places, and makes visible what is wrongly invisible, leaving justly invisible discretionary judgment" (p. 347).

Bowker et al. (1996) are here signaling what they think of as the legitimately competing claims of the local and the global. As we have already seen in her observations on infrastructure, Star recognizes the different extensions of action, spatially and temporally, and the complications that arise in reconciling their different logics. This is a theme that is strongly emphasized by Giddens, and in Chapter 7, we return to develop our own interpretation of its consequences.

The hitch is this: There is no perfect classification scheme. Instead, organizations mostly thrive, in spite of the multiple contradictions engendered by inconsistencies in work and its classification, because of what Star—borrowing from Strauss, Fagerhaugh, Suczek, and Weiner (1985)—calls *articulation work*. Articulation work is "work that gets things back 'on track' in the face of the unexpected, and modifies action to accommodate unanticipated contingencies" (Star, 1991, p. 275, also cited in Star & Strauss, 1999). By definition, then, articulation work cannot be classified (because if it could be it would not be unexpected or unanticipated). There is always a residual tension between the imperative of classification (managing a large system) and the imperative of articulation to make things work (activities in small systems).

Classifying is thus anything but neutral in its social effects. It carries with it "a politics of voice and value which is often invisible, embedded in layers of infrastructure" (Bowker et al., 1996, p. 345). In other words, classification systems are inherently political. They typically involve negotiation to sort out where the line will be drawn between cross-site comparability (dominance of the classification system) and situated local initiative (dominance of articulation work). In the act of rendering one set of activities visible, or "present" to our conscious awareness, we simultaneously make another set—the work of articulation—invisible. Nowhere is this effect more evident than in the computerization of work, because "information technologies, which traffic in representations, . . . also advantage some voices and values over others, make some things visible and others invisible" (Bowker et al., 1996, p. 346).

Technology enters the picture, because its software presupposes classification of work. The whole purpose of "requirements analysis" is to classify the activities of the organization so that they can be represented in the design of the product. When technology is implemented, therefore, it brings with it its built-in classification of tasks. Implementation of such systems reflects managerial decisions, as well. Both designers and managers can be fooled by their classification systems into ignoring the value of articulation work in smoothing the flow of activity. As the vital articulation work slips through the mesh of the classification system, it becomes "invisible" (Suchman, 1995). It was, after all, the invisible work that made the Trouble Ticketing System, described by Sachs, function. Star (1991) claims that the so-called productivity paradox (David, 1989; Taylor, 1993) is one consequence of categorization: "The introduction of (often very expensive) information technology has resulted in a decline in productivity, contrary to the perceived productivity benefits promised by the technology" (p. 44).

In subsequent chapters, we return to explore further the implications of classifying as the textual modality that mediates organizational communication and explains so much of its dynamic.

◆ Conclusion

None of the perspectives we have been developing in this chapter contradicts the basic tenets of structuration theory, but they do considerably extend its reach and application. They remind us that structure is embedded not just in the "rules" that people master in mobilizing the "resources" that come into play in action but in the resources themselves, and in particular the physical world that we have reconstructed to fit our purposes. Because structure is so deeply embedded in both practices and the physical means to realize them, it is not easy to change. Latour, in particular, insists on the structuring properties of the natural world and its artificial extensions in technology and architecture. Hutchins similarly documents the embedding of culture in the artifacts that frame our activities.

We also have explored another source of structuring: in the conversational patterning of people's interactions as they deal with a practical world. The formulation of the theory by Giddens preceded most of the work in conversation analysis that was stimulated by Garfinkel (whom he cites at some length) and Sacks (whom he mentions only in passing) but that, in the interval, has become a major area of research. It has now become acceptable to see conversation as itself richly structured, as a source (not just a transmission) of knowledge, and thus as a storehouse of social structure.

We also have enlarged the concept of agency to include collectivities as well as individuals and tools as well as the tool-users. We have introduced a concept of delegation of action in the generation of agency and begun to explore its structuring effects. The notion of a head-complement relation becomes in the next chapter a cornerstone of the theory of communication we are developing. Part of that theory is concerned with how community enters into the structuring of agency. This is a theme we have no more than evoked here; in Chapter 4, it too becomes an important element of a theory of organizational communication.

We have equally opened up for investigation the concept of intergroup relationships. Giddens has little to say about the internal dynamics of organization. We have expanded his ideas to include a concept of multiple structures, competing with each other in the systemic patterns of situated collaborative groups. We have introduced the idea that structures have a history and a future. The contradictions of structure that are characteristic of organization become a motor of change.

We also have begun to explore the concept of orders of learning and how they reflect the complex interaction of levels of the organization, from the local to the global. We have considered the issue of synchronization between levels and why it might be so hard to achieve. Infrastructure, we have seen, becomes a key index of the successful achievement of learning.

Finally, we have begun to examine the role of text as a dominant modality of communication in much of the organization's transactional exchanges.

In the next chapter, we turn to integrate these insights into a theory of communication. In the chapters that follow, we see how empirical research can contribute to a better understanding of computerization as an instrumentality of organizational learning.

◆ Notes

1. Perception, in the postbehaviorist era of psychology, is assumed to be deeply interrelated with cognition; what we see is not just determined by the stimulus display available to the senses but is determined from the beginning by expectations that have an origin in cognition.

2. Note, however, that what counts as stimuli is already determined by the selective attention of the cognizer, as the previous note makes clear, and which Hutchins demonstrates in all his illustrations.

3. On August 6, 1997, a Korean airliner crashed while trying to land at Guam airport. Some 229 people died. The accident has uncanny echoes of the observations of Hutchins and Klausen. One source of confusion was the absence of a technology called "glide slope" that usually takes over as the plane approaches the landing field; it was out of service for maintenance. The recorded conversation in the cockpit indicates uncertainty over its availability, however: About 2 minutes before the crash, the flight engineer asked if the glide slope was working, and the captain first replied "Yes" and then the first officer is heard to say "Not usable." There were other sources of confusion. For example, air traffic controllers have a computer program that is supposed to track "minimum safe altitude" of incoming flights and issue a warning if they are too low, but in practice it is frequently "desensitized" to minimize "nuisance warnings." Similarly, in the absence of glide slope, there is a cockpit instrument designed to arrest descent at a certain height; the captain was heard to order it to be set at 1,440 feet, and yet the descent continued. Although Korean Airlines would subsequently blame the crash on "pilot error," it is evident that it was the system that broke down.

4. The concept of "affordance" was developed by the psychologist Gibson (1979), who argues that Nature furnishes possibilities for action—rocks for sitting, stones for throwing, ground for walking on, trees for climbing—and that these affordances become an intrinsic part of what it means to be an aware, perceiving, active human being. Technology may or may not offer the affordances it pretends to.

5. The *New York Times* (Abelson, 1998) reported, for example, on the formation of a new Association of Independent Physicians who resist the delegation of medical decisions to "'monsters' whose only aim is to increase profits and drive up their stock prices" (pp. D1, D5). Jacobs (1992) sees a fundamental difference between ideologies of the public and private spheres of activity.

6. As Engeström (1990) understands objects, they are both that on which we materially focus our attention (such as a physical object or a task) and a purpose or aim, "both something given and something projected or anticipated" (p. 107). *Objects* that are acted on (in the first sense of the term) produce *outcomes* (the second sense, more like an objective).

4

Communication as the
Modality of Structuration

◆ That an organization is *structured,* as that term is understood in structuration theory, implies that

1. There is an established system of domination.
2. The system is legitimated.
3. It is inscribed in the frame knowledge of members, as part of their normal interpretive sense-making.

The challenge for a theory of communication that aims to incorporate these features of structuration theory is to account for just these properties.

Giddens associates the instantiation of structure with mechanisms that he calls "modalities." However, as we saw in Chapter 2, the concept of modality is not one of the better explicated features of his theory. We differ from Giddens in that we assume communication to be the basic structurational modality—how power is exercised, legitimated, and understood in communities of people engaged in a collaborative enterprise. This chapter lays the groundwork for our empirical research in setting out our conception of how communication works and how it provides the basis for organization.

The chapter has two principal sections. In the first, we propose a model of situated communication. By "situated communication," we mean simply the communication that accompanies the work of collaborative groups engaged in purposeful work. The model we present makes two assumptions. First, it assumes that communities of work are in fact discourse communities, in that they use language constructively both to make sense reflexively of the circumstances in which they find themselves and to organize their own activities to develop a collaborative response to it. Second, we argue that, in the process of developing such a collaborative response, they organize themselves by forming units of delegation of responsibility, in which complementary relations of agency—acting and acting-*for*—are created. We claim that such co-orientational units are the building blocks of all organization. They frequently become routine (what we call *imbricated*), but they are endlessly subject to recall, depending on circumstance. Communication is the modality by means of which such relations form, are revised, and may be contested.

The second part of the chapter takes up the question of how situated group work comes to be integrated into the network of relations that leads to the constitution of the organization as itself an actor. Using the same model as before as our starting point, we show how organization emerges through a sequence of translations whereby groups are transformed from situated contexts of work into corporate actors: both subject (as agency) and objects (as components of organization). Organization thus appears as a complex overlay of two kinds of discursive universe, each characterized by its differing communicational modalities. The interface thus formed between communicational levels is a potential source of contradictions. Many of the results of implementations of I/CT that we described in Chapter 1 exemplify how such contradictions may serve to explain their dynamic (and why they encountered difficulties). The chapter concludes with an examination of some of the stakes arising out of the local/global interface.

◆ Situated Communication: "A Talking Out of Text in the Circumstances of a Conversation"

We begin by inviting you to join us in performing a thought experiment. We are going to consider the sequence that initiated the situation in Operations, as reported by Suchman (1996), in two different ways. The segment of dialogue as she described it goes like this (the pauses and other punctuation can be ignored for our purposes; they are there to attest to the scientific rigor of the research):

1. Radio: Operations::ah(.)

2. (pilot) Four seventy one?

3. Ops A: (4.0) Rrahhh. [struggling with radio]

4. (.2) Four seventy one.

5. Radio: Yessir would you send

6. somebody out here the::ah(.) [Ops A looks to video monitor]

7. agent working the *jet*way here

8. is running around with their

9. *hands* up in the air (.2)

10. Ops A: //[laugh]

11. Radio //obviously

12. doesn't know how to work

13. //the uh: (.8) stairways or

14. can't get it to work (one).

15. We need some help.

16. Ops B: //Must be Sarducci [looks to monitor]

17. Ops A: Will advise. [looks to PP, or passenger service planner]

18. (1.0)

Our thought experiment has two parts. First, imagine that you are either physically present in the Operations Room as this exchange is going on or looking at a videotaped version of it. Suppose also that instead of it being a "mid-sized metropolitan airport in the United States," this is all taking place in Pakistan and you do not speak the language (the version shown previously is a later rendering into English, not a faithful transcription of the original transaction). The only parts of the exchange that will be accessible to you are the "offstage" comments such as "looks to monitor," "looks to PP," or "radio." You will understand something of what is going on, but only something. For example, you probably will guess that this is a work conversation. You will be able to arrive at this conclusion for two reasons. First, it is clear that the circumstances are those that typically characterize work (uniforms, equipment, disposition of the room, attitudes of people that connote concentration on something, absence of idle chit-chat, and so on). Second, the interaction between the people in the room and the disembodied voice to which they are responding has the form of to-and-fro talk that is one of the defining properties of conversation, as an impressive body of research stretching back now more than a quarter of a century has made clear (the work of the field known as *Conversation Analysis*).

So you, as the observer, will know it is collective work and that it is a conversation—what Goffman (1963) called a "focussed gathering"—but you will not know exactly what it is about (for example, you will not be able to tell that the voice is that of an airline captain, although you might guess). You would not be able to say with much accuracy, afterward, what the "situation" was.

Now let us take a second step in our mental experiment. Suppose that it occurred not in Pakistan but indeed in a mid-sized American city. However, you are not present, and you do not have immediate access to a videotape of the episode (which, for us readers, is in fact the case). You have to rely on Suchman's (1996) account for whatever you know about the situation. Suppose in addition that, instead of this segment appearing in an article written by a well-known and respected ethnographer, supported by marks of typical ethnographic framing (such as the punctuation to indicate pauses), we were to tell you that this is an extract from a Hollywood script proposal—or it could be for a new television series, let us say a humorous take on aviation, a sort of *Ally McBeal* with a twist.

Now it is not a conversation at all, or at least not a "real" conversation, even if it should eventually get acted out. It is just a segment of script—a piece of text. There is no "real" situation, for the moment, other than the one dreamed up in the head of the author, even though you now understand perfectly well, unlike before, what the situation is! There are no pilots, no supervisors, no ramp crew, and you could not possibly be sitting in on the situation or (until it is actually produced as a film or TV show) be viewing it on videotape. And Lucy Suchman would be turned into what John Van Maanen (1988) said an ethnographer really is: a teller of tales.

How did you know, based on a script, what the situation was? Again, two factors supply the explanation. First, there are the words people were using: *operations, agent, jetway, hands up in the air, stairways* (as in "working the stairways"), *help, advise.* These communicate because you can link them with what linguists call a *common ground* of *frame knowledge* (Goldberg, 1995; Werth, 1993): You know about airports, and radio communication, and how stairways are used to get passengers off planes, and what throwing your hands up in the air means, and how impatient passengers get when there are delays. Scriptwriters count on your frame knowledge, even when they toss in a bit of jargon, such as "Four seventy-one," because it adds that little extra touch of authenticity (as long as you recognize it as technical talk, of course).

Second, the script unfolds in the way it should: following lines that you recognize as characteristic of stories, such as a dilemma, a call for help, some perplexity as to how to respond. You are ready for what follows because stories are supposed to work this way. It is your ability to recognize these kinds of sequencing patterns of turn-taking as meaningful that linguists claim calls on "construction knowledge" (Goldberg, 1995).

82

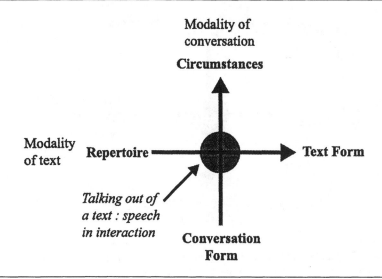

Figure 4.1. Communication as the Intersection of Axes of Conversation and Text

What are we trying to show by this little thought experiment? Our point is this: Human communication occurs at the intersection of two modalities—conversation and text. Deprived of access to its text (talking and other linguistic expressions, such as writing), conversation still has meaning—but not its usual meaning. This is the Pakistani airport illustration. Similarly for text: Taken out of conversational context, it is reduced to its essential textuality—a resource for communication, but not communication itself. This is the Hollywood script illustration.

Communication thus supposes a talking out of text in the circumstances of a conversation. The talking out supposes not just an actant (a speaker) but also at least one reactant (a listener). To illustrate, imagine communication as occurring at the intersection of two axes, one representing conversation, the other text (see Figure 4.1).

The sense of this figurative representation of communication is as follows. Conversation is framed by two parameters: (a) *circumstances* (of time, place, occasion, persons, materiality, etc., the basis for the "situatedness" of which Suchman writes) and (b) *conversation form* (the need to maintain an orderly back-and-forth sequencing of speaking as part of the dynamics of interactive talk, in the absence of which conversational coherence becomes impossible). Text is similarly framed by two parameters: (a) the existence of a *repertoire* of

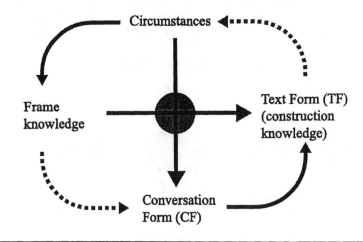

Figure 4.2. The Construction of Sense (Interpretation of Circumstances) and the Organization of Talk (Creating a Basis for Collective Action)

basic frame knowledge that forms the common ground of the communicators (without which they have no shared basis for the interpretation of events) and (b) *text form* (the syntactic and other generative rules that must be respected for communicators to produce a comprehensible string of language and thus to speak intelligibly and be understood).

Sense-making, of the text-dependent kind we automatically do unless we find ourselves in the unusual circumstance of a Pakistani airport, involves two orders of mapping: (a) of circumstance onto *frame knowledge* and (b) of patterns of interaction (what conversation analysts call *adjacency pairs*) onto *construction knowledge* (see Figure 4.2). Frame knowledge is simply the sum of acquired understandings that makes it possible for us to recognize a situation and to formulate our interpretation in language (as the captain and the operations room crew were struggling to do in Suchman's 1996 case study). Construction knowledge is that branch of understanding that permits participants in a conversation to interact both by producing comprehensible strings of language ("agent . . . running around with their hands up in the air") and knowing how to address speech to someone else in such a way as to produce a desired effect on them ("Would you send somebody out here"). It is more than simply knowing how to formulate sentences; it means being able to frame explanations, give direction, argue a point, tell a story—all the forms of expression that language furnishes to structure the flow of interaction and lend it an intrinsic meaning.

When the mapping has been accomplished as a collective achievement mediated by interaction, two distinct but interrelated (and interdependent) features of communication will emerge:

1. *Cognitively,* a situation has been produced to which the participants are now co-oriented, in that their understandings of the circumstances are sufficiently aligned to have established for themselves a basis of coherent conversation.
2. *Pragmatically,* a basis of collective action has been created, in which roles have been negotiated (or reinforced) and the aligning of an agent-to-agent relationship is under way (what we earlier called the formation of a head/complement system of agency).

Two of the duality conditions of structuration are now accounted for, at least in principle: There is an emerging system of domination (a head/complement system of agency), and the situation is understood in the categories of frame and construction knowledge that form the semantic underpinning of the group's verbal interactions. It remains to be shown how such a system is legitimated (we return to this issue later in the chapter). The motivation for the structuring is the necessity for the group to respond to events, not as a disparate collection of individuals but as a collaborative unit (a point on which both Suchman and Hutchins insist, as we saw in Chapter 3).

What initially had been a two-dimensional space or communication potential is now transformed into a one-dimensional vector, in which communication is seen to mediate the passage from a reading of a situation into a resolution of it (solving the problem of the malfunctioning stairways, for example), and thus a basis of collective action: *fact* to *conclusion,* mediated by *acts of speech.* It is this that Hutchins (1995) refers to as *distributed cognition.* A single collective agency—a power to act together—has been produced.

It is by such a mapping of one dimension—situated interaction—onto another—text—that circumstances are transformed into a "situation" and the conditions are created for the processes of distributed cognition necessary to deal with it (see Figure 4.3). Specifically, (a) the elements of circumstance are given a name and in this way matched with available frame knowledge; and (b) the patterns of interaction that are characteristic of all species interaction—not just human—are interpreted semantically, and the meaning of behaviors, as well as the identity of those who generate them, is produced. In other words, a theory of situated communication is also a theory of distributed cognition, and vice versa.

Following the analytical scheme of Marr (1982) and Hutchins (1995), communication can be analyzed as (a) *mediation,* in the usual sense of that word—

FACTS ────────► **ACTS OF SPEECH** ────────► **CONCLUSION**

Figure 4.3. The Transformation of Facts Into Conclusion Through Interaction

how information is physically displayed and exchanged (face-to-face, by phone, radio and television, in Suchman's example); (b) a representation of a situation in some code or language—verbal, graphic, or whatever (the *symbolic* function of communication)[1]; and (c) entering into the problem-solving process itself and how it thus mediates (comes to direct) collective action in a situation (for example, it furnished the only means by which the personnel in the Operations Room could play an effective role in the minidrama unfolding on the ramp because they were connected to it only electronically, not physically). This is the *essential* function of communication.

The essential function of communication, in other words, is about speech as action. But action, as Giddens points out, involves the exercise of power. To explain why communicative action generates relations of domination, we introduce the concept of agency.

The Centrality of Agency in Communication Theory

A fundamental difference between our interpretation of the theory of structuration and that of Giddens, as we have seen, is in how we understand the terms "agent" and "agency." Giddens thinks of agency as individual action. We think of agency as acting-*for* someone or something. An agent is the actor-who-acts-*for*. It is in the acting-*for* that structuration occurs—how relationships of interdependence and domination form and are sustained. Acting-*for* is organization in the making.

Consider again the minidrama reported by Suchman (1996). The operations crew has been galvanized into action by a call from the arriving pilot, and their attention is now focused on getting the stairway reactivated. We describe this as an *A-B-X* unit. The object, repairing the stairs, is *X*. The agent whose activities are being described to us (the operations team) is *B*. But *B* is acting for a waiting airplane crew and their passengers. They are *A*. We could say that a communication unit has formed, for the duration of the crisis, based on acting and acting-for. Newcomb (1953) called this a *co-orientation system,* and we believe it to be the building block of organization (see Figure 4.4).

Let us consider some of the properties of the *A-B-X* unit.

86

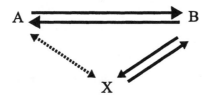

Figure 4.4. The Concept of a Co-Orientation System

Agents may be collective as well as individual. The components of an *A-B-X* unit are defined by the structure of relationships and not the other way around. Objects, for example, are defined by the purposes of agents. An object is something to which we do not attribute intention; it is the target of an intention. An agent, *A* or *B*, is defined both by the objects that are their preoccupation and for whom they act (or who acts for them). Whether *A* or *B* is a single individual, a collaborative team of workers, or a corporation is not fundamental.

To act, one must have the status of agent—acting for someone or something. Agency exists only in its *A-B-X* connections. Because the *A* and the *B* in any given relationship are both agents, it follows that the *A* in one relationship must be the *B* in another (otherwise *A* would not be an agent because he, she, or it would not be acting for). The pilot acts for his crew and passengers (his *B*-ness, because he acts for), but in his dealings with operations he is the one making a request (his *A*-ness, because he asks someone else to act for him). Similarly, the operations crew is responding to the call from the aircraft (*B*-ness) but initiates the call to ground crew (*A*-ness). This recursive transfer of agency explains a second property of co-orientation.

Co-orientation has characteristics of a fractal.[2] A fractal is a repetition of structure at finer and finer degrees of scale. We began by describing the situation as an aircraft making a request of operations. But it was in fact Ops A that the Captain spoke to—two individuals, each representing their community of discourse in that transaction. Then both Ops A and Sup got in touch with someone in ground crew. Now a new *A-B-X* unit forms: Operations-Ground crew—two communities of discourse linked by talk. Then Sup phones the other airline to request a loan of stairs. This produces another *A-B-X* co-orientation—two companies interrelated by the request for assistance. Then Sup has PP (passenger service) make a phone call for him. Here, the *A-B-X* unit is individual-to-individual, but it is embedded in a larger unit: Operations-Ground Crew.

Although some of these relationships may be interpreted as interpersonal—Sup and PP, for example—even there institutionally defined identities are involved. Some relationships involve whole work groups: the airplane crew, the operations team, ground crew. And some are corporate: one airline asking a favor of another. And there are virtual actors involved as well: the passengers, for example.

The *A-B-X* concept, in other words, is generic, a tool of analysis intended to point to the communicational characteristics of a situation. It describes the formation of an agency relationship, wherever that occurs, and whomever or whatever it involves. The importance of highlighting agency is that it is in the negotiation and renegotiation of the agency relationships that organizing occurs. From these considerations, a third principle follows.

Agency relationships tend to become imbricated. Imbrication means quite simply the arranging of units so as to overlap like the tiles on a roof. An *A-B-X* unit illustrates a form of layering, in that, for example, the aircraft crew cannot complete the unloading of their passengers without the contribution of ground crew in making sure the stairway is in place for the passengers to disembark—an imbrication of agency. Ground crew presumably mobilizes its own agencies. Some of those agencies are human; some are not. And so on. On the fractal principle, the imbrication of agencies can be as dense as one likes (or can design).

Co-orientation explains the constancies in organizational performance—why structures persist when they become imbricated. The principle of co-orientation thus appears to us to be a powerful tool in explicating the structurational principle of the propagation of structure in systems of interaction. We return to the issue of imbrication shortly.

Narrative Theory and the Structuring Role of Time

An important dimension of structuration theory, as we have seen, is the role of time in structuring activity. One way that time functions to structure events is by its narrativization. The sequencing of Suchman's (1996) episode, for example, can be seen as a trajectory. The failure of the stairs led the captain to contact Operations, and they in turn were led to communicate with the ramp crew, with maintenance, and with another airline. In this unfolding drama, the participants moved progressively from an assessment of the facts, to an exploration of possible solutions to the problem, to an eventual resolution of the situation, and—breathing a sigh of relief—back to routine. The event thus had a structure. It is, as embodied in Suchman's account, the structure of a *narrative*. She founds her analysis on the telling of a story.

Narrative structures are built around the core of a *transaction*. In its simplest form, a narrative unfolds in five steps (Greimas, 1987; Groleau & Cooren, 1999):

- A breakdown occurs, requiring constructive action.
- A principal engages an agent in the service of performing some task (this is the initiation of the transaction, and it may or may not imply negotiation of terms, persuasion, seduction, threats, promises, etc.; in effect, a head-complement relationship is established, aircraft/operations, for example).
- The principal's agent (Operations, in our example) assembles such skills, helpers, tools, and knowledge of the situation as may be necessary in the performing of the task (a phase of the narrative that frequently involves the formation of secondary principal-agent relationships—stories within stories).
- The agent (or perhaps the agent's agent, or the agent's agent's agent) carries through the action.
- The breakdown is resolved, or not, to the satisfaction of the requester, and the agent is compensated, rewarded, thanked, or otherwise acknowledged or punished (the sanction completes the transaction).

This is a structure that is endemic to narrative analysis. It applies straightforwardly to Suchman's incident: There is a breakdown; the skipper of the plane engages the intervention of airport operations; the latter, as agent, mobilizes a number of subagents; and the principal performance (repairing the stairs) is carried through, to the satisfaction of all. Suchman presumably chose this incident for analysis precisely because it had story characteristics. How to form a narrative is part of frame knowledge, part of how and why language serves as a modality of structuration (Giddens's "interpretive schemes").

What Is Meant by *Situation*?

What do we mean by the term *situation*?

Consider again the Operations Room and the minicrisis that was occupying its attention in the episode Suchman (1996) analyzed. On the one hand, there were already what might be called *circumstances*: certain people with a certain history, the physical layout of the room and of the airport in which it is located, a range of sophisticated communication equipment, a set of activities that occur in a fairly regular pattern throughout the day and night, and so on. These we take to form the relatively constant background of the work group and its field of operations: a taken-as-given. On the other hand, there is a purpose that, to at least some degree, has temporarily galvanized everyone in the room and focused their attention on resolving a problem that has arisen: the breakdown of the stairs. It is the existence of this focus of attention that we take to be the motivation for speaking of circumstances as transformed into a situation.[3]

The components of a situation include (a) a focus of attention or "object," (b) resources to be mobilized, and (c) constraints to be respected.

The stairs, whose breakdown results in the upsetting of the usual uneventful unloading process, are normally a taken-as-given part of the infrastructure. They have become

a. A focus of attention and a locus of purpose precisely because they have ceased to be what they usually are—a resource to be automatically called up in the accomplishment of a task, unloading the passengers. They have been transformed from an out-of-awareness part of a given technology into a goal, and other resources will now need to be called into play. By their having become a goal, they in turn determine

b. which other circumstantial elements will be relevant to the situation (maintenance, ground crew, another airline).

All those elements are "downstream," potential instrumentalities to resolve the situation. The passengers impatiently waiting to get off the plane and the aircraft crew dealing with them constitute a third element of the unfolding situation. That is the "upstream" part of the equation:

c. That part of the organization for whom it is the operations room that is seen as a resource to be mobilized.

So although all these different elements are part of the situation, we can distinguish between (a) what is to be accomplished—the goal; (b) that which may be called on to accomplish it—resources; and (c) other constraints in the situation, such as the need to disembark the passengers, assist them in making connections, clear the ramp for the next flight, and so on. (It is because there is an upstream and a downstream that we know the system is imbricated.)

When the stairs stopped working—broke down—they then became an object of conscious care with properties that needed be addressed. Now they had become *present-at-hand.* As Winograd and Flores (1986) wrote, "Objects and properties are not inherent in the world, but arise only in an event of breaking down in which they become present-at-hand" (p. 36). The stairs became "stairs" (for purposes of communication) only when, to again cite Winograd and Flores, they "presented themselves" as stairs in a breaking down or, to put it another way, in a state of *unreadiness-to-hand.*

It is in this sense that Engeström (1990) speaks of an "object," that part of the situation on which attention is focused because it needs attention. But note, however, that as the stairs became present-at-hand, they simultaneously made salient some otherwise *ready-to-hand* parts of the Operations team's physical and social environment, including maintenance crews, impatient passengers and pilots, and other airlines. These elements of the situation were normally also transparent—for purposes of ordinary work, invisible—but they now had to be consciously addressed by those in the team. Because these had also become present-at-hand objects that could be activated instrumentally, they were now a focus of attention. Similarly, such secondary considerations as passenger irritation, missed airline connections, and delayed landing schedules now became salient.

Finally, we have to take account of one other element in the situation (and which contributes to defining it as a situation), namely, the Operations crew itself. This is what Engeström designates as "subject," but because sometimes that which acts is both human and nonhuman, we prefer to use the neutral term *actant.* So these are the elements: a problem resulting from a breakdown, an operation to repair the source of the breakdown (which implies the mobilization of resources, a goal on which attention is focused), an actant, and an instrumentality by means of which the resources can be put to effect).[4]

We can now define what is meant by the *situatedness* of communication: Communication is that process by which objects and their properties (things to be consciously addressed) are made present-at-hand in a system of distributed cognition.

This definition makes it clear that communication occurs in a situation but is not the situation itself. Instead, communication is that process by which what had previously been ready-to-hand (imbricated agency) is transformed into present-at-hand for those whose attention is being focused on a common goal-object.

Imbrication as a Principle of Structuration

Giddens always has been clear on the relation of practical to discursive knowledge. Most of what occurs as activity is routine, not requiring much in the way of active discussion or even conscious attention. One of the challenges that presents itself to a communication theory of structuration is how to represent the structuring effect of routine work in a manner that is consistent with other elements of the theory. We address this problem by introducing the concept of imbrication.

To be imbricated, as we have said, means to be arranged so as to overlap like roof tiles or shingles, the scales of a fish, or the leaves of a tree. In such a structure, each tile has its own integrity, but it is the interdependence between tiles—each of which both supports and is supported by others—that explains the capacity of the roof, or skin (of a fish), or foliage (of a tree), to form a shield of protection against the elements—to provide shade from the sun, for example, or protect against the rain. Applied to organizational analysis, we understand this to be the way that interagency relationships are interleaved to form a durable organizational infrastructure.

Nobody (or no thing), we have been saying, would be able to do their job in an organization if there were not many others doing theirs. A single flight of any large modern airliner supposes the ongoing actions of thousands of agents—probably millions, if all the working parts of the aircraft and airport and rental agencies and ticket offices, and so forth, are counted. But all these agency relationships quickly become, as Suchman (1995) puts it, "invisible" in ordinary circumstances of work, a taken-for-granted background of "infrastructure." This is the indispensable grounding of tiled agencies quietly functioning away, out of sight and mind, that nevertheless makes the organization work. All this imbrication is, in Heidegger's (1959) term for it, *ready-to-hand,* becoming visible only when there is what he calls a *breakdown* (*Geworfenheit*)—a failure of one of the indispensable tiles.

Our use of the term *imbrication* is intended to emphasize the tendency in organizations to proceduralize agency by making its operation automatic. Installing machinery is a way to imbricate agency because, once in place and working, it performs reliably on demand. System designers are currently preoccupied with the development of agents who can perform the multiple tasks that are required to make Internet communication a reality. A major objective of technology, typically, is to imbricate agency. But once imbricated, one generation's technology becomes an impediment to the acceptance of the next (Star & Ruhleder, 1996). Imbricated structures are resistant to change. That is the natural strength of this form of organizing—but also its weakness.

A Dialectic of Control

If communication, as the realization of agency through interaction, invariably exerts power, it might be expected to generate resistance. Communication

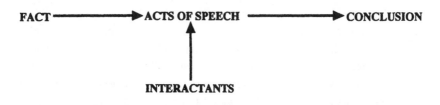

Figure 4.5. Communication as a Transformation of Fact Into Conclusion Through the Mediation of Speech Acts

thus has an essential polemic dimension, what Giddens calls a *dialectic of control.* It is here we return to address directly the question of that property of language that explains its capacity to serve as a modality for the instantiation of structure.

Consider the pattern that underlies Figure 4.5, abstracting from circumstance.

Figure 4.5 is inspired by Toulmin's (1988) model of practical argument. What we call "fact" in Figure 4.5, he refers to as *grounds,* and our conclusion is termed by him a *claim.* That which supports the making of a claim in the face of a given set of facts—what we call "acts of speech"—is what he terms a *warrant.*[5]

In other words, we are saying that, as a group or discourse community works its way through from the facts of a situation to a conclusion as to what to do about them, it is reasoning. The group is constructing, not a logical, but a practical argument. How it does so is going to be clearly distinguishable from the way in which a single individual reasons his or her way through to a conclusion, but the two patterns nevertheless share a fundamental basis: dealing pragmatically with situations.

The triplet "Fact (Grounds) (→) Acts of Speech (Warrant) (→) Conclusion (Claim)" is a form of text that can be traced back to a classical pattern of Greek logic, an *enthymeme.* The speech acts of a working group in conversation convey the warrant of an argument precisely because of the "modalizing" property of language—its capacity to assert fact and conclusions with varying degrees of epistemic and deontic effect (Toulmin also employed the concept of modality).

Modality in communication theory (Taylor & Van Every, 2000) is a linguistic category that conveys the concept of the attitude, or orientation, of a speaker with respect to what he or she is speaking about. It conveys the idea of the position of the speaker with respect to a situation. Attitudes to the facts of a situation exemplify *epistemic* modality; attitudes to the conclusion exemplify *deontic* modality.

Both epistemic and deontic modalities are normal features of everyday spoken language, a property of text but also an instrument of communication (Bybee & Fleischman, 1995). When Ops B says, "Must be Sarducci," he is speculating about a fact, an instance of epistemic modality. When the captain says, "Would you send somebody out here," he is making a request, or pointing toward a conclusion, an instance of deontic modality. So as people speak, they are constructing a kind of practical argument. Thus, speech acts that convey a warrant exercise authoritative power. In Giddens's terms: They establish a "rationalized" basis of action.

But, as Toulmin (1988) pointed out, a warrant is never a guarantee of acceptance: It may be countered by a *rebuttal*. There is an intrinsic dialectic of control in organizational communication. Warrants highlight elements of the situation that justify action (and thus create a present-at-hand), and rebuttals call attention to other features of the situation that render the conclusion problematical. What is to be made present-at-hand, in other words, is always potentially controversial.

In none of the conversational exchanges we have been citing, either those of Suchman or of Hutchins, was there an instance of what would usually be thought of as an argument. There is no good reason to suspect there would be. In locally situated systems of distributed cognition, many people typically have access to the facts. Furthermore, they have culturally engrained knowledge of the appropriate response to them, as Hutchins and Klausen point out is the case for airline pilots. The result is that if there is ambiguity about the facts, it typically is resolved by brief interchanges rather than by argument. Similar considerations apply to the coming to a conclusion. Not only is the "correct" course of action usually more or less understood by all, but the role of hierarchy in such groups is precisely to reduce the risk of time-consuming argument in normal work situations by attributing to one "position" the privilege/responsibility of primary actor.[6]

However, we will discover another, more subtle form of rebuttal. Not all rebuttals need to be expressed verbally; one can also "vote with one's feet." Practical argument has as its object to move people to action by persuading them the situation demands it. Not to be so moved is a practical, as opposed to a discursive (to employ Giddens's category), strategy of rebuttal. Suppose we interpret arguments for the necessity to computerize the organization as a persuasive strategy on someone's part (let us say, because we have already introduced this literature, BPR). Management is persuaded. In a sense, a conversation has been established around computerization. The working collaborative groups we consider, however, have little effective means to rebut the argument discursively. However, they can "rebut" it practically, by their nonadoption of the technology. Rebuttal is a way of conceptualizing computerization that we explore in later chapters.

The Importance of Community

One implication of our theory of action is the transformation of individual agency into group agency: Through communication, the collaborative group becomes an actor and is treated as such by others. When that has occurred, the A whose agency is represented in the actions of the individuals in the group, the Bs, is the group itself. The group has attained the status of what Engeström (1990) terms a community. In his schematic representation of activity (Figure 3.6), community figures as an essential node. We interpret his community-subject-object triangle as what we mean by an A-B-X system. What he shows as a subject-tool-object relationship we think of as an imbricated A-B-X component: subject as head, tool as instrumental complement.

The effect of interpreting community as an agency is to explain the concept of division of labor, in that every member of the group relates to his or her community and thus comes to have a role. In stable contexts of work, such a division of labor tends to become institutionalized and thus to express a rule of the relationship, much as Engeström hypothesizes. As we shall see, the same type of transformation, from individual to community, applies to the analysis of the organization as a whole.

Ontological Assumptions of a
Situated Theory of Communication

The situated view of communication implies a number of ontological assumptions, of which the following are most evident:

- "Facts" are not facts in a void; facts are *facts* because they point to what is to be regarded as salient in a situation.
- That which is *salient* (present-at-hand) is so because it is relative to a situation; the rest of the circumstantial world in which an activity is occurring remains transparent—ready-to-hand—during the course of the activity and thus informationally irrelevant for the time being.
- All activity is oriented; it follows that facts are *facts* because they are related to an eventual conclusion; the definition of *fact* is always specified by its relation to the purposes of the stater of the fact and conclusion—the *actant*.

♦ Communication is both in an activity and an activity in and of itself; in its role in an activity, it serves as one instrumentality among others for the carrying out of the activity (notably in facilitating a collective focus on a common present-at-hand); in its character as itself an activity, it consists in the use of language to make salient the facts of the situation (that which is present-at-hand) and to orient attention to a conclusion.

♦ The actor's power to act through communication is mediated by language, which furnishes the essential instrumentality of all communication.

♦ The situational role of communication is ended when the breakdown is resolved, and is understood to be so by all.

"Enactment" and the "Dance of Agency": The Outward Reach of Collaborative Groups

Pickering (1995) imagines scientific research as a "dance" of agency: scientists act and nature reacts, to produce an ongoing dialogue of scientific investigation, or what he calls a *dialectic of resistance and accommodation.* Weick (1979) developed a similar idea in his organizational theory of enactment: He sees action and cognition as a coupled system of act/learn in which people's actions produce the environment to which they subsequently orient. The communication that links a working group to its environing organizational context may similarly be thought of as "enactment," or as part of a continuing dance of agency, even though the "environment" in question is the rest of the organization—mostly other conversations (Figure 4.6).

Figure 4.6 shows two additional effects of the communication sequence that we have not mentioned before: (a) the circumstances have been affected by the actions of the group; and (b) the form of the conversation, including the identity and position of interactants within it, has been reiterated. By *dance of agency,* then, Pickering (1995) means the cyclic character of action. In one phase, knowing precedes acting; in the other, it follows.

For Pickering (1995), what scientists or system designers discover or design depends on what they have learned already and how they now set up the conditions for further inquiry (the topic of our Chapter 5, in which we enter a design laboratory to see how software systems are developed in two contrasting cultural contexts). Of course, it is true that the circumstances to which people respond are already framed by the ongoing involvement of people in the activity in which the circumstances arise. A breakdown in passenger unloading is already framed by airport operations. But it is equally the case that, as Weick (1979) pointed out, circumstances are selected by managers and organizations through their proactive interventions (the supervisor's call to another airline, for example).

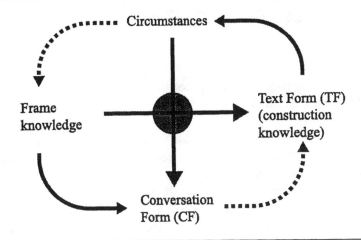

Figure 4.6. The Consequentiality of Communication

Groups have an outward reach because they affect circumstance, and this same circumstance may link them to others in the organization.

Similarly, the "form" of the conversation is dictated in good part by circumstances There are, as Bakhtin (1986) was among the first to observe, "speech genres." The conversational patterns of an operations room in an airport, the navigation team on a naval vessel, or the crew of a commercial airliner are specific to the kind of circumstances those different organizations encounter. Out of the fund of potentially relevant understandings possessed by some working community, circumstances serve to highlight—bring to the foreground of attention—some parts of their frame knowledge, whereas others remain virtual. Frame knowledge includes awareness of what the conversation is about, who participates in it, and what identities they are expected to assume. The roles that people are called on to play there are part of their established frame knowledge. Identities, in other words, have a contextual dimension and are sensitive to circumstance.

What we now explore is the communicational implications of a group's tie to its larger organizational context, mediated by circumstances. An organization, after all, is composed of more than any one unit of situated activity or ongoing conversation. It is an interlinking of conversations, joined to each other through shared circumstances. The result is the construction of units of co-orientation and collective action involving, not just individuals, but groups and the organization itself. Because of the larger context, interfaces are created between groups, each locally situated, and between the local and the global—the trans-situational.

◆ Theorizing the Extended Communication Networks of an Organization

We assume that the same model we have used to explain locally situated communication is applicable to the more extended networks of the organization. There are, however, three qualifications to be taken into account.

First, although situated work is typically preoccupied with the mobilization of allocative resources, organizational networks are more concerned with the mobilization of authoritative resources. Although each mobilizes both allocative and authoritative resources, the mix is different. Each level, local and global, depends on the other. The result, we argue, leads to what Giddens calls a "dialectic of control."

Second, the actors who participate in the intergroup communication network have a different status from those we have met until now. As corporate actors, they represent groups, in one manner or another. The constitution of the organization as a unity, as opposed to its components, brings into play both cognitive and pragmatic modalities that are distinct from those deployed locally. Of particular interest is the manner in which the organization must be created as an idea and how that idealization informs its strategies of control.

Third, text assumes a mediating role that is different in the extended network from that it plays in situated work. In the context of situated work, text is just people speaking; in the larger context of the organization, it becomes an actant. The text that preoccupies us in this discussion is that which forms the basis of computerization.

Organization as a Metaconversation, or "Conversation of Conversations"

An organization can be thought of as a dense overlay of many conversations, each oriented to some phase of activity. Boden (1994) used the expression *a lamination of conversations.* Krippendorff (1998) employed the term *an ecology of conversations.* Whatever the nomenclature, the concept is the same: a flowing, constantly evolving intersection of universes of talk in which people are caught up. It would be hard to contradict Boden's contention that the basic material out of which organizational reality is fabricated is situated talk, or conversation. It is where the meaning of events is negotiated and collective action engendered. The question of how such discursive universes link to each other, however, is what we now address. We do not want to focus on the conversations any longer but on the structural connections that link them. We are not so much interested in the processes by which conversations take form and become interrelated as in the structuring effect that follows as they do.

The Organization Considered
as Itself a Unit of Action

Consider organizational communication in the context of our model (Figure 4.6). First, the "circumstances" that apply are those that confront the organization as a whole, no longer any particular subset of it (e.g., competition from other firms or countries, government law and regulation, or sweeping technological change). Second, the "conversation" must be conceived as a conversation of conversations—a metaconversation (typically, involving levels of management and policy-making). "Conversation form" can no longer be assumed to function only according to the rules of face-to-face interaction. The participants in this larger "conversation" speak for conversations (represent them), and much of the interaction is mediated by textual characterizations of groups and their work (e.g., statistics, reports, or projects). "Frame knowledge" here relates to corporate identities and issues (the nature of the organization, the structure of the hierarchy, corporate policies, etc.). Similarly, "construction knowledge" incorporates assumptions about the interaction appropriate to corporate actors (e.g., how to deal with other departments). Institutional constraints enter the picture; rules and procedures become important.

Nevertheless, in spite of these significant differences, the organization confronts the same basic challenge as the small work group: how to transform a situation into a result ("fact" into "conclusion") and itself into a coordinated collaborative actor. The corporation-wide system of discourse also can be conceptualized as a form of distributed cognition. It too needs to reflexively monitor the flow of events and, using its accumulated frame knowledge, generate a rationalized interpretation of its own actions. It too needs to mobilize the actions of its members to produce a collective response to circumstances. As in the smaller group, the mobilization of action generates a hierarchy, or system of domination, with this difference: It is not just individuals, but groups as well, that are being structured. The organization too achieves a mobilization of action by the formation of co-orientation (*A-B-X*) units and depends for much of its routine performance of activities on the imbrication of head-complement relations. It

99

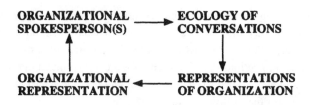

Figure 4.7. The Embedding of Levels of Discourse To Form an Organization

too comes to be accorded the status of agent: The organization becomes an actor and can position its community in interaction with other actor-networks in the larger society. Finally, its processes too are subject to the principle of a dialectic of control, a dynamic of "resistance and accommodation."

An interface between two levels of communication is created, each with its special self-organizing properties. At one level, communication occurs in the way we have been describing in the first part of this chapter: as a critical enabler in the performance of tasks, in a situated world of local circumstances. At the second level, communication occurs as a linking-up of all these locally situated discursive universes into one enveloping metaconversation. We visualize as a cycle the interface that this embedding of one level of discourse within another produces, a cycle in which the local is successively translated into the global and the global into the local (Figure 4.7).

Because the cycle is an unbroken system of interlevel translations from one domain of communication to another, we can in principle take any of the elements of Figure 4.7 as our starting point and read the cycle either clockwise or counterclockwise. Suppose we begin from the multiple conversations of locally situated work and proceed clockwise. In one way or another, those conversations must be translated into "representations" if they are to figure in the global metaconversation, either as objects of attention (what other people talk about, manage, plan, or design) or as subjects (corporate actors who make their influence felt through the intermediary of spokespersons who assume the role of agents). The effect is analogous to the dynamic we discussed earlier: There are interactants (domains of work represented either cognitively, pragmatically, or both) who confront a situation (that of the organization) but have yet to organize themselves into a collective system of action to deal with it. For the organization to emerge as an actor, therefore, these disparate representations must resolve themselves into a single representation of the situation, which is that of the organization-as-a-whole. Here, the notion of distributed cognition again applies:

Only when, through whatever interactive means, the organization has cognitively recognized its circumstances and transformed them into a situation can we say that the organization has a view. And if it has no view, it is not yet an actor capable of being attributed an intention. One further step remains: the alignment of organizational actors into a system of action, which expresses itself as a single voice (the cognitive representation transformed into a pragmatic representation).

When the communicative process is complete, the organization is enabled to perform as an agent, or actor-network (i.e., one that speaks for and to the multiple interactants that compose it).

The other "interface" of local and global is represented by the upper line of Figure 4.7. It is an interface because, from the perspective of the organization-as-an-agent, the conversations of its multiple component-situated universes of discourse constitute part of its circumstances (and not just its composition). Similarly, for those caught up in the situated world of work, the discourse of the larger organization is part of their circumstances—an exterior influence to which they have to pay attention along with others, such as those emanating from other actors, including other parts of the organizational complex.

We could equally well read Figure 4.7 counterclockwise. The situated universes of discourse of an organization assume a background of corporate resources and a shared infrastructure. The "organization," as a socially constructed entity, assumes an ideological basis in the frame knowledge of its society. The modern corporation or government department is an invention of the last century and a half, an idea that has emerged in parallel with its pragmatic realization as a system of people and technology. That idea is nurtured by an ongoing dialogue involving both theoreticians and practitioners (basically the domain of management and administration science and of the sociology of organizations). And, of course, none of this would have any meaning in the absence of the reconstruction of the basis of organization in the day-to-day activities of its members.

Figure 4.7 thus describes a system with deep cultural roots. It is, as much as any technology, a historically situated artifact, a product of the collective enterprise of a particular society. That it is an artifact constructed out of communication constitutes its singularity, but in other respects it is merely one more development in an unbroken chain that links us back to *homo faber*—humankind as indefatigable craftsperson. It is still being designed, computerization being no more than an instrumentality being put to work toward that end.

There are, we observed previously, three factors to be taken into consideration in reading the dynamics of the interface described in Figure 4.7.

Dialectics of Control

Giddens observed that power emerges from the mobilization of resources. Both local and global communities mobilize resources, but they differ in kind and importance. For the collaborative group, allocative resources are typically concrete, involving actual technology and focused on practical objects. For the larger organization, allocative resources typically take the form of capital: administration of the budget and management of the accounting system. The result is a dialectic of control. Local groups depend on global for their infrastructure. On the other hand, the global depends on the local for work and, ultimately, for profit (private sector) or performance (public sector), in the absence of which its sources of capital risk drying up.

Another kind of dynamic may be observed for authoritative resources. The global organization is supported by an elaborate institutional framework with roots in economics, politics, law, and ideology, all of which serve to sanction its exercise of authority. On the other hand, as Barley (1996b) observed, people who work in specialized fields of expertise (e.g., technicians and professionals) develop kinds of knowledge that lend their practice an authority that escapes the usual discipline of organizational hierarchy. In a time of intense investment in technology, such authority inevitably transcends the bounds of any single organization and becomes a component in a different kind of dialectic of control: the exercise of authority in the day-to-day (a feature of each of the four studies we used as illustrations in Chapter 1, incidentally).

A Polemic of Perspectives

An organization is a very special kind of object/subject. As an object, it has no substantiality. It is associated with a physical infrastructure of offices, shops, networks, and technologies, but, in and of itself, it is none of these. Fundamentally, it is no more than an idea, a construction of the imagination (Morgan, 1986). As a subject, it is no more than an actor-network, a contingent alignment of agencies in response to certain circumstances. Such an alignment presupposes an ongoing reconciliation of perspectives that are more or less compatible, one with the other. There is always something like a contest of influence—an argument (to refer to our earlier discussion) in which not everyone's representation of organization is accorded equal weight (Deetz, 1992).

Latour (1987) theorized how some representations come to develop alliances and become accepted, whereas others are sidelined. The goal is always to have one's own representation "black-boxed" (i.e., become so much a part of "what everyone knows" that it is simply taken as an unquestioned given). There is thus an element of rhetoric involved in the many-to-one translation of representations shown in Figure 4.7. At issue is power—the power to direct the organization in certain ways and away from others. At the end of this chapter, we illustrate how computerization enters this ongoing debate as one of its topics.

The Role of Text in Constructing
the Identity of the Organization

As long as we think of the linking of conversations as an intervention of an individual, such as the captain, we remain in the domain of interaction in which intention is negotiable. Text, unlike conversation, categorizes and thus assigns intention to an agent. As it does so, it creates objects (nouns, and verbs, notably). It is true that the "objects" in question are no more than symbolic, but we should be careful how we interpret the expression "no more." That "no more" is actually quite a lot.

The categorizing processes of language, enabled by textualization (including its realization as speech), are what give groups and their members the status of objects. As we pointed out previously, the script of airport operations that Suchman supplied in her study gives it a kind of reality that unmediated-by-text direct experience could not match. Because events can be described in text, one conversation can figure in another vicariously. We will never have been physically in the operations room of that airport, but, through the text, we know about it. That present-but-not-present conversation has been reified—made a *res,* or thing.

Once some conversational domain of activity has been reified, it now exists as a textual object that can be manipulated (and may figure in design). Because the textual representation of a group translates both it and its activities into categories, and because categories typify rather than specify, the translation invites the formation of equivalences. It becomes possible—perhaps even inevitable— to make generalizations across several activity centers by treating them all as members of a single class—let us say, to pursue our former illustration, all airplane crews and all airport ground operations.

To frame the issue in terms of the software development case study used as an illustration outlined in Chapter 1 (Hovey, 1992), the objective of the developers, from the perspective of the working community, was the imposition of a single standard for every operation in the entire enterprise. As we saw, the user community reacted without much enthusiasm. From the contrasting perspective of the designer (and management), we might argue differently that, not surprisingly, although the across-the-board standardization was unsuccessful, it was only be-cause the generalization was not right. But this hardly implies that standardiza-tion per se is a bad thing. The company was already standardized (we would say imbricated) in many respects. In fact, if it were not, it would never have attained the scale of operations it had.

◆ Communication, Contradiction, and Computerization

If an organization is the complex intersection of discourse communities we have described, and if their interface relationships are typically characterized by a di-alectic of control, then individuals might be expected to find themselves fre-quently at an intersection of contradictory pressures. To be an actor, we have ar-gued, one must be an agent. To be an agent, one must act for someone or something. To have nothing to act for is to have no reason to act. The problem is that people typically act-for in different ways, depending on the context. And even in a single context, people may find themselves acting for different agen-cies (e.g., see Engeström's [1990] example of doctors who respond to both pro-fessional and administrative exigencies, even within the context of a single inter-view, cited in Chapter 3).

One of the individual's interfaces is the group. We have argued that the con-text of collaborative work creates an alignment of agencies, within which the in-dividual figures as a component. Individuals work for their groups (a well-known source of morale among soldiers in wartime is group cohesion). Or indi-viduals may identify with the community where they live and find themselves acting for it or their family. Professionals see themselves as representatives of their discipline. Employees may be dedicated to working for their company, or their agency of government. One can work for the benefit of one's clients, or cus-tomers, or patients—or simply for humanity. One can be motivated by one's reli-gious beliefs, or by a cause.

We have not introduced a co-orientation model to reduce the complexity of human motivation, because it is clear that human identities emerge as a subtle interplay of motives and a rich fabric of identification with a variety of commu-nities of discourse. In the chapters that follow, we consider a different facet of the phenomenon of intersection agency relationships: the contradictions that sometimes mark the group/organization interface, focalized by an implementa-tion of I/CT. As a preliminary introduction, it is useful to flag three intersections of agency that, in some circumstances, may produce contradictory pressures.

These intersections are professional versus administrative, process versus function, and local versus global.

Tensions That Arise From Contradictory Professional and Administrative Imperatives

A powerful motive in the conduct of work is the sense of belonging to a community of people who share a unique expertise and code of ethics. Of course, such consciousness of community and the loyalty it generates may be found anywhere, but it finds its most notable expression in the professions. It is there that, in addition to a shared pride in some special skill, the autonomy of the work community is enshrined in socially sanctioned institutional arrangements, affecting entry to the exercise of the skill and subsequent conduct of its practitioners. The result is sometimes a contradiction of professional and administrative imperatives (illustrated in Chapter 1 by the case of the new medical technology in which the medical doctors simply opted out, citing professional ethics). In Chapter 5, we consider a different aspect of professional agency: its role in orienting the design of systems.

Tensions That Arise From Contradictory Process and Function Imperatives

One of the effects of organization is to structure relations between communities of work in certain patterns. Such a pattern is found where one department regularly performs a specialized service for others. It is assigned, in organizational logic, a function that it is both authorized and required to perform. For the departments who are its clients, the function is merely one (imbricated) component in its process. In Chapter 6, we explore some of the dynamics of this relationship and the role of computerization in both supporting and transforming it.

Tensions That Arise From Contradictory Local and Global Imperatives

This is the most salient of all the contradictory pressures, and it permeates almost every discussion of the dynamics of computerization of work. We have already evoked the source of the tension in Chapter 3: the push to standardize operations on the part of management (I/CT as prime instrumentality of standardization) versus the need for flexibility and native ingenuity to deal with the inevitably contingent circumstances of everyday work (I/CT as simply a tool to be employed as needed by skilled people). Perspectives on this tension are to be found in each of the chapters that follows. To conclude this chapter, we summarize a famous local/global debate that picks up several themes to which we already have alluded, including the role of text in global communication processes.

◆ The Suchman/Winograd Debate

The Suchman/Winograd debate took the form of an exchange of articles between two of the stars of the field, Lucy Suchman and Terry Winograd, published in *Computer Supported Cooperative Work* (Suchman, 1994; Winograd, 1994).

In a way, it was surprising to find these two in such disagreement, because both were associated with books (Suchman, 1987; Winograd & Flores, 1986) in which they had expressed serious reservations about the then-dominant view of computing as a control technology. Both had argued for a broadening of perspective to include consideration of how people cope with the contingencies of working life. However, there was already a difference between their respective positions, in that the Winograd and Flores book included a description of a software product, called The Coordinator, that was intended to serve as a support for group interaction. It was this software application that was to become Suchman's (1994) target.

As Suchman (1994) describes The Coordinator, it is "a mechanism for the prescription of *a priori* forms of social behavior" (p. 177). What she is referring to is the application's basis in speech act theory. Speech act theory is a conceptualization of communicative action as constructed out of exchanges in which one partner exerts what is called an "illocutionary force" on another, through the medium of speech, by expressing an intention. An act of speech, thus conceived, might, for example, take the form of a request (intention: get someone else to carry out an act). It might be a promise, or a commitment (intention: the speaker intends to carry out an act). It could be a compliment or, alternatively, a complaint (intention: to express an attitude toward an act already carried out). It could be a statement of belief (intention: to express an attitude to a state of the world).

Thought of in this way, communicative action mediated by speech would explain how the most fundamental links of organization come to be negotiated: transactions, hierarchy, sanction (positive and negative), and so on (Taylor & Van Every, 2000). The Coordinator's software aimed to (a) offer a categorization of acts of speech that people were encouraged to use in interacting with each other in a computer-supported environment; and (b) provide the means by which commitments, once entered into by participants, could be subsequently scheduled and managed. It was precisely this "emphasis on the encoding of speakers' intentions into explicit categories" (p. 178) that drew Suchman's fire because, she asserts, it "carries with it an agenda of discipline and control over organization members' actions." Instead, she argues for "an appreciation for and engagement with the specificity, heterogeneity and practicality of organizational life" (p. 178).

We have already seen in Chapter 3 what Suchman (1996) means by the "specificity, heterogeneity and practicality" of organizational life in the airport operations room example. It is how people deal with the contingencies of work. She clearly does not object to technology, as such; in fact, the world of the airport she describes is saturated with technology. It is the idea that somehow the spontaneous processes of human conversation can be captured in a set of categories, and then reproduced in the written code of a software system, that she faults.

The Coordinator was among the first attempts to capture the logic of human conversation in software (Grudin, 1990). For the most part, previous software products had dealt with information-processing activities such as those performed by individuals and with the transmission protocols by which information gets passed around in an organization. The Coordinator, by contrast, had as its focus not only the interaction process but its structuring in the text of software. It is the notion that the kind of negotiation in which people in organizations engage could be reduced to text that Suchman found outrageous.

A close reading of the argument of Suchman (1994) makes it clear that the issue, as she sees it, turns on the translation of conversation into text, and vice versa. For her, "conversation analyses underscore the irreducibly interactional structuring of talk" (p. 179). She sees "a speaker's intent as shaped by the response of hearers" (pp. 179-180). She argues for a "'radical indeterminacy' of the unfolding course of human interaction" and for "intractable uncertainties in accounting for the 'illocutionary force' of a given utterance" (p. 180). To translate a conversational dynamic (in which the meaning of a speaker's utterance is determined retrospectively, in the to-and-fro of interaction) into a category system (to reduce it to text, in other words) is, she thinks, to miss the point. The Coordinator must assume that knowledge of intention precedes its expression in speech. Structuration theory, as we have seen, makes a different assumption, namely that knowledge of intention is constructed reflexively and interactively, as a kind of negotiation.

To adopt speech act theory as a basis for system design, she believes, is to inscribe a text-based theory of intention into the coded instructions of a computer program and, in so doing, impose a straitjacket on the normal play of human interaction. It is "categorization as discipline" (Suchman, 1994, p. 181). And, consistent with other writings of hers, Suchman sees a hidden managerial agenda "to tame and domesticate, to render rational and controllable the densely structured, heterogeneous texture of organizational life" (p. 185). The Coordinator is "a tool for the reproduction of an established social order" (p. 186). And software designers have been "cast into the role of designer not only of technical systems but of organizations themselves" (pp. 186-187).

Winograd (1994), in his rejoinder, agrees with Suchman "that no systematic account can fully capture the richness of mental life or social interaction" (p. 192). It is, he says, "a dangerous form of blindness to believe that any representation captures what is meaningful to people in a situation" (p. 196). On the contrary, he argues that The Coordinator is nothing more sinister than an accounting tool. It is true that "it uses a formal structure in which regular patterns of language acts are associated with the content and time of requests, commitments and declarations of completion" (p. 192). But this, he goes on, is an inevitable consequence of using software, because the latter only works "with fully rationalized typologies (be they bits and bytes or knowledge bases)" (p. 193). Writing software, after all, is writing (Shore, 1985). But the same criticism, he contended, would be equally true for an accounting system to track profit and loss in a firm. In fact, the utility of a system such as The Coordinator is likely to become evident only in certain kinds of contexts—especially large and complex organizations.

As he says, "When people interact face to face on a regular day to day basis, things can be done in a very different way than when an organization is spread over the world, with 10,000 employees and thousands of suppliers" (p. 194). He immediately concedes that, in his experience, The Coordinator seems to work better in the management of engineering change in a large manufacturing division than as a communication tool in a research laboratory (p. 195).

But no matter what the system, it will only work successfully with the participation of the people who live in the context being represented: "Organizational design succeeds when it is grounded in the context and experience of those who live in the situation" (Winograd, 1994, p. 195). Once you have transcended the Suchman image of "an epic struggle between the forces of discipline and the forces of resistance" you are back to "dealing with interactions among people" (p. 196). Here, The Coordinator, like any other technology, might or might not prove to have its uses. Winograd ends by echoing (with more than a tinge of sarcasm) Suchman's fervent desire to "embrace an appreciation for and engagement within the specificity, heterogeneity and practicality of organizational life" (p. 178).

The Suchman/Winograd debate thus once again highlights the theme of this chapter, namely, the ongoing dynamic of translation involving the contrasting mediations of conversation and representation (Figure 4.7). It points with particular clarity to the role of computerization in this dynamic. Once integrated into work routines, technology becomes no more than another agency in the continuing adaptation of the group to its circumstances. As Hutchins (1995) emphasized, technology participates in the processes of work in a totally natural way when it is part of the situated intelligence of the working group. It is only when technology has not yet made itself part of what Star called infrastructure that the "fit" becomes problematical. It is then that the contrasting logics of "organizational, explicit" and "activity-oriented, tacit" (Sachs, 1995) lead to the kinds of incomplete implementations of technology that we alluded to in Chapter 1.

The real struggle, then, is not between technology and situated work but between the contrasting imperatives of the local and the global. Technology becomes one of the means by which global considerations of standardization and proceduralization intrude themselves into the situated world of ordinary work.

It is in how they respectively visualize organization, as a meshing of local and global, that the real debate between Suchman and Winograd is to be found. Suchman (1994) thinks of "an agenda of discipline and control over organization members' actions" (p. 178). She spoke of "ordering devices, used to organize the persons, settings, events or activities by whom they are employed or to which they refer," and she contrasts this with "acts of resistance involving a taking back of naming and assessment into indigenous categorization schemes" (p. 182). She associates technology with "disciplinary practices" and "administration of power" (p. 183). And it becomes for her "a contest over how our relations are ordered to each other and by whom" (p. 188). She echoes Star's reading of systems of classification as how the organization is categorized to become an "object" of management.

In response, Winograd (1994) mocks this

> sociopolitical drama, in which the villains (corporate managers and their accomplices: organizational development consultants and computer scientists) attempt to impose their designs on the innocent victims (the workers whom the managers want to "tame and domesticate"). (p. 191)

Winograd readily concedes "the unpleasant constraints of modern bureaucratic society, with its powerful organizations and lack of concern for the individual" (p. 191), but he argues for a different vision of the organization as "a web of conversations and commitments among the people inside and outside the organization" (p. 194). Like it or not, he says in effect, big organization is with us, and we need to develop ways to "keep track" of its intersecting commitments. Hence, technology.

◆ Notes

1. In systems development, as in communication research, this has sometimes been taken to be the principal function of communication: messaging, or information transmission.

2. For a quite different interpretation of the company as fractal, see Warnecke (1993).

3. The distinction we are making between "circumstances" and "situation" is motivated by an insight of Heidegger (1959), the difference between ready-to-hand and present-at-hand (*zuhanden, vorhanden*). In the normal course of events, as Suchman (1996) emphasized, the circumstantial world that framed the activities of the people in Operations was largely transparent. As long as the stairs functioned properly, they were just there—part of a system that could safely be left out of consciousness, because they automatically came into play when they were needed, the object of somebody else's attention, perhaps, but not of the Operations personnel. For the latter, they were, by Heidegger's definition, ready-to-hand.

4. Note that the goal already figures in the definition of the situation, as well as the operation (and the technology) that intervenes to realize the goal. This is a logical consequence of the structurational principle that activities become meaningful through monitoring and rationalization.

5. van Eemeren, Grootendorst, and Henkemans (1996) use the term *data* for *grounds*. The term *evidence* is also frequently employed to refer to grounds, or facts.

6. Which also poses its risks. At least some air crashes have been attributed to the reluctance of first officers to correct their chiefs, even when they know the latter to be in error, so strong is the hierarchical relationship.

5
Technology Development: Writing Organization

◆   In the last chapter, we reported on a debate in which one of the participants accused technology of being an "ordering device" associated with a "disciplinary practice." Her view has a basis in fact: When a computerized system is implemented in the workplace, what looks to people like a machine is actually a text—software written by some community of designers, located in a certain cultural context, situated at a particular time and place. That text is not neutral; it imposes an image of work that, when it is implemented as technology, triggers a cyclical process of organizational learning and identity reconstruction.

The other participant in the debate was more sanguine, seeing in technology no more than a useful accounting device, a device to enable the linking of large networks in the complex organizational world of today.

The debate invites us to look more carefully into the characteristics of technology and the view of work and organization that presided at its design, to be inscribed into its software code. We argue in this chapter that technology, like science, is a "hybrid" (Latour, 1993, 1994), a complex historical interweaving of material and subjective elements that is not easily disentangled. How a technology develops is partly a matter of the constraints imposed by the physical world of objects and partly an issue of social process and the vagaries of human networking. It is a product of social construction developed through a process of variation and selection, subject to cultural influences and assumptions about the nature of society and organization. This chapter, in other words, is an exploration of the system development practices that go into writing technology.

It is easy from the outside to imagine that the development of computer technology is driven by an inexorable logic of substituting better-performing systems for quickly obsolescing machines and that all machines are developed according to identical formalist principles. We explore instead the idea that technology is, at least in part, a social construction. To show how the technology designed to support collaborative work incorporates many assumptions that are deeply cultural and social, we examine two contrasting approaches in one of the newer areas in computer design that has come to be known as *groupware* or *computer-supported cooperative work* (CSCW). Our attention is focused on two design groups—one in Denmark and the other in Japan—who have been building on the specifics of their own technological, cultural, and institutional realities to produce a product for what they take to be its eventual users. One feature stands out. Although both societies are inheritors of a common fund of knowledge available to every software programmer, whatever their nationality, the product of these two design communities is in other respects highly distinctive.

The comparisons we draw encompass not only the designers' approaches to their development practice but also their relationship to their professional peers and the culture of their society. We conclude with a brief reflection about technology as one kind of text or "surface" among others on which human intentionality comes to be written.

◆ The CSCW Design Challenge

CSCW systems are communicational in spirit. They are meant to support complex situationally determined tasks, everything from boardroom meetings to telephone conversations to shared work. Among the contexts foreseen by designers are interactions occurring at the same time and in the same place (meeting facilitation), at the same time and in different places (teleconferencing), in the same place but at different times (team rooms, work shifts), and in different places at different times (e-mail, collaborative writing and design, workflow management). And, of course, there is a plethora of mixed systems.

Confronted with so many possibilities, the CSCW designer is obliged to make choices, to prioritize which kind of activity to support. Whatever the route taken, questions are raised: How is cooperative work articulated? How are tasks defined and coordinated? How are information spaces shared? And how do organizations and technologies adapt to each other?

Not surprisingly, there is considerable variety in the "solutions" designers develop in response to these and similar problems. In addition to the considerable variety of perspectives ranging from engineering, to software, to social science, and even to philosophy that coexist under the CSCW umbrella (and that have generated their own tensions[1]), regional differences also have been evident. North Americans, for example, seem to favor an empirical approach and a focus on product development and small-group applications. Europeans, on the other hand, are generally more theoretical or philosophical in orientation and put emphasis on the user organizations and organization systems. Japanese presentations to international CSCW conferences have without exception involved video-mediated communication and large-screen displays.

The Genesis of the Research Project Described in This Chapter

The regional and intellectual diversity in the CSCW community furnished the seedbed—and motivation—for the field research project we are about to describe. It led us to ask how technology comes to incorporate assumptions about organizing and the way work is done. We asked ourselves whether systems development might not reflect the social organization and culture of the designers as much as, or even more than, the wired-in properties of a standard computer and conventional protocols of system design. The evidently divergent tendencies reflected in work done in Scandinavia versus that done in Japan, for example, become an invitation to cross-cultural research. Why not find out how the technology is developed where it is being developed? This is what one of the authors of this book (Heaton, 1997) set out to do.

Our purpose was not to draw any broad conclusions about culture and technology but simply to illustrate, by concrete examples, how differently the "same" CSCW technology can be conceptualized and how institutional and cultural frames come to influence not just the design process but the very technological product that is its object.

Dimensions of Culture

Hofstede's (1980) investigations into culture led him to propose that it is possible to identify broad cultural predispositions (the "collective software of the mind," in his words) or dimensions. We selected four of his dimensions along which to distinguish between cultures:

1. The extent to which an unequal distribution of power is accepted and even expected.
2. The relative importance of individualism versus collectivism.
3. The degree to which masculine roles are clearly delineated from feminine.
4. The level of tolerance of ambiguity, or how people cope with uncertain or unknown situations.

Hofstede's (1980) research points to a continuum for each of these dimensions, with Japanese culture typically most distant from Scandinavian, and North American falling somewhere in between. He found Japan, for example, to be high in power distance, low in individualism and high in collectivism, very high in gender discrimination, and high in uncertainty avoidance. Scandinavia, on the other hand, was found to be low in power distance (especially in Denmark), higher in individualism than Japan (but considerably lower than North America in that collectivism is also part of the Scandinavian tradition, although differently conceived than in Japan), very low in gender discrimination (even compared to North America), and low in uncertainty avoidance.

Given these striking differences, we hypothesized that system designers who were constructing technologies to support collaborative work would conceive of their task in very different terms in Japan and in Scandinavia. To verify our intuition, we spent March and April 1995 at Aarhus University in Denmark, May at the Royal Institute of Technology in Stockholm, Sweden, and June and July in Japan, at Keio University, with additional interviews and observations in Nippon Telephone and Telegraph (NTT; a principal site of technology development in that country).

During this time, we were able to see the machines and CSCW systems we had previously heard reported on at international conferences and to experiment with them. Our observations of design activities were mixed with frequent verbal interaction, both in the form of recorded interviews and more casual conversations. All respondents spoke English (especially in Scandinavia, where speakers tend to be very fluent). In addition, Heaton speaks Japanese (two interviews were conducted in Japanese, and she was able to sit in on technical conferences conducted in that language).

The Objectives of the Research

Our study drew inspiration from the literature on science and technology, notably as enunciated by Woolgar (1991). Rather than assume that technological artifacts are objects with fixed attributes (uses, capabilities, etc.), Woolgar argued for a different view, namely, that an object exists only in and through descriptions and practices. He sees it as being "constituted" and argues that it is never available in a purely technical state. It is, instead, the temporary contingent upshot of an ongoing interpretation by designers and users.

Our field research aimed to trace how features of the environment of the designers (the organizational structure of the designer world, professional training

114

and commitments, cultural assumptions about work and society, material constraints, intellectual and political trends, and so on) get played out in the design process. We plunged ourselves into their ongoing conversations, or what Bijker, Hughes, and Pinch (1987) have called their *technological frame.* By *frame,* these researchers mean that designers, like people at work anywhere, build on what is already established, including theory, tacit understandings, professional practice and procedures, instruments and devices, material networks, institutional support systems, and cultural values. Their workplace is simultaneously technical and social, material and intellectual, individual and political.

In turn, technological frames are part of organizational frame (Orlikowski & Gash, 1994). The challenge for the researcher is to be sensitive to the interplay of actions and frames, to give individual initiative and originality their due while remaining attuned to how the frame influences the design process at critical junctures. It becomes a matter of looking through the design conversation, with its multiple laminations (Boden, 1994), to the text that it is progressively generating. There is something like an unconscious process of "cultural creep" as designers create artifacts to fit into the cultural spaces suggested by their existing frames of meaning (Heaton, 1997, p. 61).

Methodologically, there are two dimensions of design to be explored: *ideational* and *procedural.* Ideational simply refers to the content of the technological text—the actual products of design, as well as the articles designers write to describe their work. It is here that they set out their choices and create retrospective reconstructions of what was done and why. The ideational dimension for the researcher means examining the kinds of social interfaces that are built into the systems: Why prefer one capacity or function over another? What are the kinds of social protocols that get "built-in" (e.g., what meeting style is favored: strict turn-taking vs. free-for-all, fixed beginnings and endings with all constantly present as opposed to people dropping in and out, how to interrupt, do you always reveal your presence, and so on)?

The procedural dimension is concerned with the design process as such: What are the work situations in which designers find themselves, and how do they deal with the resources and the constraints that characterize them? The design process only looks neat and tidy in retrospect. In practice, it is contingent on many largely uncontrollable (or at best partially controllable) factors, and the eventual product is as much a result of how the designers dealt with procedural crises as they arose as it is any abstract ideational parameter.

Now, let us turn to the first part of the project: the Aarhus group in Denmark.

◆ CSCW Systems Design in Denmark

There is a rich history of concern for industrial democracy in Scandinavia that predates the era of computerization. Many universities there have departments or research centers for "working life studies," not to mention government-sponsored centers and programs. Although Scandinavian trade unions historically have tended to favor the introduction of new technology and its positive impact on the standard of living, there was nevertheless concern by the early 1970s over the potentially negative effects of the radical transformation engendered by computerization. The upshot was collaboration between university-based researchers in the critical tradition with workers and their unions, in the interest of a more enlightened approach to the design and implementation of the tools and machines to be used in work.

In the course of their work together, a central idea began to take shape: that design be wedded to local realities and the practical experience of how work is done and lead to continuing interaction with the working community itself. This was a kind of "negotiation" model of systems design, combining active field-work in which researchers acted as resource persons advising workers. The emphasis was on how to adapt and accommodate existing technologies to the workplace, augmenting skills rather than replacing or automating them, with the systems people lending the benefit of their knowledge to the working community. The significance of these initiatives was to define "a new Scandinavian model" for research and development activities—which was to capture the attention of the design community elsewhere as well.

Aarhus University

Aarhus is neither the largest nor the richest university in Denmark, and it is relatively distant from the nation's capital, Copenhagen. The computer science department is also modest. Nevertheless, it is the home of a small CSCW research program that has achieved world recognition and has become influential in Scandinavia and elsewhere. The Aarhus CSCW designers are not typical of everything that occurs in Scandinavia (indeed, they even take pride in their singularity). Nonetheless, they are Danish in philosophy and style and illustrate very clearly one pole in the design philosophy spectrum—that which is centered on user participation in design.

At the time of our study (1995), the CSCW research group included three professors, one postdoctoral fellow, two doctoral students, and occasional programmers. There is, we were repeatedly told, very little hierarchy in Danish society (from the king on down). This commitment to a democratic egalitarianism is evident in the working style of the Aarhus CSCW group, who drift in and out of each others' offices without ceremony, who eat lunch together every day, and who expect their students to express themselves as freely as if they were peers. It is not just at work that these patterns are to be found: Some of the team's members live in communities (a Danish version of cooperative or commune). Furthermore, they have known each other for many years: All three of the professors had done their doctoral work at Aarhus and had spent relatively little time abroad (with the exception of one who had, as a student, visited Xerox PARC in California for some time). Their ease with each other extends, moreover, to their openness to visitors from abroad, who find themselves warmly received and invited to join in, with few apparent restrictions.

Of the three professors in the CSCW group at Aarhus, two had participated in what was known as the UTOPIA project on developing skill-enhancing tools for graphics workers in the 1980s, and, thus, it is not surprising that the group was firmly committed to the principle of design as a cooperative activity involving users. Their activity normally alternates between developing prototypes and working with users in a client organization. As one member put it, he believed ("as a Danish citizen possessing certain political points of view") that workers have fundamental democratic rights to influence the conditions under which they work and specifically to influence the development and use of technology for their workplace (Heaton, 1997, p. 83).

From this commitment to participatory design flows a further belief in the necessity of looking at individual situations and the supporting of work in actual contexts, always remaining responsive to local needs. The idea of modeling or designing from theory, such as the waterfall model we described in Chapter 1, is anathema to them. They perceive, on the contrary, every development project to be unique and contingent on the context in which it is situated. For them, there is no distinct "requirements analysis" phase in which knowledge is extracted from the people doing the work, as a preliminary to design. Instead, it is "the challenge when you go out into real life and try to make something that people should actually use" that fascinates them (Heaton, 1997, p. 84). They do not, they say, "do CSCW." Participatory design means "actual people, actual situations, actual places, actual organizations—with all the pros and cons." It is a commitment to action research, a continuous cycle of two-way learning.

Over the years, then, members of the group have worked to perfect cooperative design techniques—techniques only distantly related to conventional programming protocols. Their immediate purpose is less to produce a software artifact (in which their programming skills are tested) or to concern themselves with video bandwidth than it is to engage people at work in a critical reexamination of their own practices as a preliminary stage in the design process. Cooperative prototyping often starts with mock-ups, simulations, "throw-away" prototypes to clarify requirements, and role playing in which workers work out how they handle ordinary situations. Such insights are transcribed onto "situation" cards supplied by the researchers. Simulations may last as long as 2 or 3 days and center on work organization, skill requirements, division of labor, and cooperation at work. By exteriorizing work patterns on the cards and discussing their meaning, the researchers hope to encourage a shared understanding of the current organization with its problems and thus establish the basis for alternative organizational and technical designs.

A couple of examples illustrate the Aarhus CSCW approach and some of the practical problems for the designers that its user-inclusive philosophy engenders. In the 1990 project called *Arbejdstilsynet* (AT, or "Work Inspection"), researchers from Aarhus worked with a state agency responsible for inspecting and advising companies on health and safety matters in a cooperative design venture involving the local Aarhus branch of AT (some 50 inspectors and 10 secretaries). As first conceived, the emphasis was to be on the development of a long-term strategy for decentralized development and maintenance, supported by technology, with a focus on developing "good" designs for the office work surrounding the principal activity of inspection. Things moved ahead, and, after conducting initial interviews and observations of both office work and actual field inspection activities, the researchers began to shape a first prototype, which led to a 3-day seminar, based on organizational simulation and mock-ups of the eventual system. One month later, the prototype had been installed on a 2-day trial basis at the AT site, and this, in turn, led to another half-day seminar to develop an action plan aiming to iron out both organizational and technological implications of the introduction of the new system.

With the prototyping well under way, their work was suddenly curtailed when the larger organization to which the local branch of AT belonged decided that the entire organization would henceforth use networked PCs with MS-DOS as its operating system (the Aarhus group would have preferred Macintosh). The Aarhus research group now found itself no longer doing prototyping for a new system but acting as consultants in facilitating the introduction of the PCs. Their new role was to take on the tasks of selecting hardware and software and tailoring the purchased applications to the needs of the clients, as well as training workers in the use of WordPerfect text editing for DOS (not Windows). Over the year, as the workers became more comfortable with using the system and fashioning it to their own needs, the Aarhus group's involvement was phased out.

In a second example of their participatory activities, in 1994 the Aarhus group collaborated with a much larger European Community two-phase team effort having the objective of developing generic CSCW applications, in this case producing a CSCW framework and design shell for applications and network infrastructure. Operationally, the assignment involved three "demonstrators" including collaboration via live video, distributed work via a global "window," and the support of mobile computers. The Danish contribution was tied into an ambitious construction project, involving some 400 employees located in four sites. The Aarhus designers were responsible for designing hypermedia-based links for third-party applications, applicable for all three demonstrations. As they saw it, this would require reconciliation of the distributed central system with the local work group, especially the integration of local planning detail.

Consistent with their customary way of working, the Aarhus team headed out into the field to organize a workshop to generate "visions" on how to overcome identifiable problems and bottlenecks. Their objective was the development of a coordination tool, using object-oriented design and hypermedia techniques. The system they evolved was intended to allow users to link up with the software applications with which they were already familiar as well as to encourage them to create their own linkages, using hypertext, to switch smoothly between individual and cooperative work and between different tasks throughout the day.

By 1995 (when we visited the project site), the system was being installed and significant problems had emerged. No one was actually using the system (beyond taking part in demonstrations). As one researcher put it, "they're all floundering around down there" (Heaton, 1997, p. 98). Of the eight people involved in the test group, two were about to leave and had no incentive to learn the system. The key person was expert in the archiving of documents but was totally ignorant of computers. And although the project was being paid to try out the system, the actual users were being paid no bonuses. Finally, there were technical glitches: The Aarhus group had believed the project was using the Windows NT platform, whereas they were actually using Windows. The designers had planned for Word (rather than WordPerfect) and Excel (which the users did not use). Microstation, a graphics program used by some engineers at the head office in Copenhagen, was not used on the site. At that point, the Aarhus team shifted into problem-solving mode and, when our field research concluded, were proposing a number of solutions, both technical and organizational, to get things back on track.

We have gone into some detail in describing the work of the Aarhus research group, not because they are typical of everything that occurs in Scandinavia, but because they illustrate very clearly one pole in the design philosophy spectrum—that which is centered on local work practices and on user participation in design. With this cultural specificity in mind and some idea of how it enters into the design process and its products in Denmark, let us now take wing and fly halfway around the world, to Japan.

◆ A Different Research Environment: Japan

Keio University

Keio is one of Japan's leading private universities. The CSCW research going on there is to be found in the Matsushita Lab in the Department of Instrumentation Engineering ("Matsushita" is the name of the professor who heads up the program, not the electronics company). There are two professors, both Keio alumni (including Professor Matsushita), 11 doctoral students, and 39 master's students working on a variety of projects linked to CSCW (or, as it is more often called in Japan, *groupware*).

Physically, the lab consists of two very crowded rooms, stuffed with papers, books, and equipment. The building is old and dilapidated, and there are teacups, plates, and food or candy wrappers strewn around here and there. One of the rooms has a double row of about 20 computers back-to-back down the center, with a few more along the walls and the MAJIC setup installed in a corner (we come back to MAJIC shortly). The other room, used primarily by the doctoral students, has about 10 desks with computers on them arranged with low partitions or piles of books to divide the work spaces.

There is always someone there. Students often work 12- to 16-hour days, including weekends, and some even sleep in the lab. One distinctive Japanese touch: Near the door is a space where people entering remove their shoes, put them on a shoe rack, and don slippers. The two professors have their own offices across the hall, both largish rooms but crammed with papers.

Keio, like Aarhus, is collectivist in its working style, as Hofstede (1980) observed, but the differences are even more marked than their similarity. At Keio, for example, there is no drifting in and out of the senior researchers' workspaces. Here, the hierarchy is clear and unambiguous: It is the senior professor who decides, and everyone else, including the associate professor, who obeys. The other side of this coin is that the professor may not be much aware of all that the students are doing until the work is presented to him. So, in a way, there is a good deal of decisional latitude (especially because, given the numbers, it is obviously the students who do most of the work).

There are other differences: The Keio group is much more male-oriented, the only exception being three master's students (and, of course, the secretaries). The intensity of the collectivism is also even more marked than in Denmark. In Japan generally, and not just at Keio, researchers are accustomed to share telephones and offices and to work in teams, in large and frequently noisy rooms where everyone pretty much knows what everyone else is saying and doing.

Researchers see both advantages and disadvantages in this arrangement. On the positive side, the result is easy sharing of information and a minimum of personal aggrandizement, because everybody knows where ideas originated. Perhaps as a result there is a different attitude to what is secret or "company confidential" than would be found elsewhere. No one in Japan, we were told, really believes in confidentiality; no one expects to be sued for leaking a secret. (Perhaps one secondary consequence is that although privacy is a key research issue in North America, there is no equivalent concern in Japanese research circles.) On the negative side of the ledger, the clatter and distraction of a crowded room make it hard to concentrate and tend to encourage conformity (and to discourage idiosyncratic thinking).

And one more striking difference from Denmark: the technical orientation. In Japan, what immediately strikes the outside observer is that the systems, many of which display impressive engineering complexity, are all up and running, even those of the students.

CSCW Systems in Japan

At the time of our field research, the showcase technology at Keio in CSCW research was a desktop conferencing system called MAJIC.

MAJIC owes much to its origins in a line of research initiated at NTT that began as TeamWorkStation and then evolved into ClearFace and then into Clear-Board. The idea for this system can be traced back to a concept that was circulating in the corridors of Xerox PARC in California in the 1980s. Imagine a communication situation (such as a small seminar) in which people are working together in developing some idea. They have a whiteboard. One of them goes to the board and begins sketching out a concept, mixing graphics and talk as they do. The others concentrate on what is being drawn, but they also pick up signals from the speaker, including a whole gamut of nonverbal and paralinguistic cues. Someone else then takes a turn at the board, adding or changing some feature until the group is satisfied that they have gone as far as they can for the moment. The CSCW design question becomes, Could you simulate this situation using technology so that the participants would not all have to be in the same physical space and could even, ultimately, participate in the seminar while seated at their own work desks? It was this issue that an NTT lab under the direction of Ishii set out to address. It forms the background to the MAJIC project.

On the principle (that has become an article of faith in CSCW circles in Japan) that "no new piece of technology should block the potential use of already existing tools and methods" (Ishii & Miyake, 1991, cited in Heaton, 1997, p. 148), the initial system aimed to support users' traditional work practices, not to supplant them, by integrating both computer applications and pencil and paper drawings. Providing the means to accomplish this objective means resorting to a very high bandwidth technology: video (note the contrast with Denmark, where the research we were describing there was relatively sparing of expensive bandwidth). Live video image synthesis is employed to capture individual workspaces (both computer screens and physical desktops) and to display them in layers on a computer monitor, thus allowing users to combine workspaces and to jointly draw on and modify the images displayed there. In this initial technology, the faces of the collaborators are shown in separate windows beside the shared workspace.

The systems that followed, ClearFace and ClearBoard, introduced a further refinement: the ability to use the same screen space to show both the drawings the participants were working on and the faces of the people working on them. To understand the principle, let us return for a moment to the whiteboard illustration. The whiteboard is opaque, so that it reflects back what is drawn on it and nothing more. The participants, however, have no difficulty, given the flexibility of human peripheral vision, in simultaneously remaining aware of others' expressions, and everyone is at least subliminally conscious of the physical shared context in which the encounter is unfolding (the room and its furnishings). All this information goes into successful communication.

ClearFace and ClearBoard treat the "board" (i.e., the screen of the monitor) as if it were at one and the same time a reflective surface on which people can draw and a window through which to follow the expressions of others involved in the exchange. The designers had concluded that people have no difficulty in switching focus between the two layers, the screen and what lies behind it (a concept of selective looking); of talking through and drawing on a transparent glass window. In other words, the designers were rethinking what it means to interact in an "interpersonal space." The system was meant to allow people to share an information space while remaining sensitive to facial expressions and gestures. It also opened up the potential for manipulating background information in such a way as to convey an impression that the participants are in a shared working environment.

One step in technological development leads to another. Like its predecessors, MAJIC is centered on the question of visually shared workspace, but with some of the earlier problems solved. Unlike ClearBoard, it is designed as a support system for teleconferencing. Its central component is a large (4 feet × 8 feet), curved, semitransparent screen on which the images of the people with whom you are interacting appear. The MAJIC unit has a workstation with a recessed, tilted monitor, two video projectors, two video cameras, two directional microphones, and two loudspeakers. Video images of the participants are projected onto the screen. Each participant sees a frontal view of the others taking part in the teleconference; the edges of the different images even overlap slightly.

The Keio research exemplifies rather well a continuing preoccupation of Japanese CSCW researchers with the nonverbal dimension of communication. Part of this can be explained as a concern with gaze. In Japan, direct eye contact may be considered a sign of impoliteness. On the other hand, in a nation in which direct speech is much less highly valued than in North America, sensitivity to atmosphere and nonverbal expression is a crucial skill. The Keio researchers are quite explicit about this:

> When we have discussions in face-to-face situations and people approve of a statement, we can tell by their attitude, tone, eye movements, gestures and so forth, whether or not they approve wholeheartedly. It is difficult, on the other hand, to estimate how strongly they approve when we read only the minutes without attending meeting. Hence, one of the purposes and/or advantages of face-to-face meetings is that all of the participants are aware of the speaker's intent and the other listeners' reactions based on both verbal and nonverbal communication. (Okada, Maeda, Ichikawa, & Matsushita, 1994, p. 385, cited in Heaton, 1997, p. 154)

The result is a focus on such factors as the symmetry (or asymmetry) of posture and body orientation as important cues, how gaze can be used as a means to control a meeting, or how to simulate natural interaction distance on screen. The other concern is with creating an appropriate background, so that the participants, although widely separated geographically, seem to blend into a common space (an illusion of seamlessness). The designers aim to eliminate the actual background altogether and replace it with an artificial one that can be chosen to create a desired mood, to relax or inspire. It is a technology, in other words, in which elements of virtual reality are beginning to appear.

◆ Institutional Settings

It should be obvious from even these summary descriptions of CSCW research in Scandinavia and Japan that the term *CSCW* is itself little more than a catchword. The products of research in the two environments we have briefly portrayed are so different that they seem to reflect totally divergent images of what cooperative work might amount to. In Denmark, adaptations and innovations based on current software practices require only a modest investment in expensive bandwidth and complicated hardware. In Japan, the emphasis is on ambitious and expensive machinery requiring extensive bandwidth, skillfully engineered but whose utility in actual contexts of practical work remains to be seen. What we want to now propose is that such divergence is reflective of the basically hybrid character of design, in that it can be traced back to a mixture of influences, some technical, some social and cultural.

We already have alluded to one such influence: the pervasive Scandinavian commitment to socially responsible technology development. At the limit (as in Aarhus and in some other contexts of Scandinavia, but not everywhere), this involves recruiting the labor union movement in programs of participatory design. Not only is this element missing in Japan, but there the link with the user is often so tenuous as to appear nonexistent. In a sense, the Japanese "user" is the designer himself (there are few "herselves" in the design circle). This is a significant difference, and it indexes different cultural values and social attitudes. We now want to carry the analysis somewhat further, to consider some more subtle influences on the design process.

How Aarhus Fits Into the Institutional Setting of Danish Society and the CSCW Community

Aarhus's Computer Science Department was formed in 1969. Members of what is now the CSCW research group were active in support of work in collaboration with trade unions beginning about 3 years later, in 1972. It was a marginal group to begin with, located in a university that had a reputation of being "radical" if not downright Marxist. And yet within the space of a few years, it has become a "star" in the CSCW firmament, featured in international conferences.

The Scandinavian environment is perhaps particularly propitious for such upward mobility. Scandinavia is not a country but a loose association of nations sharing similar languages, a long (and sometimes troubled) history of coexistence, and a set of democratic traditions that have much in common, inclining every one of them to social democratic forms of government. But there is no central power. None, even Sweden, is large enough to dominate the others.

Furthermore, Scandinavia is located within Europe, and Europe, although now committed to a degree of central bureaucratic administration and common economic institutions, remains in other respects a loosely coupled federation, often uneasily cooperative at the level of working committees, such as those responsible for sponsoring technological research. Again, although there are hierarchies, their hegemony is diluted by the seemingly endless multiparty negotiations that have become a prominent feature of contemporary European existence.

Such a loosely joined environment provides room to maneuver for talented and ambitious actors, such as the group at Aarhus has proved to be. Their success, in other words, has been far from accidental. We can draw on Latour's (1993) theory of translation (cf. Chapter 3) to explain how the historical accident of working in collaboration with trade unions—part of the Scandinavian, Danish and (more specifically) Aarhus context—could have been progressively transformed into one of the members of the group becoming a principal adviser to the Danish government on information technology, and the group itself attaining a position of world recognition.

Their success story rests on the production of texts and involves a rhetorical strategy of enlisting a growing number of allies in the production of what will eventually become a shared text for a complete network of researchers. Although their work in the field with ordinary people, solving mundane problems involving established software applications, seems less glamorous than the usual show-and-tell of I/CT promotion, they turn it to their advantage by generating convincing texts.

The reports of their work are all marked with three qualities that produce a kind of official version of the participatory design story: (a) a consistent and convincing reinterpretation of the group's own history of design work in conjunction with other major projects in the participatory tradition; (b) a theoretical grounding in philosophical reflection and activity theory (Engeström, 1990); and (c) a pattern of citation that attests to a growing tradition, one that is "so tightly knit that the authors of a new paper know that they can draw on a bank of references to support their claims with no danger that the reference will dissociate itself if a skeptic checks back" (Heaton, 1997, p. 169). This all begins to pay off when others join in on the citing, which has happened. As participatory design has gained in popularity, the writings of the group have acquired legitimacy, even to the point of becoming "classics" in their field. Reference to the Aarhus activity has now become inevitable in any discussion of the subject of participatory design.

As Aarhus's influence has grown, so have the means available to it, including financing and personnel. This, in turn, has encouraged it to undergo a subtle shift of emphasis from a preoccupation with fieldwork to an increasing focus on more technical work, using its acquired skills in object-oriented programming and hypermedia for which it has become known. It is no longer part of the radical fringe.

How Keio Fits Into the Institutional Setting of Japan and the CSCW Community

It is often said that Japan is a network society. Clearly, a prominent feature of Japanese social life is its pervasive interdependence, which carries over to continuity in interinstitutional as well as interpersonal relations. Links between professors and companies, for example, involve reciprocal obligations that go far beyond the individuals involved. Individuals typically act as representatives for their companies or universities, and rarely only in their own name. People meeting each other for the first time immediately face a problem of "positioning": Each of the interactants first has to determine who the others are (senior professor? junior associate? research head? graduate student?). Business cards take on an importance as identity cues to a degree not imitated in North America. It is the person's role, not the person himself, who is addressed.

Rank is of vital importance, as is belonging (or not belonging) to a given group (to not belong is to have no positioned identity). It is uncommon to contradict someone of senior status, even in the frankest of exchanges. The signs of hierarchy are omnipresent—who sits where at dinner, the depth and duration of bowing, who goes through the door first, and so on.

This interdependence carries over to relationships between companies, government agencies, and universities. Again, there is an extensive web of interrelations at the institutional level. Although universities depend on government for financing, it is usual for private firms to fund research in university labs. The Matsushita Lab at Keio, for example, receives funding from between 30 and 40 companies, including major support from 6 or 7 of them. Other support comes in the form of donations of state-of-the-art equipment or sponsorship of invited researchers from elsewhere.

The benefit is less in direct transfer of research results from university to company (most companies have their own much better financed and staffed research facilities) than in other more subtle forms of recompense. One of these is in the channeling of university graduates to selected companies. In addition, because university professors, as independent experts, may play an important advisory role in public policy (e.g., Professor Matsushita sits on some 40 committees), companies expect to benefit from their eventual intercession in policy matters. This is not an exceptional circumstance; in Japan, the maintenance of personal relationships is perceived as an essential step to social peace.

These observations are not simply those of the outsider. Japanese quite consciously and explicitly see themselves as having a distinctive national culture, which they themselves freely analyze. Professor Matsushita has reflected deeply on the question and shared with us how it might affect principles of CSCW design. Among the specific characteristics he sees as particularly "Japanese," and which would be unlikely to duplicate the rags-to-riches saga of Aarhus, are these:

1. The Japanese economic style favoring prearrangement in advance to agree on a "fair share" for each, in the interest of an equitable outcome, in which all can flourish.

2. The Japanese approach to interaction that favors the development of strong interpersonal relationships and "quiet cooperation" as opposed to overt decision making.

3. The importance of context and face-to-face communication, given the ambiguity of the Japanese language.

4. The Japanese tendency to see unfolding events as influenced by many elements and to take a long-term perspective.

5. The importance of togetherness and solidarity rather than promotion of one's own opinions.

The Japanese context does not, of course, eliminate networking of the opportunistic kind (in a certain sense, it makes it inevitable), but the forging of network links occurs in a more muted way because of the already existing pervasive interdependencies and the tendency to conform to the established norms.

Within this world, the nurturing of bonds takes precedence over lobbying for additional resources, and, to follow Matsushita's reasoning, the role of text is quite different: less to persuade than to record. Researchers there struggle to mimic Western styles of article-writing because the more common Japanese mode is a report written in serial, diary style: First we did this, then we thought,

127

then we tried, and so forth. Theorizing and ideological positioning of the kind found in the Aarhus literature are conspicuously absent.

The Keio lab, unlike Aarhus, is thus a highly conservative environment. Everyone has been trained in engineering; there is little interaction of any significance, for example, with social scientists, and there is little concern for the integration of technologies in the "situated" circumstances of ordinary work. Perhaps as a consequence, the emphasis is on the engineering of functionally workable systems. Japanese researchers know that their reputation is in the perfecting of existing technologies more than in innovating startlingly new ideas for design, and their CSCW work is an "exception" in which they take pride. People do see themselves as cogs in a larger wheel (and, to some extent, they accept themselves in that role more than do those in Scandinavia). The chronicle of TeamWorkStation to ClearFace to ClearBoard to MAJIC is fairly illustrative of a design process in which each phase of development becomes a platform for further refinement. The continuity is striking, not just in one laboratory but in the design community as a whole.

One result of this tight knitting of developmental trends in Japan (or at least so it appears to the outsider) is the emergence of a distinctly Japanese style and content of design. It was evident from interviews and from attendance at conferences (where the interventions were in Japanese, not English, and thus not tailored to meet visitor expectations) that CSCW researchers share a belief that, being Japanese, they are different and that groupware products for use by Japanese must be adapted to the particularities of their culture. It was a repeated leitmotif: Science and technology may be culturally neutral or universal, but designing a groupware system, they acknowledge, cannot be approached in the same way as designing a television. Furthermore, they suggest that CSCW systems should not attempt to do everything. In a culture in which context is so crucial to the interpretation of meaning, there is a limit to how effectively even the richest video medium can supply the vital cues—the sort of information that any office context furnishes, even when it is only perceived at the level of peripheral awareness.

◆ Technology: An Ideology of Organization?

Pickering (1995), as we saw in Chapter 4, developed two analogies for comprehending the logic of technological development. The first, which he called a *dance of agency,* refers to the iterative process whereby the technologist constructs a system and then looks to see how (or if) it works. Typically, something is not quite right (e.g., it is not possible to integrate pictorial data stored electronically); so now the researcher makes a change to the system to correct what seemed like a deficiency; again, the system performs and the researcher observes; again, another change follows; and so on, in principle ad infinitum. This is the ongoing interaction between subject and object, each in its different way having its own in-built kind of agency.

On the basis of this image, Pickering made a second observation. He thinks of the objective partner (e.g., the system software) to the dance as a *surface of emergence* on which is inscribed, progressively, the designer's intentions. This is a cumulative image of design whereby the designer is always working with a system or surface that already bears the marks of those who have worked on it earlier. Those marks both constrain and enable the choices of what can be added or modified and yet do not totally control the outcome. Each designer, in the particular way he or she chooses to proceed (e.g., by emphasizing one element of software capacity over another or by privileging a certain set of social protocols in the design to support work), adds his or her own traces to the surface. And so it goes, with the additions of the next person who works on it, and the next after that. Technology, in other words, is a text on which human intentionality comes to be written (and where it also can be read).

To put this observation in the communicational and structurationist terms that we have been developing, technical activity typically involves the development and articulation of received culture (what we have called *frame knowledge*) to solve practical problems. The activity is thus a mix of formal modes of symbolization and tacit, local knowledge, acquired over years of practice in association with others of the same professional bent. There grows up a body of knowledge around "what works" and what does not, much of which has been developed by trial and error. This knowledge affects designers' decisions (conscious or not) to go in one direction or another, to pursue one line of inquiry, or to change focus. Thus, whatever emerges as "technology" in any given context can be explained both by the surface of emergence the researcher inherited or chose and the instrumentalities he or she put to work to construct new artifacts on it (the dance of agency).

Given such an explanation of technology development, it is not surprising that we found CSCW systems originating in Scandinavia to differ from those of Japan, and vice versa. Their surfaces of emergence were very different in the first place: already installed systems in an ordinary working environment in Denmark, and abundantly funded engineering laboratories in Japan. Similarly, the ready-to-hand instrumentalities were profoundly different (even though training in software engineering skills is the common property of both). In the Danish group, such instrumentalities include a mixture of technology, philosophy, and sociology and a reliance on techniques of social animation they have developed to facilitate interaction with workers. In Japan, on the other hand, instrumentalities include a mixture of software and hardware engineering practices, undiluted by sociological influences. In Scandinavia, iterative design models and usability testing are integral components of basic computer science education, and philosophy and ergonomics are common subjects. In Japan, basic computer science and engineering is weighted much more to mathematics and physics. General cultural and ideological orientations are also in play. You could hardly develop computer systems in Scandinavia without reference to workers' self-determination, whereas in Japan the designer cannot escape the need to "be Japanese."

◆ Society as a "Surface of Emergence"

But this is only part of the explanation. There is a further component that Pickering emphasizes much less that we can call the *social surface of emergence*. It is a dimension of which we also must take account in explaining why CSCW systems are designed differently in different contexts. In addition to how they construct material artifacts, we need to consider how designers situate themselves in their respective professional and societal environments.

Modern science has from the beginning required that the act of experimentation and observation be witnessed by others for it to be considered authentic (Latour, 1993). To communicate one's interpretation for validation by peers is part of the responsibility of being a professional. However much designers might act disinterestedly in applying their professional and background knowledge to build better systems, they are nevertheless also performing for, and being judged in their performances by, other members of their community. By building systems, by solving practical problems in contexts of work, and by talking about them and writing about them, designers situate themselves in their communities, professional and otherwise.

A-B-X Again

These two communities, Denmark and Japan, illustrate very well what we mean by *A-B-X*. Each is intensely caught up in the practice of design. This is the

B-X dimension. It has its own internal dynamic and logic that Pickering thinks of as a dance of agency. But these same designers have a career to make. They relate to communities that are sometimes disciplinary (articles for journals, presentations to conferences, collaborations with codevelopers, participation in the affairs of the profession), sometimes client-oriented (both government and industry, although with different emphases, depending on the context), sometimes user-oriented (in Aarhus, especially), sometimes social and political (as citizens and contributors to national policy-making). This is the *A-B* dimension.

Each dimension supplies the context for the other. What we call the *A-B* dimension of situated action constitutes the organizational framework of all the work the designers do: its motivation, its means, and its legal, financial, institutional, and regulatory envelope. On the other hand, it is the sum of all the *B-X*s that add up to an *A* in the first place. A society is constituted by the layering of its situated processes.

This is simply the structurational thesis in a slightly different guise. What our case studies point up is the strength of the interaction between the *B-X* and *A-B* dimensions. When we focus in tight on design work, the process is found to have its own systemic logic. Each new design becomes in turn a surface of emergence on which designers build another generation of artifacts. In Scandinavia, participative design began in Norway and then was picked up in Sweden and Denmark, so that, by the time our study was undertaken, there was already an unbroken quarter-century tradition of this work. The designers had been learning—what participative or negotiated design means and how to realize it in practice. In Japan, we saw how each new technology became the basis for yet another: an accumulation of artifacts, each bearing a family resemblance to its predecessor. But the differences between the two environments can also be explained by the very different social, cultural, philosophical and political premises on which the designers were building: an *A-B* reflected in the *B-X*. The Danish technology reflects a deep concern for democratic process and a view of work as self-management. The products that result tend to stay close to current work practices, eschewing more radical innovations. The Japanese technology is different, imbued with a preoccupation with the subtle dynamics of interpersonal interaction. It too aims to incorporate into its design the situatedness of work, both by building in assumptions about what people do at their desks and how their meetings unfold in more collective settings. These are "technical" differences, but they reflect deeply engrained cultural assumptions about sensemaking, the exercise of power, and what is legitimate in a social setting.

The technologies, in other words, are structuring devices.

◆ Note

1. Bowker, Star, Turner, and Gasser (1997) referred to the "great divide" between perspectives.

6

Dialectics of Control in a Tiled Organization

◆   In earlier chapters, we outlined a communication-based version of structuration theory that can provide an original platform for thinking about technology and organization. Both organization and technology, we have argued, are constituted in communication as negotiated representations of coorientational relationships of object and agency. In this chapter, we proceed to illustrate several of the principles of our theory with respect to a study we conducted (Groleau, 1995) into the implementation of computerized technology in an office setting—the purchasing department in a merchandising firm.

◆ The Purchasing Department

The research site in question is a purchasing department in the headquarters of a large commercial firm, a publicly owned for-profit corporation—a combination common in Canada. The corporation has some 2,000 employees (of whom about half are located at the central office). The purchasing department consists of 10 employees, including a director, a head of operations, three purchasing agents and two "technicians," a secretary, and two typists. The group occupies one large integrated office space, whose physical disposition is shown in Figure 6.1. Note how the physical layout of the room reflects the statuses of the people in it: director and the secretary who occupy a slice of the room with distinctive markers of position—walls and desks—typists near the filing cabinets and supplies, agents and technicians seated in order of seniority (James more senior than Georgie) and/or functional specialization. Suchman (1996), we have seen, remarked on the manner in which physical space reflects group culture, but she does not emphasize to what extent hierarchy is embodied in that materialization.

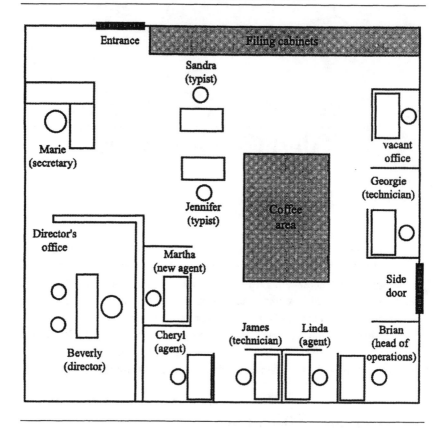

Figure 6.1. The Locations of the Purchasing Department Employees

The department handles most of the purchasing for the corporation: furniture, stationery, laboratory equipment, clothing, security services, audio-visual (AV) equipment, petroleum products, and so forth—everything but the supplies for its core business, transportation services and real estate. Any order for $200 or more goes through them.

The company purchasing function consists of a relatively formalized process of transactions in which the purchasing agents and clerical staff receive requisitions from client departments, solicit bids from suppliers, analyze bids and select suppliers, and, finally, prepare purchase orders that finalize transactions with the suppliers. Company procedure for choosing suppliers and receiving and evaluating their bids must be followed to the letter. To purchase items at the lower end of the cost scale (from $200 to $5,000, for example, agents are allowed to contact possible suppliers and receive their bids by telephone. As the value of the requisitioned items rises, however, supplier selection becomes more formal, requiring written invitations to bid and deadlines for receipt of written bids. At the top price level (items of more than $200,000), a request for submissions must be published in newspapers, and bids are opened publicly in the legal department.

Similarly, company policy also specifies levels of authorization that are required for the various levels of purchases. Although the departmental head of operations can approve those of less than $10,000, purchases of between $10,000 and $50,000 must be approved by the departmental director, those between $50,000 and $200,000 by the vice president of the division in which the department is located (Public Affairs), and those of more than $200,000 by the executive committee of the corporation (the president and two other members of the board of directors).

Relations with the internal clients of the department—those in need of supplies—are also governed by strict rules. Any purchasing requisition (PR) must be submitted on a standardized form that specifies who is issuing the requisition, the date, a delivery address, desired date of delivery, budget code, estimated cost of the item or items, and a description of the merchandise in question. In addition, the form has spaces for authorization by appropriate officials in the requisitioner's department; again, the level of authorization required depends on the importance of the order, but typically two approvals are required.

The normal procedure to process a requisition goes as follows: Once a PR is received in purchasing, it is evaluated by the head of operations, Brian (all names are fictitious), who then redirects it to one of the agents, either Marsha, Cheryl, or Linda or to a technician (Georgie or James). Technicians' functions are limited to handling blanket orders (i.e., the ones for which a supplier already has been identified for a given category of frequently purchased goods, such as stationery, usually for the period of a year). For biddable items (and certainly for those of more than $10,000 not covered by an established agreement), the requisition is directed to Cheryl, for construction equipment, petroleum products, printing services, messenger services, security services, snow removal, and gardening; Linda, for computer equipment and supplies, office furniture, and professional services; and Martha, for uniforms and other clothing, carts, elevator equipment, communication, and AV equipment. For very complex requisitions, Brian himself handles the process.

135

Brian completes spaces reserved on the form for the departmental use: name of the responsible agent, purchase method to be used, and code for the eligible suppliers. The file is then forwarded to the agent. There is a daily meeting of members of the department, which provides for an exchange of useful information, especially if some complication is expected. Brian strongly encourages a friendly ambience in the group; he prides himself on his people skills.

Names of approved suppliers are entered by keypunch operators into a database on a central mainframe computer (a corporate service) located not in the department but in accounting (accessed via a terminal). The only computer in the department prior to the project we were studying was a machine on the secretary's desk used for generating statistics. Consulting the database is, in principle, obligatory for orders between $50,000 and $200,000, although this policy was not always respected. For less than $50,000 (and even for the larger requisitions), agents typically consult their files on previous purchases (they walk over to the filing cabinet and pull the file on already processed orders identical to the category on which they are working). They then use their own cardex system to locate potential suppliers. For orders of more than $200,000, the publishing of a request for submissions in newspapers means anyone can submit a bid. Open competition is, in fact, obligatory, because this is a public corporation. Once a bid has been accepted, the paperwork—now a file with attachments—is transferred to the secretarial staff to write up a purchase order, which is then dispatched to the selected supplier.

This is roughly how the purchasing service worked prior to computerization (we come back later to consider what computerization changed). Although purchasing employees did their best to follow company policy and approached their responsibilities very much as a team effort, their department suffered from an unfavorable image in the corporation. It was known to be overwhelmed with paperwork, continually behind on its deadlines, and not very efficient (or perhaps very *in*efficient would be more accurate!).

There was truth in the criticism. Departmental analysis and preparation of documents, for example, involved considerable duplication of effort. The database on which suppliers' names and addresses were recorded was a chaotic shambles, with companies sometimes identified by two different names, addresses that were no longer valid, ineligible companies still there, and others that should have been entered had not been (the updating was sometimes as much as 2 years behind schedule). It was not a pretty picture, a prime candidate for computerization, in fact. But before we turn to the impact of computerization, let us first consider the department's activities in the perspective of the theory we have developed in previous chapters.

◆ Theoretical Considerations

In Chapter 4, we outlined a theory of communication based on the concept of situation. We conceived purposive activity as a double translation in which some group of people who share a common fate and are caught up in certain circumstances (a) successively transform those circumstances into a meaningful situation (*cognitive dimension*) and (b) organize themselves to act as a collective agent to resolve it (*pragmatic dimension*). In resolving it, they generate a distribution of responsibilities within the group (what Engeström described as a *division of labor*). We observed that such purposive activity has a structure that conforms to the principles of narrative: from "breakdown" to resolution. Text acts as a mediator by means of which the conversational situation is transformed into a focused response.

The organization is itself, we observed, a conversation of conversations, and the role of organizational communication is to link two or more of them into a network. We then pointed out that the linking produces *A-B-X* systems of co-orientation, with *A* and *B* occupying head-complement agency positions, and *X* as their common, or "boundary," object. The agents *A* and *B*—the respective *conversations,* from the perspective of their own internal dynamic—become, in interaction with other communities of discourse, transformed into collective actors: *actor-networks.*

A common feature of such *A-B-X* relationships is their tendency to become imbricated—encrusted by rules and procedures and mediated by technology. Although technology may be merely one agency among others in our theory, it figures primarily in imbrication. This is so because machine artifacts have no inherent intentionality, independent of their being harnessed to or offering possibilities to human purposes.[1]

Finally, we observed that organizational communication has an irreducible polemic dimension. No matter how imbricated a system may be, the potential for conflict is always present, because alternative and potentially incompatible representations coexist in all organizations as an inherent property of the processes that produce organizational identity in the first place (see Figure 4.5).

The Purchasing Department Reexamined

The purchasing department case can now be rephrased to illustrate these principles. First, as it has been defined in the organization, the purchasing function cuts across two workplace conversations: from client departments to the purchasing department (intraorganizational) and from the latter to suppliers (extraorganizational). Second, the rules laid down by management produce a co-orientation system in which *A* is the client department, *B* is the purchasing department, and *X* is the requisitioned supplies. Third, the purchasing activity is what links the two conversations, and its components can be seen to be those of narrative:

- There is first a breakdown, requiring constructive action (a department needs supplies).
- An *A-B-X* relation forms: An agent is engaged by a principal in the performance of a task (purchasing department by client department).
- The agent assembles such instrumentalities as may be required to perform the task, including delegation of responsibility to "helper"-agents, that is, purchasing agents and technicians.
- The agent carries through the task (negotiations with suppliers).
- The breakdown is resolved (the supplies are delivered).[2]

The agents here are primarily collective (departments) and secondarily individual (at the actual level of performance, members of the purchasing department). Technology enters as a facilitator of imbrication: the forms, files, correspondence, and so forth.

Three further observations are in order.

Different Orientations to the Object

First, although the respective conversations are linked by a common implication in an activity and a shared boundary object (the requisition for supplies), the principal actors' representations of the activity are different:

- For the client (the department placing an order with the purchasing department), a situation is created when it is realized that some good or service has to be ordered because there is a need for it that current stock cannot satisfy. The situation will be resolved when the order is filled and whatever was requested has been delivered.
- For the purchasing department, the situation is initiated by the arrival of a requisition form that has to be dealt with by finding a supplier (vendor), issuing a contract, and filling the order.

Purchasing has thus become an obligatory step (that we call a *tile*) intervening between the client and the vendor, an intermediate (and indispensable) agency posed between source and destination, a transaction within a transaction (Figure 6.2).

| CLIENT REQUESTS PURCHASING |
| PURCHASING SELECTS SUPPLIER |
| SUPPLIER DELIVERS GOODS |

Figure 6.2. Purchasing as an Intervening Step ("Tile") Between Client and Supplier

In this transaction, each of the collective actors (departments) is responding to a different perception of situation, even though purchasing is acting vicariously as an (institutionally authorized) agent for the requisitioning department, its in-house client. For both, the *object* (in the sense of what their attention is focused on) is concluding an agreement with a supplier, but for one (the client), finding a source of supply is merely a means to an end. For the other (the agent), getting a contract signed with a supplier is the end, and everything else its members do within their department is a means to the attainment of that objective.

Process Versus Function

This leads us to our second observation. A means-end disparity of perspective is an example of a well-known distinction that we have discussed elsewhere (Taylor, 1993) between a *process link* and a *function link* to some object. For the client *A*, the acquisition of supplies via a contract is secondary to its main purpose in the organization: a component of process, but not an end in itself. For the agent *B*, choosing the supplier is primary. Indeed, it is the object that defines its function—*B*'s raison d'être. Within its own domain, *B* becomes *A*: head, rather than complement.

The means-end bifurcation of object orientation is a logical consequence of any principal/agent or head/complement transaction (Figure 6.3).

Now, taking the operation of purchasing in isolation from its transactional imbrication in the larger process of ordering and delivering supplies, we see that within its own process there are embedded functional components: Brian's routing of requisitions, the agents' handling of particular requisitions, the secretarial tasks of typing up contracts, and so on. The divergence of process and function linking is a matter of perspective: One agent's process (purchasing as an activity in and of itself) is another's function (a component of an activity).

The narrowing of focus that accompanies preoccupation with some function is a phenomenon well known in the classical literature on administration and management. This narrowing of focus has been termed *displacement of goals*

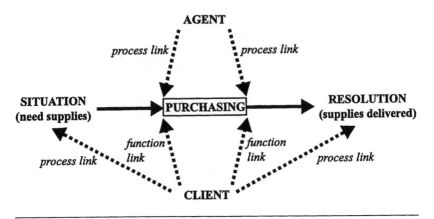

Figure 6.3. The Contrasting Perspectives of Function and Process

(March & Simon, 1958; Taylor, 1993). As we saw in Chapter 1, business process reengineering sees itself as a strategy to overcome the (dys)functional preoccupations with turf that ensue from a preoccupation with a specialized task.

Dialectics of Control

Our third observation is that although the relationship is imbricated, it is also contestable, in that the client departments are unhappy with the service they are receiving. Given that the enlisted purposes of an agent are always likely to be more or less consistent with those of the client (Latour, 1994), contradictions may arise, as they did in this case. Purchasing was failing to respond adequately to its clients.

There is, in other words, a consequence to the branching of process and function into distinct perspectives. Looked at from a structurational view, the issue becomes one of access to allocative resources. The institutionally authorized agent for ordering supplies is the purchasing department. Its ability to mobilize key allocative resources is the source of the department's power. This control over allocative resources (the buying power of the corporation) is translated into a decisional power where the supplier is concerned (an *A-B-X* system in which purchasing is *A* and suppliers are *B*).

The client/agent relationship, on the other hand, involves an authoritative resource. The issuance of the requisition by the source department has a directive effect (purchasing is bound to follow through on the order, and it is thus, technically, a resource to be called on by other departments). However, because pur-

140

chasing is legitimately entitled to take a decision as to who is eligible to be the supplier, and on what terms, it exercises, by procuration, the ordering department's authoritative power. There is, in other words, a complex system of *domination,* to use Giddens's (1984) term, at work here. The exercise of one order of power is contextualized or embedded in the exercise of others. None is unconditional.

The purchasing department is thus a component in a dialectic of control (Giddens, 1984). Although constituted as a service department, its indispensability as the intermediate step in the ordering of supplies, and thus its control over vital allocative resources, afford it a nontrivial position of power. It can block a requisition originating with the client (by heel dragging, requests for additional clarification, etc.). Inversely, it can facilitate the process. On the other hand, its client departments have their own strategies for bypassing it (e.g., breaking up an order into components small enough to avoid the requirement to go to purchasing).[3]

If conflict remains latent in such an organization, it is because the mobilization of resources has become proceduralized—encrusted with rules, both formal and informal, explicit and tacit. The process had been *sanctioned* by the organization and thus was constituted as *legitimate.* Furthermore, the character of the transactions that are involved, and the identity of those who engaged in them, has become part of the meaning system of people who worked in that organization. They had been integrated into frameworks of *signification* (frame knowledge). People's titles and job descriptions are as much artifacts of their activities as their tools or the physical organization of their workspace.

So there was, in fact, a kind of uneasy balance of power manifested in this case study by the considerable dissatisfaction in client departments with the quality of service offered by purchasing and by repeated requests from purchasing to management for additional personnel (which had been uniformly rejected in the period leading up to our case study). It was a stand-off—one that is not untypical of densely tiled and proceduralized organizations everywhere. But it was obviously an unstable equilibrium, and a situation ripe for transformation. How, then, would computerization fit into this picture?

Computerization as an Agency of Change

The goal and the effect of computerization in an organization is to address a problem as being one of "function." The object-oriented programming briefly described in Chapter 1, to take one illustration, aims to encapsulate some function so that it can be called up on demand and will perform the desired service -

reliably—automated purchasing, for example. In this sense, process and function are perceived as compatible goals of programming. The object of system design is to make the function so efficient that it becomes totally unobtrusive—just a part of the processes of the taken-for-granted infrastructure. And supporting the efficiency view of system design is an implicit premise: that interagent relationships can be uniformly treated as an issue of allocative rules and resources for their deployment. The issue of mobilization of authoritative resources, however, simply does not arise. This is where structurational analyses branch away from more conventional views of organizational process and permit us to address the issue of power and the strategic mobilization of resources that is implied.

The Structurational Point of View

Consider the context of purchasing. That which lent to the department and the individuals working in it not only their power but also their very identity as organizational people was their unique ability to mobilize key allocative resources. Remove that privilege, and they cease to exist as identifiable actors. This logic applies to the department as a whole (supposing the purchasing function to be totally computerized) but also to individuals within the department who might discover that their function had been usurped by a computerized interloper. This is the menacing side of computerization.

On the other hand, with computerization, new functions appear and new roles for people emerge. Either way, the configuration of power shifts and with it structures of signification (who does what, who is what, *what* is "what") and legitimation (who is authorized to do what, following which procedures). So computerization is not a purely rational transformation; it is also a political event. Our analysis of the computerization process in the purchasing department aims to capture this dimension.

◆ Computerization and Politics in the Purchasing Department

The Genesis of the Computerization Process

It was the new head of purchasing, Beverly, who was instrumental in getting the operations of purchasing computerized. Her appointment actually came as a shock to some members of the department, especially Brian and Cheryl. The previous director, not long before his departure, had strongly intimated to Brian, who had extensive experience in purchasing, that he (Brian) would be new head. He further led Cheryl to understand that she would be promoted to Brian's old position of operations director (a management rank, unlike the unionized agents).

Beverly's nomination (she had no prior experience in purchasing) was interpreted as the parachuting of an interloper, particularly by Brian, who was nearing retirement and for whom promotion would be the cap of his career (and a boost to his pension). So relations between Beverly and Brian were cool, a chill that was certainly still very much in evidence during our field research: Brian's resentment had not evaporated.

We do not know what considerations led to the decision to name Beverly to the position of director, but there are some clues. The first we have already mentioned: the less-than-enviable performance of the department and its repeated calls for more staff to cope with its overwhelming load of paperwork. Another factor may well have been the location of the department, not in Finance (where you would normally expect to find it), but in Public Affairs! Why it had been exiled to Vice-President, Public Affairs (VP-PA), none of our informants seemed to be quite sure, but the consequence was that the department's divisional VP displayed little interest in its operations.[4] The third factor was the personality of Beverly herself. A professional accountant by training with a variety of managerial experiences in the firm, she was identified as a coming organizational star. She, unlike Brian, used words such as *productivity*. She was being fast-tracked. The situation in purchasing may have seemed a good way to let her show off her ability to manage.

All this is speculation, of course, but the fallout was clear enough. Beverly was an innovator, by temperament as well as vocation. This is a corporation that had institutionally, over the years, developed a culture of promoting from the inside, by lateral transfers. Professional training as the key qualification was the exception rather than the rule when it came to hiring. Most people had acquired the skills they had the hard way, by experience. In filling a position, seniority typically counted more than qualifications, with the result that the overall level of educational attainment was below average. Where promotions were involved, the corporation often behaved like a closed shop. Brian may thus have had some justification in feeling that he was entitled to the position, given the culture of the firm.

Beverly, still young (approaching 40), with a lively, outgoing personality, identified with a different philosophy: dedicated to recruiting new blood, getting more people with a university education into the organization, and hiring on the basis of the specialized skills needed for particular tasks. She was little inclined

143

to get bogged down in the day-to-day nitty-gritty of forms management (in which Brian was easily more competent than she). She took it, she told us, to be her challenge to turn the performance of the department around and to make it into a more productive unit. The obvious way to accomplish this goal was to substitute a more efficient way of handling requisitions than the paper morass it had for so long been—to computerize operations, in other words. So she set about doing just this. A little more than a year after her arrival (May 1991), an initial phase of computerization was already a fait accompli.

How to realize her objective was not at first self-evident. Although company policy specified that expenditures in computer equipment should be compensated by reductions in staff, Beverly had no intention of cutting positions. Instead, she made a different argument, claiming that computerization would pay for itself because of the increased level of service the department would be able to offer. She even made a virtue of their reputation for poor performance. As she pointed out in her plea for resources, people who are constantly running to stand still have no time to investigate sources of better prices. As a result, the corporation was paying premium prices for its supplies—a *dis*-economy that needed to be corrected. It is a sign of her dynamism and her salesmanship that she was able to persuade the company she had a point and get it to back her initiative.

Management did so, however, with some strings attached. It made no sense to buy existing off-the-shelf software, they pointed out, because these incorporated both purchasing and accounting in a single product, and the organization already had an accounting system. Furthermore, there was a project afoot to introduce some major changes in accounting practice for the whole corporation in the "near future" (which, in organizational language, means anything from 1 to 5 years), so the budget she received would be modest, and for limited goals. Given the constraints, she turned to the in-house computer programming division for a simple software to support departmental operations.

The computer division asked that she name an experienced person from the department to work with them in designing the system. Brian was asked first but he declined, somewhat sourly, on the grounds that his presence in the department was indispensable. The next in line was Cheryl, who accepted with alacrity (she already had some prior experience with the implementation of a computer system). Although she too had suffered disappointment when Beverly was named, her failure to get promoted was easier to rationalize than it had been for Brian. In any case, Cheryl was a cheerful, positive kind of person who was delighted to assist Beverly in the changes she was introducing. So she was named the "pilot" of the project and designated both to collaborate in the design and to shepherd the implementation of the technology into the department, when that took place.

The New System

The system the designers developed was predicated on the premise that all computers in the department would be networked to provide a common database. It was intended to systematize procedures to get a better handle on the flow of requisitions and contacts with suppliers. Targeting the bottleneck of coordination of supplier/order data, the system consisted of "components" for generating, verifying (making the necessary computations), and printing purchase requisitions, requests for prices, orders, and records of purchase requisitions. It also generated, verified, and printed lists of suppliers, specifications, and potential bidders, as well as statistical compilations for regularly scheduled reports.

Implementing the System

After months of development, the system was finally implemented. Three computers were placed in the department, one for the use of typists and two for the agents and technicians (the machines were located in the coffee area). One full day and a half was devoted to giving employees an indoctrination into the new technology, with a system designer and the pilot, Cheryl, as guides to its functions and uses. A week's experimentation period was declared, and employees were strongly encouraged by Beverly to become familiar with the system. To this end, she authorized overtime for anyone interested in learning its capabilities. But, in fact, there was little take-up of her offer, and employees went about their business pretty much as before.

Following the initial trial period, everyone was instructed that henceforth they would be required to enter all incoming PRs into the computer database. The early results were not very satisfactory. For one thing, unaccustomed to working with a computer keyboard and baffled by its programming logic, agents continually complained to the pilot that they had "lost their data" so that Cheryl was repeatedly called on to come to their aid. An even worse problem was the location of the workstation. Every time some supplier phoned in to verify the status of one of their bids, the agent had get up from his or her desk, go over to the workstation, and—if it was free!—verify the information on the computer, and then return to his or her desk to deal with the supplier. It took almost a month for the system designers to realize that this arrangement was not going to work, whereupon they scrounged enough machines so that every agent would have his or her own computer. Finally, the system was fully operational.

How successful was it? Some of our fieldwork was conducted in the department 18 months after implementation, so we had a fair view of its integration into the work scene. The director, Beverly, declared herself satisfied with the increase in productivity of the department, even though she was frustrated by the continuing reliance on paper trails. She had conceived, in her own mind, of a "paperless office," and it had not happened. Our own observations confirmed the gains in efficiency (the typists were no longer submerged under piles of text to be typed because the "print" function of the computer had eliminated several steps in the process). On the other hand, there was still discomfort in using the technology among some of the agents, and, more important, most of the functions foreseen by the designers had not been operationalized. Overall, then, it was a success, but not a dramatic one. Not all of the department's problems had vanished.

◆ A Structurational Explanation of the Computerization of the Purchasing Department

This case study is less than an exciting instance of computerization: a smallish work group, responsible for a rather banal back-office task, introduced to a technology that was far from state-of-the-art, leading to an outcome that was neither a total success nor a complete failure. But the very ordinariness of the case study is why we elected to use it as an illustration of structurational thinking in practice. Our conceptualization is one in which the structures of computerization are filtered through the institutional constraints and systemic practices of a multitude of disparate users, of whom the purchasing department is just one small example. But, if we credit the structurationist arguments of Barley (1986) and others, those "small" (locally situated) systemic practices are where the realities of computerization emerge.

A Changed Work Environment

People's physical surroundings, for example, are not just a place where they work but are, in a real sense, partners in the construction of a response to events (cf. Suchman's airport case study). In the purchasing department, it was the files that were the dominant structuring agency. The work of a purchasing agent is situated both physically and temporally by the files—his or her surface of emergence. The arrival of a requisition is not treated as an isolated event, naked of context. Instead, the first thing the agent does is to see what happened the last time, for a similar category of order. Out come the files and (before computerization) the hand turns to the trusty cardex sitting on the desk. Similarly, every time some supplier phoned up to inquire on the progress of selection of a bid, back would go the agent to the files. The files become not just an adjunct to action but an intrinsic part of its performance. It was as if the files could talk.

Computerization was meant to change this. One of the components of the new system was supposed to make it possible for the agent both to consult what had happened in earlier requisition cases and to track the progress on current requisitions—on screen. But, unfortunately, it proved to be one part of the technology that failed to deliver. Our observations of the department's work patterns, already more than a year after the implementation of the system, revealed that agents still relied, almost exclusively, on hardcopy printouts; they almost never used the screen to retrieve data. They were constantly walking over to the filing cabinets and pulling a file.

There were, we discovered, two reasons for their preference for paper. First was the complexity of commands needed to get at the computer storehouse of information, which took them some time to master. Second, the computer screen was an inadequate presentational device when documents had to be compared (as they always did when it came time to compare bids).

Consider first the complexity of the command system of the computer. To access a request for proposal (RFP), the first step was to identify the supplier and, once that was done, to bring up all the purchase orders for that supplier. Noting the number of the appropriate purchase order, it was then possible to access the required RFP and bring it up on the screen. But now only one RFP was available, so that to compare the price offer of this supplier with others, the agent would have to go through the same routine for the competitors. If the bidder was on the phone, this meant going back and forth from one document to another—a laborious and time-consuming operation on the computer—and embarrassing for the agent. How much easier to just print everything out and then flip through the paper copies, even while the conversation was going on. Or get the file.

Similarly, if you wanted to compare bids to come to a decision as to which was the best offer, why not just lay them all out side by side on the desk in front of you and let your eye do the scanning from one to the other? The work of the agents depended on their capacity to visualize patterns, to create links between various types of information, and to evaluate a situation using the normal pattern recognition skills of a human being (a capability that continues to challenge artificial intelligence). In this respect, the physical layout of their workspace was still more useful than the new technology, even if it had an improved set of access commands.

When we questioned the head of the department on the issue of the information segmentation that computerization had unwittingly produced, she expressed astonishment. She had certainly noticed (and been disappointed by) the continuing reliance of the agents on hardcopy (how could she miss it, given their multiple trips to the filing cabinet?), but she had put it down to a lack of computer power and the resulting slow response of the machine. It had not occurred to her that, however powerful the database and efficient the command system (obviously it could have been improved), the computer screen has limitations as a display device. Furthermore, no one in the design cycle leading to the development of the system had given much thought to the view of reality that the computer offers and how it might affect the conduct of work.

There was one other effect of computerization that needs to be highlighted. This was how it affected the distributed intelligence of the work group (Hutchins, 1995). In the precomputer era, RFPs and orders were typed up by the clerical staff and, although the typing function had become the principal barrier to a reasonable level of productivity, there was one advantage: The typists as well as agents were fully informed on the state of each project. When suppliers called for an update, they frequently could provide the required information. After computerization abolished this step in the process, however, the clerical staff no longer knew the status of projects. From the point of view of Hutchins, when certain information became less available to all members of the group, the former mutuality of work was removed as a backup security.

On the other hand, computerization resulted in new sources of information, or, as Giddens referred to them, new allocative resources. For the first time, it became feasible to use a computerized list of possible suppliers, indexed by their specialty according to industry codes. With the new capacities of the system, purchasing could also now take on the task of informing client departments of due dates for renegotiation of blanket orders instead of leaving it up to the departments to keep track of their deadlines.

The Human Dynamics of Implementation

Our study also provides a modest illustration of the dynamic role of contradictions in organizational process (Engeström, 1987, 1990). To see why, we need to fill in a bit more context.

The company in question, we noted at the beginning of the chapter, is a kind of hybrid institution, much more common in Canada and the Scandinavian countries than it would be in the United States: a publicly owned and managed commercial for-profit enterprise. As a public agency, its first preoccupation is the maintenance of an appearance of transparency and open process: Bureaucratic process is intended to guarantee that everyone who deals with the company may do so on an equal footing, without special privilege. The meticulous proceduralization of the purchasing function, with its carefully written rules and regulations and its multiple forms, is meant to guarantee fairness. The voluminous files are a proof of transparency.

But the company had for some time been under pressure to become more efficient—to behave more like a profit center, in the private sector sense of that term. Like many other corporations over recent years, it had been talking the language of productivity and better service to its customers. If you were listening, you would hear two voices: one, bureaucratic, concerned with correct procedure and "transparency"; the other, entrepreneurial, preoccupied with customer satisfaction.

It is the contradictions in an organization that lead to change; and to this might be added that, conversely, computerization not only reflects the inherent contradictions that characterize most, if not all, organizations (even the most ostentatiously single-minded) but that it further creates a context for change. We take the new computerized supplier database as an example.

Restructuring the Organization: The Supplier List

The new system contained a component that made immediately available to agents the master list of suppliers that had been kept, not very efficiently, in the central database. When the workload of the typists began to slacken, one of them, Sandra, with long experience in the department, elected to take on the long overdue job of updating the database. She began phoning suppliers to make corrections to the addresses, one by one until, finally, she had reduced the list from 4,000 to about 2,500. She eliminated repetitions, verified that the companies were still actively involved with the department, made sure the business codes were accurate, and so on. She made herself into the unofficial keeper of the supplier list. And, because one of Beverly's selling points for the new system was that it would encourage agents to broaden their range of suppliers to make sure they were getting the lowest price, Sandra's efforts had high priority with her.

Now an anomaly became evident. On the one hand, there was some friction between the agents and the secretarial staff over the division of responsibilities. In the past, when the typists were laboring under a tidal wave of documents to be completed, the agents did most of their own photocopying and faxing. Now, as the agents were doing work that previously had been done by the secretarial staff, and because the latter were, if anything, underworked, they felt the typists should take on these tasks. The typists, however, claimed this was not in their job description. On the other hand, because of the priority assigned by Beverly to Sandra's new task, she was given an authorization code or security clearance level that entitled her to access corporate sources of information that the agents did not have. Sandra thus put in a request to have her status upgraded, because she was now doing a more responsible task. When Beverly demurred, Sandra appealed to her union.

This is a minor incident but it merits some consideration. Earlier in the chapter, we observed that although purchasing was a "function" from the perspective of other departments, within the department itself there were also functions making up parts of the purchasing process. One such function was the supplier list. Prior to computerization, it was little exploited and not associated closely with any single individual's role. Sandra's initiative changed all that. She made the list into an indispensable allocative resource, replacing the individual agent's card files, something to be consulted by everyone in the course of carrying out their task. Sandra also transformed privileged access to an allocative resource into the basis of an enhanced *authority*. If her move were successfully *legitimized*, it would change her role and her status—a transformation reflected in, to use the structuration framework, a modification of the *significance* of her position.

We would suggest that the entire experience of computerization that we have been analyzing can be seen as a set of variations on this same theme. For example, there was a movement in the corporation to relocate some of the functions of the purchasing department into the client departments. Purchasing countered this movement by reiterating the necessity to avoid "crony capitalism" in a public corporation. And computerization did do something to improve the purchasing department's strategic position in this contest (especially because it could now remind departments of the necessity to have blanket orders renewed since it finally had up-to-date information on the state of the budget, which previously had been missing). In this case, computerization tended to reinforce an established system of tiling.

Within the department, the effects of computerization were more variable. We have already cited the case of Sandra, but we could equally have used that of

Cheryl as our point of reference. Cheryl leapt at the chance to become the pilot of the computerization project. She became the person who already had implementation experience, the person who worked with the computing department (and thus a repository of secondhand technical knowledge), and the person to whom everyone turned for assistance when the technology actually arrived. She, like Sandra, turned access to an allocative resource into access to an authoritative resource and, in doing so, effectively usurped Brian's position as the moral leader of the group.

To put this in structurational terms, most action has unintended as well as intended consequences. But this also suggests a revision of Giddens's distinction between allocative and authoritative resources. It would lead us, in fact, to a more "situated" view of resource. When a resource is a function, it is always allocative (because that is what functionality means). But a resource is only functional in a given context. When one varies the context, what seemed allocative in one perspective now reveals itself to be authoritative in another.

◆ Conclusion

Earlier (in Chapter 1), we quoted Grint et al.'s (1996) critique of Business Process Reengineering (BPR) and its implicit assumption that management is rational, not political. Before we consider their criticisms, let us briefly see how BPR might have dealt with the purchasing department bottleneck.[5]

The "rational" solution to the inefficiencies of purchasing in this corporation, from a BPR-type perspective, is simple enough: Do away with the department entirely! (Hammer & Champy, 1993). At least for contracts of less than $200,000, why not delegate the responsibility for purchasing to the client departments (for more than $200,000, there are legal constraints)? Each department submits its estimated expenses for the year as part of its budget, and, once approved, it is entitled to approach vendors directly and to negotiate terms with them. There is, of course, the risk of scams but, motivated by the desire to stretch the budget to its limit, there is also the possibility that departments would make better deals than the purchasing department, with its more bureaucratic procedures, had before.

The issue of central control remains. This is a public corporation, susceptible to having its performance sanctioned by its political masters. Two strategies seem possible to ensure control over the purchasing process. On the one hand, current technology opens up the possibility of transparent process, in that the purchasing procedures followed by departments, once automated, would be open to inspection. But this, in turn, presupposes an overlook function and a department to do the surveillance. So we risk ending up with interdepartmental friction of a new kind.

The second strategy sounds more constructive. It supposes that the work begun by Sandra is expanded. Purchasing mutates into an intelligence operation and becomes more "customer-oriented" (with other departments as its "customers"). The central database becomes a resource that provides an abundance of information on available vendors, their products, prices, previous performance, customer evaluation, and so forth. Using the facility of the Internet, vendors are encouraged to contribute directly by updating information on their products and prices. But this does not really answer the control problem. And it risks producing wide disparities between departmental practices—anathema to a public corporation.

All this assumes, of course, that the management of a corporation is guided by strictly rational considerations and that they take seriously the necessity to deal with the situation in purchasing. As we have seen, it was not clear they did in the case we were studying.

The Critique of BPR

The critics of BPR offer a different view of management as *essentially* political. The location of the purchasing department under the VP-PA was an effect of politics. The choice of Beverly as director was a political act. Cheryl's assumption of the role of pilot was a political act. Sandra's taking the supplier list in hand was a political act. The interdepartmental and interdivisional dynamics of the corporation were political processes.

We argue that the root of the struggle for power, which is the essence of politics, is focused on the function-process tension. It is a consequence of the dynamics of co-orientation and the continuing negotiation of A-B-X relationships. Functions emerge as a consequence of the identification of an allocative resource and the association of an individual or group with its exploitation. Functionality in this sense is the origin of "turf." Computerization enters the equation precisely because it can lead to the discovery of new or enhanced allocative resources. When it does, it alters not just the pattern of exploitation of allocative resources (which is the rational dimension of organization) but also the mosaic of exploitation of authoritative resources.

The outcome will never be fully predictable, at least in the short term. The newer the technology, the less predictable its consequences will be. Many of the contradictory findings in the field, we believe, can be traced back to this instability: a technology whose potential cannot be predetermined but must be used in real work situations before its properties can be assessed.

In Chapter 1, we outlined four hypotheses that attempt to explain the mixed results of experiments in computerization. It is instructive to ask now what enlightenment each adds to our analysis of this case study.

- ◆ Hypothesis 1: There are limits to what computerization can accomplish. The problem with this formulation is that it assumes that *computerization* has a fixed definition. In the case we have been analyzing, it is clear that the system that was implemented could not do all the things it had been designed to do (notably in its display functions). But this does not mean some other more sophisticated system (offering split screens, for example) could not. What we tend to think of as a unitary phenomenon, computerization, is in fact anything but.

- ◆ Hypothesis 2: The principal roadblock is the bureaucratic administrative patterns of the past. There is no question that the purchasing department was mired in procedure, but it is not at all clear that reengineering eliminates bureaucratic procedure. What it may well do is displace the internal dynamic of power-sharing. And it is far from self-evident that a "customer orientation" is consistent with such a dynamic.

- ◆ Hypothesis 3: Politics is inevitable. There is no question that politics played a role in the unfolding drama of the purchasing department, from the president of the corporation all the way down to Sandra. But once we have said this, it is hard to say what is thus explained about the success or failure of implementations of technology, other than that rationalist projects (including some of those described in Chapter 1) are unrealistic. Computerization in most organizations that we have studied is much more piecemeal and incremental than BPR promises, as a "revolution."

- ◆ Hypothesis 4: The technology is not yet perfected. That was certainly a factor in this case study. But this raises a fundamental issue: What does it mean to be *perfected*? Star and Ruhleder (1996) see the success of a technology as measured by its transformation into infrastructure (what we think of as imbrication). They argue that it is "experimentation over time [that] results in the emergence of a complex constellation of locally-tailored applications and repositories, combined with pockets of local knowledge and expertise" (p. 132). Because of this, they think that "highly structured applications for collaboration will fail to become integrated into local work practices."

What we seem to be in the midst of, then, as a society, is a phase of progressive transformation—of work practices, of organization, and of technology. It is a transformation that occurs at the working level, such as we have been describing in this chapter, but it is also part of how organization is changing. In the next chapter, we explore a different dimension of this transformation: the tension between local and global.

◆ Notes

1. This point is related to Gibson's (1979) idea of *affordance* discussed in relation to Star's concept of infrastructure (cf. Chapter 3).

2. System designers working in the language/action perspective (L/AP) have developed a model of a business transaction known as DEMO (Dynamic Essential Modeling of Organization) (Dietz, 1994; Steuten, 1998) with similar capacities. A transaction (e.g., booking a hotel room) is conceptualized as evolving in three phases: (a) negotiating the conditions of transaction, (b) executing the agreed-on service, and (c) evaluating the result.

3. A recommendation favored by the proponents of BPR, to relocate many of the purchasing functions in the client departments (Hammer & Champy, 1993), would seem to indicate that this particular dialectic of control is endemic to large bureaucratic organizations.

4. There were politics involved. The VP of Public Affairs was regarded by the corporation as a valuable resource because of his public credibility (according to our interviews, he had "a vast network of contacts"). But the functions he directed were too small to justify making them a division; they easily could have been handled by a department. Putting purchasing under his jurisdiction was one way to give his division greater weight (and because it was one of the corporation's principal links to the environment, there was some plausibility to the move). On the other hand, the VP of Finance had under his control not just financial services but the computer department, as well. An aggressive, domineering man, the addition of yet another key service to his sphere of control may well have posed a threat to other members of the executive council, who feared the concentration of too much power in his hands. This is at least strongly suggested by our interviews, although we made no attempt to verify the situation further.

5. We acknowledge the helpful comments of Jodie Pryor on the relevance of BPR to this case.

7
Explaining System Integration

◆ The key concept of structuration is duality of structure. By *duality,* Giddens means to reject the usual essentialist notions of organization, technology, and group as entities in their own right. Instead, each is seen as already embedded in the practices of ordinary life. That which we are accustomed to think of as *organization, technology,* or *group* is constructed in the ways we organize our interactions, mediated by what Giddens calls *modalities.* It is the modalities that account for the structuring effect, in three ways. Through the quotidian production of human conversations, we generate a meaningful set of situations (structures of *signification,* for Giddens), an articulation of coordinated agencies to deal with them (structures of *domination*), and principles of admissible behavior as set down by one's community (structures of *legitimation*).

Nonetheless, the notion of modality is among the less well explicated elements in Giddens's theory. Giddens argues that the structure of society is embedded in the "rules" we follow to manipulate the "resources" we mobilize in establishing a practical world of action. He locates the inscription of structuring rules in the "memory traces" of individual actors and in the habits of behavior and interaction they are accustomed to follow. Chapter 3 explored alternative conceptualizations that are less individual-based than his.

In Chapter 4, we outlined what we consider to be a more plausible hypothesis: that rather than residing in the habits of individuals, structures are built into the artifacts (including texts) that people produce in their dealings with a practical world. The environment in which we live is constructed. We are encompassed by our artifacts, and they actively channel our activities. As Latour argues, the world of activity is a mixture of human and nonhuman (technological and artifactual) agencies—a *hybrid* blend. The consequence is a dynamic of structuring in which people's action is continually informed by the agencies of their "tools" (Engeström), or "rules/resources" (Giddens), or "technology" (Star). But those same artifacts and technologies are merely the product of some previous structuring activities and, thus, the carriers of one generation's learning to another (Hutchins). There is, in other words, no point at which organization is quite organized, or technology quite designed. Duality implies movement, open-endedness.

The theoretical question we now address is how to reconcile structures that are global, in that they inform multiple conversations, with those that are local and specific, in that they inform only one conversation. Giddens (1984, p. 28), for example, distinguishes between social integration ("systemness on the level of face-to-face interaction") and system integration ("connections with those who are physically absent in time or space"). Each involves what he calls "homeostatic causal loops and reflexive self-regulation." Much of work activity is locally structured—socially integrated. How may we then account for the structuring at a more global level as well—system integration—and for the articulation of the two levels?

We argued in Chapter 4 that communication is the modality that accounts for the integration of the local and the global. The mediating property of communication is text. The singular characteristic of text is in being simultaneously symbolic and material. As symbol system—spoken language—it is a carrier of epistemic and deontic modality (Taylor & Van Every, 2000) and thus mediates the structuring activities of interaction, whatever their location. As an artifact—recorded speech or writing—it is separable from its context of production and thus mediates communication between conversations. With recording, the text artifact possesses what we have called elsewhere "degrees of separation" (Taylor, Cooren, Giroux, & Robichaud, 1996). It thus becomes the instrument of structuring both local and global forms of integration. In Chapter 5, we explored the idea that computers are carriers of text. By implication, they are part of what constitutes the modality of structuration.

The consequences for research of this mediating characteristic of text are what we explore in this chapter. To introduce the question of how to conceptualize the structuring modality of text, we describe an analysis conducted by Star and Ruhleder. We then consider three major examples of research on computerization inspired by structuration theory and consider the degree to which each has managed to capture the dynamics of both the local and global. In the second part of the chapter, we present our own communicational analysis of a case study of technology implementation that illustrates how techniques of inscription (text) built into a technology become an instrument of structuring at both levels.

◆ Structuring the Local and the Global

In Chapter 3, we introduced Star and Ruhleder's (1996) concept of infrastructure. Their ethnographic exploration and analysis of the initial phases of customizing a large-scale software system for a group of scientists convinced them that a technological system cannot simply be imposed. It only becomes infrastructure for people in their work practices when embodied in their activities and organization. Infrastructure "occurs," Star and Ruhleder maintain, when the tension between local flexibility and global standardization is resolved—whenever a balance is achieved in technological development between local practices and organizational change. The "when" of infrastructure is a technology that has come to be taken for granted by the people who use it. Infrastructure is the moment when they see the technology as merely one of the means by which their work is carried out (p. 114).

Through what processes does a transformation of technology into infrastructure occur? Taking their lead from Bateson's (1972) classification of the different "orders" of learning according to their increasing levels of abstraction and complexity, Star and Ruhleder's answer is that such change is a matter of learning. Star and Ruhleder identified three orders of learning that are simultaneously in play for both users and designers when a new technology is under development in the workplace.

First-order learning issues are factual ones. These include such problems as access to machines, taking first steps to get started, developing computing skills, and modifying work routines, all of which can be resolved in a fairly straightforward fashion by means of additional information, training, and redistribution of resources.

Issues of a second order of learning are more abstract and continue over a longer time frame or cycle. They stem from the unknowable effects of the use of a new technology, such as whether the best choice has been made, or the possible consequences it may have for how the tasks that a group carries out are organized, or for a group's rules of interaction and collaboration. The resolution of these issues is more than a matter of resource redistribution. It requires ongoing coordination and negotiation between users, designers, and management.

Third-order issues of learning about the system are the most political because they center on the very nature of work and of the organization itself. This is the level at which the long-term or far-reaching implications of computerization are raised: its effects on the values and norms of the organization, on occupational categories and status, and on the partition of responsibilities and turf. As it becomes infrastructure, according to these authors, the technology simultaneously constrains and enables the orders of learning and is also being structured by them.

Though not explicitly structurationist, Star and Ruhleder's (1996) analysis captures very subtly the structuring dynamics that occur over time as work practices, technology, and organization come to mutually define each other. As an analysis, it is coherent with a communicational perspective on learning. Now let us consider some more overtly structurationist versions of similar cases.

Structurationist Perspectives

A number of scholars from communication, sociology, and sociotechnical studies have in the past few years adopted a structurationist perspective to understand the relation between technology and organizational change. Structurationist-inspired research has emphasized the mutually constructed duality of the human use of tools—that technologies are both created by human action and also used to accomplish action (Orlikowski, 1992). The result, especially in fieldwork studies, has been to make empirically accessible the reciprocal processes occurring between technology and work practices, including design, at the level of local system integration. The challenge that remains is to encompass the global along with the local in a single analytical frame. This is no simple feat, and it is not surprising that, in practice, much of structurational research ends up by privileging one dimension at the expense of the other.

Adaptive Structuration Theory

Our first example based on structurational premises consists of an influential body of experimental research on the use of group support system technologies. Communication scholars Poole and DeSanctis and their associates (DeSanctis & Poole, 1994; Poole & DeSanctis, 1990, 1992; Poole, Holmes, & DeSanctis, 1991) propose what they call "adaptive structuration theory" (AST) for studying the "interplay between technology and the social process of technology use" (DeSanctis and Poole, 1994, p. 142). They justify their choice of experimental design as a counterweight to more qualitative studies on the same theme, enabling them "to develop methods that can handle more extensive samples and permit systematic comparison of cases and structured analysis" (Poole & DeSanctis, 1992, p. 7)

The key to AST thinking (Griffith, 1999) is that the advanced technologies have a double structuring effect: the structures that are integrated into the technology and those that result from people's perceptions and use of it. Technologies, DeSanctis and Poole (1994) argued, trigger "adaptive structurational processes" that can lead to "changes in the rules and resources that organizations use in social interaction" (p. 143).

AST research has centered on the implementation of an integrated system of communication and decision-making software known as a group decision-making support system (GDSS). A GDSS is intended to provide technical support for groups who have been brought together for the purpose of evaluating data related to a problem or task to arrive at a collective solution. The work of Poole and his colleagues assesses the use of a particular GDSS still in development, using as subjects small groups of students (3 to 5 people in each).

The AST approach conceptualizes the structure of the GDSS technology along two dimensions: its *spirit* (e.g., the general intent of the technology, favorable to democratic decision making) and the specific *features* it offers (e.g., method of voting). Both spirit and features are treated as independent variables (Poole & DeSanctis, 1992, p. 13). The take-up of the system by the groups (which of the "features" or functions they choose to exploit, which they ignore) is called *appropriation*. Appropriation is interpreted as an indicator of Giddens's modalities of structuration: "structures-in-use" (i.e., system dynamics) (Poole & DeSanctis, 1992, p. 11). A category system of types of appropriation is developed to yield a set of independent variables, with analysis based on the coding of transcribed group protocols of interaction. Findings support the view that "the technology alone cannot guarantee improvements but that these are tied to how groups appropriate the technology into the interaction system" (Poole & DeSanctis, 1992, p. 43). The effect of a technology, in other words, is mediated by the structural properties of the user group and emerges in the group's interaction.

The researchers associated with Poole and DeSanctis have generated a stream of meticulously conducted research findings over a period now extending over more than a decade. AST has provided the theoretical base for complementary research on user-implementer understanding of the technology (e.g., work on technology user triggers for sense-making by Griffith, 1999; see also Orlikowski & Gash, 1994) that have added to our understanding of both task group process and its link with particular technological design features.

A question remains, however, whether what they have been studying is structuration in Giddens's sense of system integration. For one thing, their work clearly falls under the heading of what Markus and Robey (1988) term *variance research* (DeSanctis & Poole, 1994, p. 132; Poole & DeSanctis, 1992, p. 16): identification of independent variables of technology structure, the group's internal system, and other sources of structure (the task, the organizational environment). Similarly, social interaction is viewed as a phased appropriation of features of the technology and decision processes. It is true that there is an attempt to take account of "emergent sources of structure" and "new social structures," but the experimental conditions themselves limit the possibility of internal structuring. Outcomes are properties interpreted by the researchers, such as efficiency, quality of decision, degree of consensus, and commitment. Organizational change is analyzed as a linear movement of technological adoption, with appropriations that initially occur in microlevel interaction eventually being "reproduced to bring about adoption of technology-based structures across multiple settings, groups, and organizations" (De Sanctis & Poole, 1994, p. 143). It is difficult to see how a key element in Giddens's theory—the institutionalization of structure to transcend bounds of space and time (Giddens, 1984, pp. 35-36)—could be captured in what are, after all, relatively brief sequences of group interaction.[1]

To be sure, the theory of Giddens does not lend itself easily to experimental testing. It might even be fair to ask if the notion of establishing efficient causal links through the use of an experimental methodology is not inherently contradictory to the central assumptions of structuration.

Structuration and Field Research

Field research in the structurational mode, as conducted by Barley and Orlikowski and her colleagues, has focused on the structurational and reciprocal processes of social construction out of which emerge the interactive, technological, and organizational aspects of people's world. Where they differ from AST is in their emphasis. Whereas AST research is concerned with the relation between a technology and its users, Barley's work emphasizes the workplace/organization dimension, and Orlikowski's focus is on technology and organizational change.

Barley

Barley's (1986, 1990, 1996b) influential sociological investigations of technology in the workplace are motivated by his contention that technologies change organizational and occupational structures by transforming patterns of action and interaction. He prefaces his 1986 study of the introduction of a CT (computed tomography) scanner unit into two medical clinics with an initial observation that has both theoretical and methodological implications: "After two and a half decades of research our evidence for technology's influence on organizational structure is, at best, confusing and contradictory" (Barley, 1986, p. 78). But rather than see this negatively, as a failure to establish a clear *technology/ cause—organizational-structure/caused* relation, he proposes the novel idea that we look at this incoherence as a successful result—a "replicated finding" (p. 78). On this assumption, it is not the methodology of social science research that is insufficiently refined to produce the desired cause-effect relation reliably. It is the misguidedness of the theoretical underpinning of the research, based as it has been on an assumption of technology as a material cause of organizational structure.

If structure is conceived, Barley suggests, as an emergent property of ongoing action, then it is not totally surprising that it, too, will influence how technology is taken up. And if, as structuration postulates, such structures become, when institutionalized, not merely a product of but a constraint on human endeavor, then it is reasonable to conceptualize the implementation of technology into work environments as a complex process. Any theory that fails to take account of the institutional context of implementation, he warns, and Star and Ruhleder would agree, will lead to unfounded generalizations.

Barley (1986) then makes an important revision of the relation of technology to organization (p. 81) that bears some relation to Star and Ruhleder's (1996) observations on levels or orders of learning. He proposes that we view technologies as "occasions that trigger social dynamics which, in turn, modify or maintain an organization's contours" (Barley, 1986, p. 81).[2] Even if we assume, with Giddens, that structure, as he conceived it, informs social settings with patterns of signification, domination, and legitimation, nevertheless there is always room for what Barley calls "slippage" between the institutional template and the exigencies of daily life. The introduction of a new technology represents precisely, Barley thinks, the kind of "exogenous shock" that enhances the likelihood of slippage. Momentary slippages are quickly forgotten, but "when slippages persist, they become replicated patterns whose contours depart, perhaps ever so slightly, from former practice. Eventually, changed patterns of action reconfigure the setting's institutional structure by entering the stock of everyday knowledge about 'the way things are' (Berger & Luckmann, 1966)" (Barley, 1986, p. 80). At this point, the technology becomes infrastructure. (It is fair to see the results that we reported on in the previous chapter as at least a partial confirmation of Barley's argument.)

It follows logically that "identical" technologies can result in different structures, depending on the prior institutional context, but also on the hazards of local process in determining the day-to-day outcomes of interaction. The only way this can be captured in research, he thinks, is through a longitudinal study sufficiently prolonged that it allows for the investigation of how the technology is incorporated into the everyday life of the organization's members (note the contrast with the experimental method).

Barley's study illustrates how this can be accomplished. He followed, as an observer, the implementation of an identical CT scanner into two clinics, one "urban" and one "suburban," in a Massachusetts city, over a period of a year, beginning 4 months before the implementation. As it happened, both clinics purchased the same machine at the same time. A technology such as this brings together two categories of user: radiologists (of which there were initially six at each site) and technologists. The relations between these users were already established or institutionalized by previous technologies of radiography and fluoriscopy. In both medical centers, the pattern was that the radiologists (who possessed superior qualifications in diagnosis as well as technical skills) gave orders to technologists.

The introduction of the CT scanner, however, resulted in quite different patterns of learning and hence association in the two sites. In the suburban clinic, the technologists were better acquainted with the new technology than were the radiologists, and the result was a considerable increase in their autonomy and decision-making power. In the urban site, the choice was made to recruit radiologists experienced in CT scanning, and the opposite outcome could be observed: Technologists became increasingly dependent on the radiologists' expertise to the point that they left themselves open to accusations of incompetence.

The "same" technology but two very different consequences: a technology that became a valuable "resource" for the technologists to increase their power and the legitimacy of their role in the suburban clinic had exactly the opposite effect in the urban clinic. As Barley (1986) puts it (p. 106), "The scanners occasioned change because they became social objects whose meanings were defined by the context of their use." He believes that technologies "do influence organizational structures in orderly ways, but their influence depends on the specific historical process in which they are embedded" (p. 107).

Barley has continued to explore the inseparability of technology and work and organizing. In his 1996 study of technicians in the workplace, he draws an important link between changes in workplace expertise and organizational form. He raises the possibility that when subordinates know their work better than do their bosses and develop a degree of autonomy based on their expertise, then the grounds of hierarchical organizational structure and the arbitrary exercise of authority it encourages are undermined. Yet, despite these intriguing observations, Barley fails to explore further how the dynamics of local technician

organization may translate into more global or translocal organizational structures. The modalities for that duality of structure are missing.

Orlikowski

One of Orlikowski's (1988a, 1988b, 1992, 1996) contributions to structurational analysis has been to propose that it is not just the organization that evolves
on structurational principles but the technology, as well. Technology, she writes,
"is created and changed by human action, yet it is also used by humans to accomplish some action" (1992, p. 405). It is, she argues, interpretively flexible. Although it is true that, once developed and deployed, it "tends to become reified
and institutionalized, losing its connection with the human agents that constructed it and gave it meaning, and it appears to be part of the objective, structural properties of the organization" (1992, p. 406), such reification is always
open to recall. And the rigidification is not necessarily negative, in that it is what
provides "the stability and taken-for-grantedness that is necessary for institutionalization" (p. 406; and for the emergence of large organizationally based
enterprises).

But such rigidity is inherently no more than relatively permanent, and technology is forever restructurable. If it tends not to seem so, it is because the development of technology (in which, as we saw in Chapter 5, the hand of the maker is
still visible and the role of institutional constraints all too evident) is typically
separated in time and space from its use in an organizational context.

Orlikowski thus distinguishes two logical patterns, one for technological development and one for implementation (she terms them alternative modes of *design* and *use*). In the former, researchers who observe the design process are
likely to emphasize a pattern of causal links, represented in Figure 7.1 (cf. our
observations in Chapter 5).

In this framework of explanation, the explicit understanding that, indeed,
technology does reflect the design imperative is conditional on a second principle to the effect that the design process is itself set within a culture and carries
traces of it. Researchers who study the implementation and use of technology in
organizational settings, she suggests, see a different pattern of causal linkage
(see Figure 7.2).

BPR, for example, focuses, as we saw in Chapter 1, on the "enabling" capacity of technology to support (and engender) *institutional properties,* such as de-
centralization and the flattening of hierarchy. Much ethnographic and psycho-
logical/ergonomic research, on the other hand, has focused on the other link, to

163

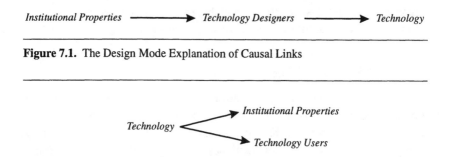

Figure 7.1. The Design Mode Explanation of Causal Links

Figure 7.2. The Use Mode Explanation of Causal Links

the *user,* portraying technology either as an enabler or as impoverishment (what critical theorists see as *disempowerment*).

Orlikowski assumes all these links to be operative in every context, to a greater or lesser degree. It is the separation of design from use over time and space that results in a difference of perspective. For example, users may be systematically discouraged (as she reports in her field research) from exploring technological innovations. It is also true, of course, that some technologies are more amenable to restructuring than are others (the CT scanners studied by Barley being an instance of a technology that was little open to revision at the point of use). On the other hand, designers may be blissfully unaware of their institutional (i.e., disciplinary) blinkers.

In the course of much of her research, Orlikowski (1992, 1996) has linked the implementation of a technology in the workplace to the processes of organizational change. In her 1992 research in a large consulting and software design firm, for example, she found confirmation for her assumption that the unidirectional technology-to-user link (the "technological imperative") was actually an effect, not of the technology, but of institutional pressure, funneled through management, and impelled by a context of intense competition. Rigidly standardized methodologies imposed on consultants served to reduce costs and eliminate experimentation. Software, which you might think to be an eminently structurable technology in a firm of computer experts, was nevertheless treated as a "black box." Individual innovation was not merely discouraged, it was actively and explicitly penalized.

Orlikowski's approach thus constitutes a further abandonment of the determinist, or essentialist, view of technology as possessing inherent properties, independent of its context of use. She sees technology as both formed by institutional properties and informing them, and she sees both technology and institutions as formed by and forming users. Nonetheless, her research does not quite manage to show the mechanisms by which the local becomes global—the dynamics and processes that link systems of integration at different levels with each other. Organizational change, though endemic, remains seen from the local level.

In the following section, using an example from our own field research, we explore how the concept of text might contribute to resolving this dilemma.

◆ The Meter Reader Study

Following an exploratory investigation in 1991 and 1992, we conducted field research from 1994 to 1996[3] into the dynamics of implementation of a new technology designed to program and monitor the work routines of meter readers in two large service utilities. The utilities delivered electricity to a mixture of private homes and commercial enterprises (one of them also handled gas delivery).

Reading meters on a regular basis to measure customer use surely constitutes an illustration of what Suchman (1995) calls "invisible work"—a necessary but unspectacular task. Given its reliance on personpower, however, it represents a considerable overhead to a utility. For this reason, it is typically a target for cost-cutting in firms that have become increasingly bottom-line sensitive over the past decade or so, especially when deregulation looms, as it did in one of the cases on which we are reporting. Industry associations regularly sponsor major conferences to consider how to streamline the humble meter-reading function. Deliberations are taken up with, among other things, new technologies designed to facilitate the task of meter reading, including telemetrics, prepayment systems, and the like.

The two companies in which our study was undertaken occupied adjacent geographic territories with similar climates. They were largely engaged in the same line of business commercially, but in other respects there were important differences. For example, one was American (we call it "Amfirm"), and the other was Canadian (which we designate as "Canfirm"). The American enterprise was privately owned and listed on the New York Stock Exchange. The Canadian company was a state-owned monopoly, although its management structure and day-to-day practices and operations were, by and large, typical of those of any major modern corporation. Canfirm was big (3.3 million customers, nearly 25,000 employees, including 550 meter readers). Amfirm was modest in size (800,000 or so electricity and 240,000 gas customers, slightly more than 4,000 employees, including 180 meter readers, but in the process of downsizing while the study was being conducted), and limited to regional operations (although its radius of operations extended to 35% of the population of the state). Canfirm had a wide variety of operations, including the development of hydroelectric sites and the sale of power. Amfirm was principally a service company that encouraged its employees and clientele to invest in company stock, an option that, by definition, was not available in the Canadian enterprise. Although Canfirm covered a wide range of regional mixes, the district chosen for our study was mixed rural and urban (Sector L, with 150,000 customers and 25 meter readers). The district selected in the U.S. study was more rural (Division P, with 37,000 customers and 6 meter readers/collectors).

As we shall see, these and other institutional differences were to play a significant role in the two technology-implementation scenarios.

There were, however, striking parallels. In 1987, both companies adopted the use of a portable microcomputer (a Portable Billing Machine, or PBM) to replace the pencil-and-paper method of recording readings that constituted the traditional technology of the profession. Implementation of the PBM required rejigging the routes so as to program into the machine the plan of the district and thus to facilitate easy entry of the data resulting from the reading of meters. In the process, routes were reconfigured to produce what was hoped to be a more realistic schedule of readings. In 1994, both firms adopted a new technology, a Hand-Held Unit (HHU, referred to in Canfirm as a Micro-Ordinateur de Main, or MOM).[4] Again, reconfiguring of the routes became necessary.[5]

The new technology offered distinct advances over the previous in that it could be programmed to simulate the route to be followed by the meter reader: street plans; identification of meter sites by street number and character of owner (private home, commercial enterprise); distances between sites; expected time required for each reading; and possible difficulties, such as limited access or presence of a dangerous animal. It also included a clock that automatically recorded the time of each reading and thus furnished a full chronicle of the reader's activities during any given day of work, literally minute-by-minute (even second-by-second, if desired). In addition, it provided for the entry of information on any particularities of the site, such as accessibility of the meter, hazards such as unfriendly dogs, and so on.

Whereas the PBM had merely automated the recording of data, the new system went further. It provided a practical means to plan and control the performance of meter readers and thus was envisaged to provide a tool for supervision and management different from the past—in essence, an instrument of micromanagement. When, at the end of a working day, the reader returned to his or her office and downloaded the data from the HHU, a full description of the performance of the route was now available for checking.

Institutional Differences

The technology may have seemed the same in both cases, but it was evident from the first day that the cultures of the two enterprises were widely divergent. Often, a researcher's initial encounter with an organization is revealing. In Canfirm, we met the supervisor and then were given authority to speak to individual meter readers, which we did one by one in the privacy of an office. When this had been accomplished, we then made our own schedule of field observations. We began a program of accompanying the selected informants on their daily routes, occasionally taking on the actual task of recording data on the MOM. Other informal meetings followed, typically beginning in the home work room as readers picked up their equipment and headed out on the routes.

In Amfirm, the pattern was very different. Here, the role of the supervisor was salient. The initial meeting with staff took the form of a group interview, with him present, frequently intervening to answer questions that had actually been addressed to individual readers. On our first full day of research, we were called to his office, and from there told which reader we could accompany. He then drove us out to where the reader was on his route and left us to carry on. Later in the day, he was on the phone to check that "everything was going okay." "Don't think anything of it," our companion remarked, "he's everywhere."

In fact, the supervisor, an ex-Army officer who had been through the Vietnam War experience, made no bones about his philosophy: There would be no slacking by members of his group. No one could end their day until every route had been completed. In a competitive world, the customer had to come first.

These were only some of the differences. The Canfirm style was bureaucratic. Routes were assigned on the basis of seniority (some readers had been there for 20 years and more) and in conformity with the clauses of the union contract. Once a reader had been named to a route, it was to all intents and purposes his or hers—a kind of tacitly understood partitioning of the turf. In Amfirm, the supervisor posted routes on a weekly basis and deliberately rotated them regularly to discourage turf possession but also to assure greater mobility among the readers by giving them an overview of the whole territory. He thought this made them more alert to potential sources of trouble. But it was also associated with another difference: In Canfirm, when a reader failed to complete his or her route, the remainder of reads was turned over to a "Rover" specially hired for this purpose. In Amfirm, when one reader could not complete a long route by himself or herself, the practice was for other readers who had finished their routes to pitch in and work together to do the remaining reads.

Not surprisingly, we observed a much stronger solidarity in the Amfirm than in the Canfirm group. Whereas the former expected to meet each other after work and on weekends for collective activities, the latter made a clear separation between work and leisure. They treasured their gossip with each other in the morning and during the lunch break, but socialization mainly stopped there.

The system of discipline could not have been more different. In Amfirm, it centered entirely on the person of the supervisor. The Amfirm trucks (the readers' "offices," as they liked to think of them) were fitted with two-way radios so that he could access them at any time they were on their route (and they him), and he could listen in on their conversations when they talked to each other. There was also a horn installed on the outside of the truck so that when they were out doing a read he could alert them that he wanted to communicate with them. The daily readings of the HHU were immediately available to him, and he studied them minutely, along with the readers' own written reports on incidents that had occurred in the day's round. He had no hesitation in dressing a reader down before the others, in public, in no uncertain terms, if he thought they had been "goofing off," as he put it (we were present for one such demonstration).

Hands-on, all the way: It was a "The buck stops here!" style of supervision. Furthermore, the company enforced regular drug checks and employed what were called "flying checkers" to spy on readers on their rounds. The atmosphere was marked by constraints and a certain oppressiveness. The company was unionized, but in an atmosphere of intense competition, the union was quite cooperative with management.

In Canfirm, the supervisor, an ex-meter reader, had a more bureaucratic role to play. For one thing, the union, a very powerful force, had been able to block any use of the MOM for purposes of job evaluation or discipline, with the result that the supervisor (at least officially) had no access to the data on individual performance. The performance data were available only to a central policy committee that, in principle, could access them for 1 month only (although that constraint was not respected) for the purpose of eventually restructuring routes to achieve greater efficiency. The supervisor's latitude in assigning routes was similarly restricted by established convention and union rules. Furthermore, the trucks were not outfitted with radios (even personal radios were forbidden, to avoid "waste of time"), so there was no way to contact employees once they had checked out in the morning. Discipline was exercised in a more formal, impersonal manner in this enterprise. Employees were forbidden, as a matter of company policy, to meet for a restaurant lunch, for example, or to foregather in any other venue (a regulation not always respected in fact).

The economics were different too, and this was evident at the level of local practice. In Amfirm, employees were entitled to purchase company stock and thus developed some sense of ownership of the enterprise. Their functions also included that of collection of due (and overdue) accounts, and they had the power (and the responsibility) to shut off service to delinquent clients. Their relationship with the customer was thus on more than one level, and they felt, sometimes evidently so, like representatives of their company and part of its promotional wing (like "ambassadors," one said). It also should be noted that in this part of the state—an economically depressed area—their job was a coveted one and offered a certain degree of prestige.

In Canfirm, the task of collection earlier had been stripped from the readers and assigned to another branch. They thought of themselves as a low-prestige function: *des liseuses de boules* (an almost untranslatable colloquialism, with derogatory overtones, meaning literally "people who write down figures from meter windows"). They were housed in the basement and felt it to be a kind of ghetto.

The company had launched a total quality campaign to enlist employees in the "performance challenge," but it was evident that this was greeted with outright skepticism by the meter readers. They were more likely to grouse about the extravagances of senior management than converse on the need to increase productivity or offer a better service to the customer. The solidarity of the group was more like a defensive reflex to guard, at any cost, such privileges that individuals had acquired over the years.

Canfirm was all too aware that meter reading was costing them too much—roughly $1.75 per meter read, as compared with a much lower figure in other Canadian companies (in Amfirm, each read cost less than $1). But the company also knew that any attempt to change established practice would be met with fierce resistance. There was an issue of "union mentality"—adherence to the status quo.

Individuals did not feel, our respondents told us, "threatened" by the new technology. Perhaps as a result, there was a certain laxity to be observed in the performance of tasks. Members of the group acknowledged this and were uncomfortable about it, but they knew that if they spoke out they risked reprisals. Union solidarity took unkindly to idiosyncratic expression of unpopular opinions. So for the moment there was a kind of stand-off while the company quietly explored other, more drastic, alternatives. Now let us turn to reexamine the different contexts, using structuration theory as our guide.

◆ Analysis: The Importance of Space/Time in a Theory of Structuration

Giddens's theory emphasizes the central importance of space and time as components of action—a centrality that he thinks his colleagues in sociology have too often ignored. They have tended to think of space and time as no more than external parameters of social practice—merely its "where" and "when." Giddens argued for space/time as a component entering intrinsically into the constitution of activity.

If all communication were face-to-face, this might be a less problematical omission (although Giddens cites Goffman on the role of space even in face-to-face interaction as evidence to the contrary).[6] To leave out of account the organizing properties of space and time in organizational communication, however, leads to serious distortions. The reasoning is straightforward. If organization-in-the-large depends on the binding of situated social practices to produce the evident systemic properties of the larger society, this could only be accounted for by the stretching out of activities to form a link between local societies. Otherwise, they would be entirely locally situated in unique—and disconnected—times and spaces. That would not be a "system."

This concept of space/time as "binding" is related to another idea of his that needs to be explained. Action, as we have seen, is *action* because it has effects (otherwise we could not explain power). But action may have (and typically does have) unintended as well as intended effects. To define action only in terms of the intentionality of the actor is too narrow a criterion. It is true that action is often correlated with intentions, and not by accident, but the action is viable in its own right, *qua* action. It is the action, with its *durée* (duration) and its extensions in space, that makes it binding.

This social elasticity of space and time is highlighted by the existence of modern means of communication. We reintroduce here Silverstone, Hirsch, and Morley's (1992) concept of the "double articulation" of television. What they mean is that, on the one hand, television is just one more household convenience, like a refrigerator, or a barbecue, or a car. It has to fit into the routinized situated practices of the family. The technology comes to constitute a part of what these authors call the "moral economy" of the household: who gets to use what and when. Alternatively, a moral economy is how the allocative resources of the household are distributed and how this reveals the authoritative resources of power.

That is one articulation—the locally situated. But the other is explained by television's role as a mass medium that connects the members of the household outward to a wider consumer economy. This outward reach of a medium is its other "articulation." The double articulation thus illustrates Giddens's idea of actions that may bind simultaneously both the local and the nonlocal.

The HHU or MOM is a case in point. On the one hand, it is a little machine that makes the recording of the meter reader's data much more handy than the old pencil-and-paper method (especially in the rain, when the paper had a tendency to get soaked). That is the local ecology of the reader—a facility for a route. But the "little machine" is also a medium of transmission of information to nonpresent actors (i.e., not present at the scene of reading, either physically or temporally). What they see is not a distant view of the figures on the meter, filtered by technology, but a record of the performance of the meter reader and a means to hold him or her to account. The effective agent in this mediation is text. What begins as an action—reading a meter—is transformed by the technology into a "reading" that is recorded in the machine and subsequently can be printed out.

This is a double articulation with more "bite" than television because it furnishes a means of surveillance. It is a way of being present in the space and time of the meter reader and to sanction his or her behavior there—a looking inward on him or her rather than a means for him or her to look outward.

Obviously, personal space is an emotionally charged zone, closely linked to the sense of identity and autonomy of the individual. Any invasion of such space might be expected to produce symptoms of stress and anxiety. Given that the technology-mediated intrusiveness was considerably greater on a day-to-day basis in Amfirm than in Canfirm, we expected much greater stress to be manifested at Amfirm than at Canfirm. To our surprise, the presence of the invasive technology at Amfirm elicited not very much reaction, and, where any was expressed, it tended to be favorable: "He's the boss, he's just doing his job." The greatest stress mentioned by Amfirm informants was the climate!

This result seems at first counterintuitive. Surely, surveillance technologies—especially surveillance technologies—might be expected to have direct effects, unmediated by institutional factors in that they affect individuals directly, at a vulnerable place in their armor.

Again, Giddens (1979) provides a clue to explain our findings. According to him, an actor's most basic sense of security, as a human being, is profoundly related to the routineness of daily life. It is the feeling that things are predictable—

a feeling that, he thinks, can be traced back to the earliest experiences in child-hood—which provides what he calls "ontological security":

> In most circumstances of social life, the sense of ontological security is routinely grounded in mutual knowledge such that interaction is "unproblematic," or can be largely "taken for granted." . . . Where routine prevails, the rationalization of conduct readily conjoins the basic security system of the actor to the conventions that exist and are drawn on in interaction as mutual knowledge. (pp. 218-219)

What seems to have happened is that in Amfirm the technology was rapidly integrated into the daily routine. For one thing, the authoritarian style of the supervisor was old news to most of the employees, who themselves had served in the military and were used to his manner of speaking and dealing with them. In its own way, military life promotes a sense of security, precisely because it is so routine. (The exceptions are those individuals who are treated as marginal, and, in the case of Amfirm, these were the female meter readers.)

Also, the Amfirm group was smaller, workers were all part of the same community, and they knew each other well. They also identified positively with their company. They had some sense of why it was acting as it was as it went through a period of downsizing. Finally, because of their additional responsibilities as bill collectors, they had a relatively greater degree of autonomy in negotiating the carrying out of their daily task assignment and a greater feeling of personal worth as representatives of the company.

So what seemed to have happened is that supervisor and meter readers had arrived at a modus vivendi—an accommodation in which people knew the limits but could still function comfortably enough within them. The sense of security was tangible. They even sometimes spoke warmly of their supervisor as someone who was tough but fair and who would go out of his way to help them when someone was sick or had a tragedy in the family.

In Canfirm, the implementation of the technology had little direct impact on the daily routine. But a sense of insecurity was omnipresent, if diffusely so. This was because the decisions that eventually would decide the fate of the meter readers as a profession would be made by people they did not even know and be handed down as fiats. The firm, notoriously, had been through a series of shake-ups and reorganizations in recent years and might be expected to experience more in the future. Although their union was a powerful actor, its capacity to protect its members was subject to the kind of pressures unions face everywhere in contemporary industrial societies under the impulsion of globalization. At least some of the meter readers were aware of the menace. One individual was critical of his colleagues for resisting heavier workloads because, in the long run, their low productivity posed the greatest threat of all to their economic security.

This analysis highlights a fundamental point about the special character of organizational action. Giddens drew a distinction between actions of short duration (e.g., to read customer X's meter) versus actions of longer duration (e.g., to carry out a weekly schedule) versus actions of longer duration still (e.g., to embark on a career as a meter reader) versus very long actions, or what he calls, borrowing from Braudel, *la longue durée,* by which Giddens means the duration of an institutionalized practice (meter reading as an institution).

Because individuals are methodologically skilled social actors and thus know what they are doing (a principle accepted by Giddens, following Garfinkel, 1967, and Sacks, cited in Jefferson, 1989), they are also capable of seeing action in the light of its different *durées.* So it is possible that although the employees of Amfirm did resent the unending surveillance of their day-to-day activities (that would only be human), this perception did not carry over to their understanding of the longer duration. The absence of surveillance of the day-to-day at Canfirm, by contrast, was countered by a much higher level of sense of insecurity over the long run, in that rumors of the imminent phasing out of meter reading had been circulating since at least our first observations in 1991.

If, as Giddens argues, action emerges retrospectively as a consequence of the reflexive monitoring of the ongoing stream of activity, then technology may make activity simultaneously available to be monitored by differently situated people, some physically colocated, some not. It follows that the same activity may figure in more than one line of action. Our study illustrates both a local and a more extended loop—from meter reader to central planner to management and finally, much later, back to meter reader.

Practically speaking, the difference between the two contexts was this. At Amfirm, the most salient return loop was short and the reaction immediate, locally generated, and invasive. On the other hand, it was tightly coupled to the routine practices of workers, and the supervisor's conduct was easily comprehensible, based on both practical and discursive frames of knowledge. There was undoubtedly a longer loop in which their activity figured as an object (probably several), but its influence was attenuated because the hard-nosed "commandant-style" supervisor was a guarantee to his superiors (and in particular to his general manager) that discipline was tight in his unit and company goals were being met.

At Canfirm, the immediate return loop was little invasive (although irritating, in that route allocation was seen to invite favoritism). But the long loop was very threatening. We recorded interviews with central analysts in which they expressed their concern for a lack of discipline among meter readers, indexed by time gaps in the records of the daily rounds. Reaction, when it came, would not be, as at Amfirm, in dribs and drabs, but drastic and unforeseeable to those affected.

The consequences of actions, then, are both local and nonlocal, and, to understand the interface of technology and organization, it is necessary to trace the binding effects of space and time, independent of the intentions that originally motivated the action.

◆ Conclusion

Our study is suggestive as to how to approach the study of the technology-organization link. For one thing, it strongly confirms the principle enunciated by Star and Ruhleder, Barley, Orlikowski, Poole and DeSanctis, and others that technology is unlikely ever to be, in and of itself, a unique efficient cause of organizational change. In use, the HHU and the MOM, although basically the same machine, turned out to be quite different technologies. In one case, it was a daily check on performance, with immediate operational implications; in the other, it was an instrument of long-range planning.

It seems likely, then, that although the two firms had followed a similar pattern of response over the decade from 1986 to 1996, their future evolution might diverge considerably. For Amfirm, the technology represented a success story in enabling them to merge two regional offices into one without diminishing the level of service, and at a significant saving in costs. For Canfirm, there were no visible economic benefits in the short term, and we could reasonably speculate that its managers would be impelled to more radical alternatives, such as experiments in telemetrics (as, in fact, has turned out to be the case: Since the study, Canfirm has moved to a form of outsourcing of the meter reading function, on the basis of pay-per-read).

In understanding the relation of technology and organizational change, researchers need to be sensitive to both the local and the extended loops of self-organizing. The reengineering literature is based on the idea that once management has chosen a strategy, and if they are tough-minded enough to impose it, a "business revolution" can be achieved. But that view is naive. If work consists mostly of the mobilization of resources, guided by implicit, tacit understandings (Giddens's "rules")—practical, not discursive, knowledge at work—then a strategy such as BPR is going to encounter grave difficulties at the level of operations (as it indeed has).

On the other hand, the ethnographic literature too often treats the local achievement of work as if it were going on in an organizational vacuum. By leaving out of account the extended line-of-action loops, this approach risks consigning itself to a conservative, antichange view of work, at a time when, rightly or wrongly, change is the norm. The ethnographic approach tends to emphasize above all what Giddens thought of as practical knowledge. This is to underestimate, in the running of any business, the role of discursively framed understandings, such as the cost to the organization of meter reading. It is true that meter reading is locally grounded, but it also figures in other conversations mediated by text—elsewhere. Text transforms the activity that is first realized in a conversation of workers into a "rationalized" medium susceptible of being exchanged over space and through time. What started as the daily experience of reading meters becomes, in a managerial text, a different reality—a written or spoken interpretation of it—discursive, no longer practical. But text, in turn, has no organizational meaning until it has been interpreted in some (managerial) conversation, which in its turn must be translated into text if it is to bind, in its turn, the conversation of work to that of management (in the form of "company policy," for example).

It is this "loop" that subtends Giddens's "dialectic of control" (which is, of course, also a dialectic of legitimation/sanction and signification/communication).

◆ Notes

1. Compare the words of Thompson (1989): "When the regularized practices structured by rules and resources are 'deeply layered' in time and space, stretching through many decades and over large or fixed domains, Giddens speaks of 'institutions'" (p. 61).

2. Although it goes beyond the bounds of this book, this view of organizational process is consistent with a self-organizing theory of work process such as we have described elsewhere (Taylor, 1995). In this view, all organizations are self-structuring, and events such as computerization do not so much determine any resulting restructuring as motivate it.

3. The study was part of our ongoing effort at the University of Montreal to map the dynamics of implementation of new technologies into a variety of milieus. The results are reported in a doctoral dissertation submitted by Martine Harvey (1998). Harvey was responsible for all fieldwork. Harvey and Taylor presented a summary of the work at the ICA conference in San Francisco in May 1999.

4. There were minor differences in the units in the two companies. In Amfirm, the machine was literally "hand-held" in that it resembled a cellular phone. In Canfirm, the unit was somewhat larger and came with a shoulder strap for carrying. In other respects, the technology was the same.

5. In Amfirm, the reconfiguring was done by a meter reader assigned to the task, and the use of topographic maps, along with other information. In Canfirm, the same task was turned over to a professional programmer, using a specialized software designed for the purpose.

6. As we have seen, Suchman (1996) argues very strongly for the structuring properties of time and space in practical work.

8
Reconciling the Interface

◆ In this final chapter, we explore the hypothesis that computerization is a complex problem of learning. Learning, in the literature on computerization, often has been pictured as an individual challenge. Our perspective is different, in that we assume that the integration of a new family of technologies—certainly any of the importance of the I/CT—triggers a process of learning at the level not just of the individual but also of the group and of the organization. If cognition is not uniquely a mental process, as Hutchins (1995) believes, but is accomplished in the discourse and practical activities of collaborative groups, then learning, almost by definition, is also a collective achievement. It is the interface complications that a multilevel learning process engenders that we probe in this chapter.

The chapter has four parts. In the first, we expand on the concept of learning. In the second, we consider computerization as a mediator of organizational levels and an intrinsic part of the problem of learning. In the third, we consider some of the things that can go wrong in introducing new computerized systems. We conclude with some general observations on the role research might play in managing more effectively the respective interfaces that computerization makes salient.

◆ Learning as an Organizational Phenomenon

"Orders of Learning" Again

In Chapters 2 and 7, as we saw, Star & Ruhleder (1996) borrowed from Bateson (1972) his concept of "orders" of learning, each order figuring as an embedded component of the next higher order. Bateson's idea can be illustrated in this way:

177

- ◆ First-order learning: Learn
- ◆ Second-order learning: Learn (to learn)
- ◆ Third-order learning: Learn (to learn (to learn))
- ◆ And so on, in principle—although not in practice—ad infinitum

Bateson (1972) phrased his exposition of the concept of orders of learning in terms of the individual. In first-order learning, people learn to respond selectively to stimuli within a context that is assumed constant: "cases in which an entity gives at Time 2 a different response from what it gave at Time 1" (p. 287). For example, a purchasing agent learns to treat a request for offers differently if it exceeds $20,000 than if it is for less (Chapter 6). Learning of this kind, according to Bateson, involves "correction of errors of choice within a set of alternatives" (p. 293).

This matter of context is fundamental. As Bateson (1972) said, "Without the assumption of repeatable context, our thesis falls to the ground, together with the whole concept of 'learning'" (p. 289). We normally assume the stimulus to which we respond has a context that, because it is constant, can be ignored (part of the "ready-to-hand"). But, argued Bateson, contexts have contexts as well, and when the context of the context changes, what previously had been appropriate responses cease to be so, because they no longer fit the new context, even though they may still be appropriate to the previous. This is when second-order learning is required.

In second-order learning, it is the context that needs selective attention (to be made "present-at-hand"): A response that is appropriate to Context A may be the wrong one for Context B. Bateson referred to second-order learning as "a corrective change in the set of alternatives from which choice is made," or "a change in how the sequence of experience is punctuated" (p. 293). A new set of responses has to be mastered. This is the kind of situation that Beverly hoped to create in the purchasing department when she began to computerize operations. By changing the context, she was aiming to break some of the old, unproductive habits of behavior and to initiate new patterns of work.

It is worth noting here the structurational implication of second-order learning. It will be recalled from Chapter 2 that Giddens (1984) sees the activity of sense-making as a "reflexive monitoring" of the "ongoing flow of social life" (p. 3). Acts, he says, "are constituted only by a discursive moment of attention to the *durée* of lived-through experience" (p. 3). He sees the emergence of the "acting self" as an effect of an embedded set of processes: "reflexive monitoring, rationalization and motivation of action" (p. 3).

For Bateson (1972), second-order learning includes "changes in the manner in which the stream of action and experience is segmented or punctuated into contexts together with changes in the use of context markers" (p. 293). Notice the similarity of language and concept: experience as needing to be segmented to be understood. The implication is this: Second-order learning is equivalent to *re*structuration of interactive patterns. Such learning indexes situations in which the modalities of structuration (signification, domination, legitimation) of the new context are in contradiction with the learned system of purposive action of the old. The purchasing agents find themselves in a bind: Many of their Level 1 learned responses now become problematical as they face the prospect of computerized operations.

Third-order learning is about rethinking the context of the context. It implies a reexamination of previously unquestioned premises. It problematizes the basis of the definition of contexts that we are accustomed to take as established—our habitual frame knowledge. It implies the capability of reclassifying contexts according to some more general principle that in effect would lead us to question the validity of our established categories. It is what would be called, in current jargon, "thinking outside the box" or "coloring outside the lines." In organizational terms, it is about rethinking the very nature of organization.

Bateson (1972) defined third-order learning as "a corrective change in the system of sets of alternatives from which choice is made" (p. 293). He sees it as "difficult and rare, even in human beings" (p. 301). We suggested, at the end of Chapter 6, some of the ways more radical change might have been envisioned—but were not—in restructuring the purchasing operations of the company. To alter well-grooved systems (even if they do not work very well) requires a great revision of established ways of thinking and doing—intellectual and pragmatic—that is not easy to do.

As we have said, Bateson (1972) is thinking individual learning. We have proposed a different basis for learning in this book, one that assumes that cognition is indeed individual but also a property of interaction, whether at the level of the group or of the organization. Following the lead of Star and Ruhleder (1996), we now explore the broadening of Bateson's concept of *orders of learning* to link it with a different concept, that of *levels of organization*.

Orders of Learning, Levels of Organization

Suppose there is a correlation between orders of learning and levels of organization. Star and Ruhleder's (1996) analysis of their case study offers at least some support for this hypothesized correlation. According to their reading,

- First-order learning involves solving problems of information distribution (users knowing about the system), individual problems of access (where the machine is located with respect to them), baseline knowledge and computing expertise (unevenly distributed among individuals), and modified work routines (e.g., learning new habits of uploading and downloading files)—all of which fall under the category of *individual* problems of learning.

- Second-order learning involves such phenomena as the "culture" of the working group (e.g., Mac vs. UNIX), group particularities that become evident within the wider network and are related to how groups address problems and how they organize to carry out tasks, and, finally, community-imposed deadlines on the structuring of work—all of which involve consideration of *group*-related alternatives, or context, from the perspective of individual learning.

- Third-order learning involves solving problems related to how work is conceived (varying disciplinary backgrounds), network externalities (the relative degree of use of the network and thus its greater or lesser utility as a channel of communication), and the reward structure implicit in a given institutional framework—all of which imply reference to the *organization* as a whole and how it establishes the contexts of group response.

The implication of learning that occurs at three different organizational levels and in three different conceptual modes (orders of learning) is that, to understand the dynamics of implementation of a new technology, we have to take account of how each level creates a learning context for the others. Suppose that first-order learning occurs at the individual level, second-order learning implies learning at the group level (because the group establishes a context for the individual), and third-order learning implies learning at the organizational level (because the organization establishes a context for both group and individual). If this is the case, then grave inconsistencies may arise. For the individual, if the group does not change, then second-order learning is made difficult. For the group, if the organization remains stuck in old ways of thinking, group (and individual) learning is blocked. As Star and Ruhleder (1996) observed, successful computerization supposes a synchronization of orders of learning with levels of organization, a synchronization that we visualize in Figure 8.1. We think of these synchronization issues as problems of *interface*.

Consider the purchasing department described in Chapter 6. With the implementation of the new system, Brian reacted negatively and dropped out of the group (took extended sick leave). Cheryl quickly made herself expert in the new system (she became the "pilot") and assumed the effective daily leadership of the group—but with a style different from that of Brian. The transformation of Sandra, a typist, was even more dramatic. As a result of personal learning, she became the group's gatekeeper to the database and, in doing so, raised the possi-

		Three Orders of Learning		
		1st order	*2nd order*	*3rd order*
	IND	Individual learns to handle a variety of tasks in a fixed context	Individual learns to adapt to new context, vary responses according to context	Individual questions context, raises fundamental questions of meaning
Three levels of organization	*GP*		Group learns to vary its response by internal reorganization, within a fixed context	Group learns to adapt to changing context, and to vary responses accordingly
	ORG			Organization learns to adapt to new context, vary responses accordingly

Figure 8.1. Synchronizing Orders of Learning and Levels of Organization

bility of a much more fundamental rethinking of the role of that previously underused resource. Her individual learning also raised issues of her status within the group. Meanwhile, the relationship of agents to clerks was in transition, with effects on the efficiency of the group. Each individual was adapting to a new context in their individual ways. At the same time, the context itself emerged out of the amalgam of their various adaptations. Second-order learning thus assumes, as we interpret it, that the "context" is both externally and internally constituted.

On the other hand, we suggested in our analysis, the process of change in the purchasing department might well have seemed more radical if the organization had been different—not merely tolerant of Beverly's initiative but already embarked on a reengineering project. The context was comparatively benign for individual learning (second-order learning), but it discouraged global adaptation at the level of the whole organization (third-order learning).

Barley's study of the CT scanner implementation reveals a similar effect of interfacing. Because of differential experience of radiologists with the new technology in the two contexts, the technicians found their status enhanced in one clinic and reduced in the other. The resulting different dynamics of the two groups could be traced back to individual learning patterns, and yet the result was a change in how the group functioned and in its subsequent performance. Organizational context again played a significant role: How management chose to implement the system had unforeseen effects.

The 911 police department dispatching system implementation described in Chapter 1 would serve equally well to illustrate the synchronization problem that may be raised by the individual-group interface. There, green dispatcher recruits unfamiliar with police work were thrust, with limited training, into a central control function affecting the entire force. They were instantly confronted with a steep individual learning gradient (as they struggled to become "police minded"), affecting their individual performance and morale. But the secondary implications were even more dramatic; not only were there major problems in interfacing the individuals' and the group's learning, there were spillover effects for the organization as a whole: issues of status, responsibility, distribution of authority, and so forth. Here, the organizational context showed insensitivity to group dynamics and problems of individual learning.

One thread appears to us to characterize all the experiences in the implementation of technology we have been describing: The interface between group level and organizational level, and between second-order and third-order learning, was consistently contradictory. In the next section, we look into some of the factors that may explain the failure of synchronization of these two levels: where the work is done, and where it is planned and directed.

◆ Computerization as an Agent of Learning

Co-orientation theory assumes that the A-B-X model applies wherever we find an interconnected system of agencies. It is thus as applicable to the analysis of corporate as it is of interpersonal relations. For example, the basic structure of most organizations can be represented as collaborative working communities (GRP) who, as part of their tasks (WORK), act as agents for the organization (ORG) in realizing its mission. Figure 8.2 illustrates the pattern.

Obviously, this is a highly abstract way of representing an organization. It assumes that the object X on which the different members of the organization are focused is the same. In a very broad sense, this is a justifiable assumption. Microsoft (A), for example, engages system designers (B) in the production of software products (X). But this way of speaking remains at such a high level of generality that it is not very helpful in explaining learning. At the level of everyday practice, the system designers have their preoccupations, as does the management of Microsoft. Fortunately, a feature of A-B-X theory is that, because it is characterized by the fractal property, broad generalizations about the overall structure of agency of an organization are compatible with much finer-grained analysis.

ORG ⇌ GRP ⇌ WORK

Figure 8.2. Collaborative Work and Its Two Interfaces

In the day-to-day of company operations, the *B-X* and *A-B* parts of Figure 8.2 are typically loosely joined. On closer inspection, the *B-X* of Figure 8.2 quickly breaks down into locally situated *A-B-X* subcomponents, in which the *B* part includes technology. People at work have their day-to-day preoccupations and a range of instruments to deal with their problems as they are needed. Similarly, in large organizations, the *A-B* part of Figure 8.2 on closer inspection exhibits multiple local arrangements, involving various combinations of the imbricated agencies that go to make up an administration.

What makes the *A-B/B-X* interface problematical is the residual assumption that *B* is an authoritative resource of *A* and subject to the latter's control. Otherwise, the domains, though linked by their global objectives, remain relatively opaque, each to the other.

How does computerization enter this picture?

Basically, to reiterate a point we have made already, computerization serves to *represent* the organization back to itself. It is a kind of representation that we have illustrated a number of times in earlier chapters. For example, the system designers described by Hovey in Chapter 1 wrote up, first in ordinary language and later in computer code, an elaborate description of what they took to be the exact particulars of how work was conducted in the telecommunications firm for which they were designing. That they got it wrong does not contradict the representational character of the task on which they were embarked. The Aarhus designers take elaborate pains to engage users in exercises designed to tease out of them what it is that they actually do at work, as a preliminary to constructing tools that might be useful in helping them to do it. Even the Keio designers, although not directly linked to any user community other than their own, believe they are capturing the real dynamics of how people interact, even while they keep their distance from actual users.

Of course, textualization—representation of situated work in a description— is only the first step in system design. The second is to construct an actual tool in conformity with the representation. Once constructed, it has to be sold and implemented. This involves system design and its interpreters in an act of representation of a second kind: serving as persuasive agent for the technology. The technology may be sold in one of two ways: either back to the people whose work was the basis of the original phase of representation or to their managers. Either way, a gamble is involved, because if the representation was not well done, the technology's chances of succeeding are drastically reduced.

More subtly, as we shall see, in the selling part of the representation the organization is itself represented back to itself, as part of the justification for the sale. Management is given a new image of itself, the organization it manages, and how management works. Here, too, the representation might, or might not, "get it right."

Technology thus constitutes a crucial mediator of the interface dynamics of A-B-X. As an allocative resource, it is intended to be a B-X enabler. As an authoritative resource, it is an instrument of intervention of management in the running of its working operations and the communities responsible for them. Let us consider some of the things that might go wrong in this dialectic of control.

◆ Things That Might Go Wrong When Organizations Computerize

Getting the Representation Right?

The first and most obvious thing that can go wrong is that the designers' representation of the actual activities is off the mark. When this happens, people try to use the technology but are frustrated because the result is a diminished capability to respond to the challenges of daily work.

The studies briefly summarized in Chapter 1 illustrate what we mean. Consider, for example, Hovey's (1992) case study of the development of a generic forms tool for the administration of a large telecommunications firm. The design process began with a "requirements analysis." A requirements analysis of the kind she was referring to in her study is constructed as a set of descriptions of tasks performed by individuals and the routes that information takes through the interconnected task network. For example, a customer's request for service may be routed to a networks department, to accounting (for billing), and to archives (for storage). The analysis is intended to capture both the information requirements and activities of individual employees and the flow of the documentation through the network.

The problem was that the analysts took no account of local or even regional disparities in practice. They treated work as repetitive individual task performance, with no consideration of the contingencies people have to deal with in the day-to-day. In fairness to the designers, their concept of the GFT was that of a modifiable arrangement of fields that could be reconfigured by employees to reflect changing circumstances. The problem was that this capability remained, for the users of the system, a pure abstraction. The process of reconfiguring that the designers conceived, including assignment of responsibility for it, had very little relation to the actual structure of group activities.

Much the same pattern could be observed in the other illustrative cases described in Chapter 1: the hospital (too impoverished a conception of nurses' work), the 911 system (a technology that was not "police minded"), and the Baby Bell (a serious misunderstanding of the interactive basis of technicians' work). In all cases, a short circuit occurred: The implemented system foresaw only first-order learning, whereas second-order learning was going to be required for the system to be successfully implemented. Each of these implementations assumed individuals would be trained; how the group would function was not part of the representation. In fact, group process tended to be seen as an aberration (Sachs, 1995).

Recent Trends in Design

The last thing we want to do is demonize system design. The challenge of designing for complex group-involved work contexts is a recent phenomenon. Dealing with interactive process at the group level is not something developers had to cope with before groupware and CSCW came onto the scene.

Many systems designers are aware of the problem. Software programming is an unforgiving medium that exacts perfect clarity in the instructions that are its working schedule, or else it blocks. Its logic permits no ambiguity. In real life, knowledge is fuzzy, and real-life situations are ambiguous or, as Weick (1979) prefers to call them, "equivocal." As systems designers De Michelis et al. (1998) observe, technology easily may become either an essential instrumentality or an inflexible taskmaster, insensitive to the immediate realities of work. When it is a taskmaster, it comports itself like a "bossy superbureaucrat" (De Michelis et al., 1998, p. 65), dictating to people exactly how they are to behave, rather than helping them.

The designers at Aarhus attempt to resolve this potential incompatibility by according priority to the lived world of work. They aim to fashion a technology that is useful, even if it is not technically perfect. Other designers, notably at Lancaster University in Great Britain, favor what they term a "design conversation," by which they mean an ongoing collaboration between designer and ethnographer. In designing a new system for the British air control center located near London, for example, the ethnographer became the eyes and ears that recorded how work was done, and the designer worked through a sequence of prototypes until one seemed to meet the exigencies of the work situation (Hughes, King, Rodden, & Anderson, 1995). Others, notably a group in the Netherlands, Sweden, and Germany who draw inspiration from speech act theory, have taken on the conceptual task of theorizing the dynamics of communicative interaction (de Moor, 1999; Steuten, 1998; van Reijswoud, 1996). Their work is an extension of that initiated by Winograd and Flores (1986), known as the language/action perspective (L/AP) (it was this approach that Suchman criticized in her debate with Winograd). L/AP theorizing bears a considerable resemblance to the co-orientational approach we have been outlining in this book.

There is, then, a continuing preoccupation with how technology relates to the context of work created by groups. It has become a developing center of interest for a number of communication scholars as well, including Poole, Jackson, Holmes, Contractor, Aakhus, and Corman. What Bowker et al. (1997) called "the great divide" in CSCW research has not yet quite vanished, but small bridges are appearing across the gulf.

Representing, Not Just Work or Groups, but the Organization Itself

All the projects we have considered in this book involved selling the system not to the working community itself but to management. The reason for this is that computerization not only describes *work* in a new way; it represents the *organization* back to itself in a new way. It thus represents at three levels: individual task performance, group process, and organization. It is this third level of representation, and the kind of third-order learning that is now sometimes claimed for it, that we now want to examine.

Accounting

A typical reason management is given to invest in a new system is that it enhances the accountability of operations by making the processes of the organization more transparent to senior administration. In very large operations, involving tens and even hundreds of thousands of employees, management can hardly know much about local activities, other than what it can read from the figures. This was the case for Canfirm, for example, that we reported on in Chapter 7. What was known about meter reading boiled down to statistics of the performance and cost of the operation.

186

What we now want to do is to consider the implication of "relying on the figures." To this end, we sketch in outline the contours of an argument developed by Boland and Schultze (1995).

The accounting innovation that is most closely associated with computerization is known as "activity-based costing." It is made possible by the vastly enhanced recording and memory capacity of the computer, to the point at which activities can be broken down into their components and information collected on the exact contribution of each to a given process of production (the Canfirm case study is a fair example). Older methods of assigning costs to products were obliged to employ more approximate methods, typically assigning the cost of some contributing service on a per-volume basis. The adherents of activity-based costing argue that their methodology gives management a much more accurate picture of the contribution of any particular product to the profitability of the enterprise and thus allows it to drop less profitable lines of development and concentrate on those that contribute most to the bottom line.

Boland and Schultze (1995) observed one consequence of this tightening of the accounting grip on performance: "In an activity based costing system, work is replaced by the notion of activity" (p. 309). The concept of work, they pointed out, implies "a job to be accomplished or a function to be performed that has a local, self-contained quality" (p. 309). An activity, on the other hand, "is a more abstract notion in which mental or physical actions of a person are identified not as a job-of-work in their own terms, but as one element in the complex assemblage of a particular product of service" (p. 309). Boland and Schultze added,

> Work takes place in a local space that is reflexive in its own terms (humble as they may be). Activity, in contrast, take place in an exposed global space, extended and linked directly to products and distance outcomes in an enterprise-wide form of reflexivity. Work is localized, passive and contained. Activity is abstract, global and extended. (p. 310)

To have a compelling appeal to management, activity-based costing needs to be clothed in a narrative that makes it relevant to its client, the manager. Boland and Schultze (1995) analyzed one such story (Cooper & Kaplan, 1988). This is a story about two firms, identical except that one has adopted activity-based costing and the other has not. Because the first firm has been able to identify accurately its product with the best cost/price ratio, it is able to rid itself of less profitable lines, and it prospers. The other firm is stuck with a mixture of profitable and unprofitable that depresses its overall profitability, and it goes into decline. As Boland and Schultze pointed out, this story has a moral:

> Variety and small volumes breed inefficiency, which is costly and therefore bad. Treating products and customers as commodities in a mass market helps management reduce the variety it faces, which is good. Traditional cost allocations hide this true reality from us and induce us to first indulge in variety and then eventually to pursue it blindly. (p. 315).

The moral, Boland and Schultze argued, is not activity-based costing but that "variety is messy, disorganized and noisy" (p. 315). The narrative constructs a kind of world.

Against this narrative, Boland and Schultze (1995) counterpose an anti-narrative in which customers begin to demand greater variety. Now Company 1 is stuck with a line that no longer sells very well, whereas Company 2 thrives, because it is responsive to the changing needs of the marketplace. It is able to build on its already existing variety to develop new and exciting product lines, whereas Company 1, which has successfully suppressed previously "unproductive" local variety, is now left struggling desperately (and ineffectually) to reintroduce it. In this story, the moral is that "only organizations with a sufficient capacity for complex interaction and coping with the variety presented by their environment will survive" (p. 317). As they pointed out, the original story was conservative in that it "presumed a world in which things will not change (except slowly and predictably), whereas our second version presumes a world in which things can and will change, and often quickly" (p. 317).

The Narrative of Computerization

We have cited Boland and Schultze's (1995) "moral tale" at some length in part because it illustrates to what extent, as we have pointed out earlier, computerization depends on representation. Usually, we have tended in the literature on computerization to look principally at how the computer represents the doing of work (and obviously how it could lead to better work performance). But this all occurs within a context, that of the organization as a whole. Now it begins to appear that the computer's other representation—that of the organization itself—may be at least as important. Because we already have been introduced to BPR, and because it has set itself up as one of the principal interpreters for management of the meaning of computerization, let us consider its narrative briefly.

The Reengineering Story

There are significant parallels between reengineering and activity-based costing, notably in portraying the new technology as a means of enabling and controlling activities. The other similarity is their reliance on narrative. Consider Hammer and Champy's (1993) influential text as a narrative. The classic elements of story-telling are all there:

- A breach or breakdown: Chapter 1 of their book is called "The Crisis That Will Not Go Away."
- Something has been lost: "American companies are performing so badly precisely because they used to perform so well" (p. 10).
- A goal is established: "Winning companies know how to do their work better." (p. 26)
- A means is established: "Reengineering: The Path to Change" (the title of Chapter 2).
- A hero is identified:

  "[a] leader—a senior executive who authorizes and motivates the overall reengineering effort. . . . The reengineering leader makes things happen. He or she is a senior executive with enough clout to cause an organization to turn itself inside out and upside down and to persuade people to accept the radical disruptions that reengineering brings" (pp. 102-103).

- He or she has helpers: a process owner, a reengineering team, a steering committee and a reengineering czar—even newly motivated and enthusiastic workers (Chapter 6).
- There is an enemy to be defeated: "Inflexibility, unresponsiveness, the absence of customer focus, an obsession with activity rather than result, bureaucratic paralysis, lack of innovation, high overhead" (p. 30).
- There is a magic object (indispensable in fairy stories): "The enabling role of information technology" (title of Chapter 5).
- And a happy ending: Chapters 10 to 13 recount successful cases of reengineering (as told by their leaders).

As a rhetorical device, BPR has a potent appeal (at least to managers, to judge by the sale of books and the number of experiments companies have undertaken). Its analysis of crisis is buttressed by an appeal to company viability; it establishes its target audience, the chief executive, as a hero; and it details a prescription, reengineering. The "potent" ingredient is narrative.

The effect is to constitute a virtual organization in which a certain view of the world is presupposed. Part of that view is about work and about collaborative groups doing work. Yet, as you read the text, it should occur to you that everything that is said about work and collaborative groups is prescriptive. At no point is any real empirically based evidence presented to support the image the authors are projecting of how work is going to be done in the reengineering corporation, other than that of conversations with chief executive officers of very large companies.

Summary

Let us now briefly pull together what we have been saying. Most of the studies of computerization we have been considering could be thought of as interface problems involving highly situated domains of collaborative work, on the one hand, and the standardizing practices of management, on the other. System design enters at every point: as a tool of individual work, as a medium of group collaboration, and as an instrumentality of corporate administration. It is, in some sense, the "all-things-to-all-people" technology of today. The problems seem to arise in the synchronization of the interfaces: between individual and group and between group and organization.

Until quite recently, computer design was focused on the individual and the tasks he or she performed (the code words were "user" and "workstation"). The collaborative character of much work was not only ignored, as Sachs (1995) reported, but actively suppressed—treated as an irrelevancy, or worse. The image of the transformed-by-technology organization that was sold to management was fashioned out of the same cloth.

Beginning in the mid-1980s, a revision of perspective began to take shape, in part because of an increasing ethnographic interest in recording the realities of ordinary work life and in part because computer design had moved into the area of groupware. The principal effect of this work was to make it evident how much of work is—and needs to be—interactive. In this revised view, making sense of a world and constructing an intelligent response to it occur within the communicational dynamics of interaction—much like the people in Suchman's airport operations or Hutchins and Klausen's (1996) airline cockpit that we described in Chapter 3. The role of the group had by and large disappeared in the literature on computerization. It has been inching its way back slowly as the forgotten variable.

This shift of perspective presents a challenge to system designers that, as we have reported, at least some take very seriously. But it also presents a challenge to organizational learning. By overselling an image to management of the computer as the great standardizer, we may well have set back the learning process. We may have created a third-order learning context that is in fact a contradiction of second-order learning.

Computerization is not just a practical issue of implementing some fancy new tools. Its power to represent is the area on which we need to concentrate. It is creating not just a new tool set but a new story line with its own special narrative assumptions.

In Chapter 1, we outlined four hypotheses intended to explain the less than totally successful track record of computerization. Each of them can be seen as a way of narrativizing the group/organization interface. In one, computerization is seen as an invasive force that threatens the viability of local self-regulating practice (this is the ethnographic tale). In a second, the middle layers of management are portrayed as a dead weight that blocks the happy reunion of workers with their natural leaders, senior management (this is the reengineering tale). In a third, it is the inevitable play of interests that sidetracks rationalistic projects (this is the political tale). In the fourth, it is a quest for the ultimate system that will be the answer to all the other problems (this is the technological tale).

Which of the tales is the right one?

That remains to be seen. The story has not yet quite been told.

◆ Conclusion: Toward a Research Agenda

Our purpose in this book has not been to provide an answer to the computerization paradox we signaled in Chapter 1. Taken separately, we observed, experiences in computerization are often disappointing. Collectively, a transformation is under way. The explanation is perhaps not too complicated. Left to themselves, people have adapted, are adapting, and will continue to adapt computer-based technology to their activities in multiple, and often highly ingenious, ways. The implementations described in Chapter 1 were not like this: They imposed a model on people, based in design principles that took little account of learning, responsiveness to contingencies, or group interaction. The result, in far too many cases, was to block natural learning.

We thus seem to be somewhere on a long learning curve whose ultimate destination is hard to foresee. If, as some believe, the new technologies are incompatible with the institutional arrangements we inherited from the second phase of the industrial revolution, the final effect of computerization is likely to be a major transformation of the shape of organization. Given the number of start-ups, mergers, acquisitions, and the resulting surge in productivity that computerization seems to have inspired, there may indeed be some validity in this speculation. That may well be what third-order learning means: an adaptation that takes place spontaneously at the level of society itself. A bit Darwinian, even: Those organizations who learn, survive; those who fail to do so, do not.

The Role of Communication Research

We are caught up in a "communication revolution," and its most important implications seem to be organizational, and yet, curiously enough, I/CT and its fallouts have preoccupied the field of organizational communication very little, until recently. This inattention to what may prove to be a historical upheaval as great as the two prior phases of the industrial revolution is now changing. There are, it seems to us, two prime areas of research that invite our serious attention.

There is first the individual-group interface. This has begun to be intensively studied by ethnographers and conceptualized by systems designers (as we hope to have illustrated in this book), but not in the context of a theory of communication. There is a crying need for communication researchers to take up this task. Implementation projects will continue to experience difficulties in the absence of better intelligence about how work is done, how technology fits with its doing, and how to introduce new technology.

There is, secondly, the group-organization interface. Here, because the study of narrative, rhetoric, and argumentation is such a central part of the traditional field of communication studies, communication scholars should find a fertile ground for productive inquiry. If we are, in some measure, to reach toward the third order of learning that Bateson described, we need to become a great deal more self-critical about the narratives that sustain practices of management and the perception of technology that they project.

If this book has stimulated an interest in pursuing these two paths of research, it will have more than amply justified the investment we have made in it. Our aim has been to present a structurational theory that is sensitive both to the systemic dynamics of human collaboration in making sense and mobilizing action and also to the role that text plays in the organizing processes of a society larger than the local. Understanding computerization as a new medium and social process as a continuing tension between locally situated practice and societally engendered structure should, we believe, be the model on which research practice builds.

References

Abelson, R. (1998, March 25). A medical resistance movement: As independence fades, doctors fight care plans. *New York Times*, pp. D1-D3.

Akzam, H. (1991). *Implantation technologique et adaptation organisationelle: Periode d'experimentation* [Technological implementation and organizational adaptation: The experimentation stage]. Unpublished master's thesis, University of Montreal.

Bakhtin, M. M. (1986). *Speech genres and other late essays.* Austin: University of Texas Press.

Banks, S. P., & Riley, P. (1993). Structuration theory as an ontology for communication research. *Communication Yearbook, 16,* 167-196.

Barley, S. R. (1986). Technology as an occasion for structuring: Evidence from observations of CT scanners and the social order of radiology departments. *Administrative Science Quarterly, 31,* 78-108.

Barley, S. R. (1990). Images of imaging: Notes on doing longitudinal field work. *Organization Science, 1*(3), 220-247.

Barley, S. R. (1996a). Foreword. In J. E. Orr (Ed.), *Talking about machines* (pp. ix-xiv). Ithaca, NY: Cornell University Press.

Barley, S. R. (1996b). Technicians in the workplace: Ethnographic evidence for bringing work into organization studies. *Administrative Science Quarterly, 41,* 404-441.

Bateson, G. (1972). *Steps to an ecology of mind.* New York: Ballantine.

Berger, P., & Luckmann, T. (1966). *The social construction of reality: A treatise on the sociology of knowledge.* Garden City, NY: Anchor/Doubleday.

Bijker, W. E., Hughes, T. P., & Pinch, T. J. (Eds.). (1987). *The social construction of technological systems: New directions in the sociology and history of technology.* Cambridge: MIT Press.

Boden, D. (1994). *The business of talk: Organizations in action.* Cambridge, MA: Polity.

Boland, R. J. J., & Schultze, U. (1995, December). *From work to activity: Technology and the narrative of progress.* Paper presented at the International Federation for Information Processing Working Conference on Information Technology and Changes in Organizational Work, University of Cambridge, Cambridge, UK.

Bowker, G. C., & Star, S. L. (1999). *Sorting things out: Classification and its consequences.* Cambridge: MIT Press.

Bowker, G. C., Star, S. L., Turner, W., & Gasser, L. (Eds.). (1997). *Social science, technical systems, and cooperative work: Beyond the great divide.* Mahwah, NJ: Lawrence Erlbaum.

Bowker, G. C., Timmermans, S., & Star, S. L. (1995, December). *Infrastructure and organizational transformation: Classifying nurses' work.* Paper presented at the International Federation for Information Processing Working Conference on Information Technology and Changes in Organizational Work, University of Cambridge, Cambridge, UK.

Bryant, C. G. A., & Jary, D. (Eds.). (1991). *Giddens' theory of structuration.* Boston: Routledge & Kegan Paul.

Bryant, C. G. A., & Jary, D. (Eds.). (1996). *Anthony Giddens: Critical assessments.* Boston: Routledge & Kegan Paul.

Bybee, J., & Fleischman, S. (1995). *Modality in grammar and discourse.* Amsterdam/Philadelphia: John Benjamins.

Callon, M. (1986). Some elements of a sociology of translation: Domestication of the scallops and fishermen of St. Brieuc Bay. In J. Law (Ed.), *Power, action and belief* (pp. 196-233). Boston: Routledge & Kegan Paul.

Callon, M., & Latour, B. (1981). Unscrewing the big Leviathan: How actors macro-structure reality and how sociologists help them to do so. In A. V. Cicourel & K. Knorr-Cetina (Eds.), *Advances in social theory and methodology: Towards an integration of micro- and macro-sociologies* (pp. 277-303). Boston: Routledge & Kegan Paul.

Chomsky, N. (1995). *The minimalist program.* Cambridge MA: MIT Press.

Churchward, M., & Bennett, J. (1993). *A guide to workflow and business re-engineering.* London: Olivetti UK.

Clark, J., Modgil, C., & Modgil, S. (Eds.). (1990). *Anthony Giddens: Consensus and controversy.* London: Falmer.

Clegg, S. R. (1989). *Frameworks of power.* Newbury Park, CA: Sage.

Cohen, I. J. (1989). *Structuration theory: Anthony Giddens and the constitution of social life.* New York: St. Martin's Press.

Cooper, R., & Kaplan, R. S. (1988, September/October). Measure costs right: Make the right decisions. *Harvard Business Review, 88*(5), 96-103.

Cooren, F., & Taylor, J. R. (1999). The procedural and rhetorical modes of the organizing dimension of communication: Discursive analysis of a parliamentary commission. *Communication Review, 3*(1-2), 65-101.

Craib, I. (1992). *Anthony Giddens.* Boston: Routledge & Kegan Paul.

David, P. (1989). *Computer and dynamo: The modern productivity paradox in a not-too-distant mirror.* Palo Alto CA: Stanford University Press.

Deetz, S. (1992). *Democracy in the age of corporate colonization: Developments in communication and the politics of everyday life.* Albany: State University of New York Press.

DeMarco, T. (1979). *Structured analysis and system specification.* Englewood Cliffs, NJ: Yourdon.

De Michelis, G., Dubois, E., Jarke, M., Matthes, F., Mylopoulos, J., Schmidt, J. W., Woo, C., & Yu, E. (1998). A three-faceted view of systems. *Communications of the ACM, 41*(12), 64-70.

de Moor, A. R. E. M. (1999). *Empowering communities: A method for the legitimate user-driven specification of network information systems.* Unpublished doctoral dissertation, Tilberg University, The Netherlands.

DeSanctis, G., & Poole, M. S. (1994). Capturing the complexity in advanced technology use: Adaptive structuration theory. *Organization Science, 5*(2), 121-147.

Dietz, J. L. G. (1994). Modeling business processes for the purpose of redesign. In B. C. Glasson, I. T. Hawryszkiewycs, B. A. Underwood, & R. A. Weber (Eds.), *Proceedings of the IFIP-TC8 Open Conference on Business Processing Re-engineering* (pp. 249-258). Amsterdam: Elsevier.

Engeström, Y. (1987). *Learning by expanding: An activity-theoretical approach to developmental research.* Helsinki, Finland: Orienta-Konsultit Oy.

Engeström, Y. (1990). *Learning, working and imagining.* Helsinki, Finland: Orienta-Konsultit Oy.

Garfinkel, H. (1967). *Studies in ethnomethodology.* Englewood Cliffs, NJ: Prentice Hall.

Gibson, J. (1979). *The ecological approach to visual perception.* Boston: Houghton Mifflin.

Giddens, A. (1976). *New rules of sociological method: A positive critique of interpretive sociologies.* London: Hutchison.

Giddens, A. (1979). *Central problems in social theory: Action, structure and contradiction in social analysis.* Berkeley: University of California Press.

Giddens, A. (1984). *The constitution of society.* Cambridge, MA: Polity.

Goffman, E. (1963). *Behavior in public places.* New York: Free Press.

Goldberg, A. E. (1995). *Constructions: A construction grammar approach to argument structure.* Chicago: University of Chicago Press.

Goodwin, C., & Goodwin, M. H. (1996). Seeing as situated activity: Formulating planes. In Y. Engeström & D. Middleton (Eds.), *Cognition and communication at work* (pp. 61-95). Cambridge, UK: Cambridge University Press.

Greimas, A. J. (1987). *On meaning: Selected writings in semiotic theory.* Minneapolis: University of Minnesota Press.

Griffith, T. L. (1999). Technology features as triggers for sensemaking. *Academy of Management Review, 24,* 472-488.

Grint, K., Case, P., & Willcocks, L. (1996). Business process reengineering reappraised: The politics and technology of forgetting. In W. J. Orlikowski, G. Walsham, M. R. Jones, & J. I. DeGross (Eds.), *Information technology changes in organizational work* (pp. 39-61). London: Chapman & Hall.

Groleau, C. (1995). *An examination of the computerized information flow contributing to the mobility of tasks in three newly computerized firms.* Unpublished doctoral dissertation, Concordia University, Montreal.

Groleau, C., & Cooren, F. (1999). A socio-semiotic approach to computerization: Bridging the gap between ethnographers and systems analysts. *Communication Review, 3*(1-2), 125-164.

Grudin, J. (1990), April. The computer reaches out: The historical continuity of user interface design. Proceedings of *SIGCHI* Conference, Seattle, WA, ACM 1990, 261-268.

Hammer, M. (1990, July/August). Re-engineering work: Don't automate, obliterate. *Harvard Business Review,* 104-112.

Hammer, M. (1996). *Beyond reengineering: How the process-centered organization is changing.* New York: HarperCollins.

Hammer, M., & Champy, J. (1993). *Reengineering the corporation: A manifesto for business revolution.* New York: HarperCollins.

Harvey, M. (1998). *Analyse comparative de deux (2) groupes de releveurs de compteurs (québecois et américain) soumis à la surveillance sur un territoire balisé* [A comparative analysis of two (2) groups of meter readers (Quebecer and American) subjected to electronic surveillance on their regular routes.]. Unpublished doctoral dissertation, University of Montreal.

Harvey, M., & Taylor, J. R. (1999, May). *Action at a distance and over time: Reflections on structuration theory.* Paper presented at the International Communication Association, San Francisco.

Heath, C., & Luff, P. (1996). Convergent activities: Line control and passenger information on the London Underground. In Y. Engeström, & D. Middleton (Eds.), *Cognition and communication at work* (pp. 96-129). Cambridge, UK: Cambridge University Press.

Heaton, L. (1997). *Culture in design: The case of computer supported cooperative work.* Unpublished doctoral dissertation, University of Montreal.

Heidegger, M. (1959). *An introduction to metaphysics* (R. Manheim, Trans.). New Haven CT: Yale University Press.

Held, D., & Thompson, J. B. (Eds.). (1989). *Social theory of modern societies.* Cambridge, UK: Cambridge University Press.

Heygate, R. (1994). Being intelligent about "intelligent" technology. *McKinsey Quarterly, 4,* 137-147.

Hofstede, G. (1980). *Culture's consequences: International differences in work-related values.* Beverly Hills, CA: Sage.

Hovey, M. (1992). *Conversation in the software development process.* Unpublished master's thesis, University of Montreal.

Hughes, J., King, V., Rodden, T., & Anderson, H. (1995, April). The role of ethnography in interactive systems design. *Interactions, 57-65.*

Hutchins, E. (1995). *Cognition in the wild.* Cambridge, MA: MIT Press.

Hutchins, E., & Klausen, T. (1996). Distributed cognition in an airline cockpit. In Y. Engeström & D. Middleton (Eds.), *Cognition and communication at work* (pp. 15-34). Cambridge, UK: Cambridge University Press.

Ishii, H., & Miyake, N. (1991). Toward an open shared workspace: Computer video fusion approach of TeamWorkStation. *Communications of the ACM, 34*(12), 37-50.

Jackson, M. H. (1996). The meaning of "communication technology": The technology-context scheme. *Communication Yearbook, 19,* 229-267.

Jacobs, J. (1992). *Systems of survival: A dialogue on the moral foundations of commerce and politics.* New York: Random House.

Jefferson, G. (Ed.). (1989). Harvey Sacks—Lectures 1964-1965 [Special issue]. *Human Studies, 12*(3/4).

Johansson, H., McHugh, P., Pendlebury, A. J., & Wheeler, W. I. (1993). *Business process reengineering: Breakpoint strategies for market dominance.* New York: John Wiley.

Jones, M. R. (1994). Don't emancipate, exaggerate: Rhetoric, "reality" and reengineering. In R. Baskerville, S. Smithson, O. Ngwenyama, & J. I. DeGross (Eds.), *Transforming organizations with information technology* (pp. 357-377). Amsterdam: North-Holland.

King, J. L., & George, J. F. (1991). Examining the computing and centralization debate. *Communications of the ACM, 34,* 64-72.

Koestler, A. (1967). *The ghost in the machine.* London: Hutchinson.

Krippendorff, K. (1998). *Ecological narratives: Reclaiming the voice of theorized others.* Unpublished manuscript, University of Pennsylvania.

Kuutti, K. (1996). Debates in IS and CSCW research: Anticipating system design for post-Fordist work. In W. J. Orlikowski, G. Walsham, M. R. Jones, & J. I. DeGross (Eds.), *Information technology changes in organizational work* (pp. 177-196). London: Chapman & Hall.

Latour, B. (1986). The powers of association. In J. Law (Ed.), *Power, action and belief: A new sociology of knowledge* (pp. 264-280). Boston: Routledge & Kegan Paul.

Latour, B. (1987). *Science in action: How to follow scientists and engineers through society.* Cambridge, MA: Harvard University Press.

Latour, B. (1993). *We have never been modern.* Cambridge, MA: Harvard University Press.

Latour, B. (1994). On technical mediation—Philosophy, sociology, genealogy. *Common Knowledge, 3*(2), 29-64.

Lave, J. (1988). *Cognition in practice.* Cambridge, UK: Cambridge University Press.

Lea, M., & Giordano, R. (1997). Representations of the group and group processes in CSCW research: A case of premature closure? In G. C. Bowker, S. L. Star, W. Turner, & L. Gasser (Eds.), *Social science, technical systems, and cooperative work: Beyond the great divide* (pp. 5-26). Mahwah, NJ: Lawrence Erlbaum.

Lynch, M. (1991). Laboratory space and the technological complex: An investigation of topical contextures. *Science in Context, 4*(1), 51-78.

Lynch, M. (1993). *Scientific practice and ordinary action: Ethnomethodology and social studies of science.* Cambridge, UK: Cambridge University Press.

Manteiro, E., & Hanseth, O. (1995, December). *Social shaping of information infrastructure: On being specific about technology.* Paper presented at the International Federation for Information Processing Working Conference on Information Technology and Changes in Organizational Work, University of Cambridge, Cambridge, UK.

March, J. G., & Simon, H. A. (1958). *Organizations.* New York: John Wiley.

Markus, M. L., & Robey, D. (1988). Information technology and organizational change: Causal structure in theory and research. *Management Science, 15,* 583-598.

Marr, D. (1982). *A computational investigation into the human represeentation and processing of visual information.* New York: Freeman.

Martin, J. (1990). *Information engineering* (Vols. 1-3). Englewood Cliffs, NJ: Prentice Hall.

McPhee, R. (1989, May). *Structure, agency and communication: Linking micro- to macro-analysis.* Paper presented at the annual conference of the International Communication Association, San Francisco.

McPhee, R. D., & Poole, M. S. (1980, November). *A theory of structuration: The perspective of Anthony Giddens and its relevance for contemporary communication research.* Paper presented at the annual conference of the Speech Communication Association, New York.

Mestrovic, S. G. (1998). *Anthony Giddens: The last modernist.* Boston: Routledge & Kegan Paul.

Miller, P., & O'Leary, T. (1993). Accounting expertise and the politics of the product: Economic citizenship and corporate governance. *Accounting, Organizations and Society, 19*(2-3), 187-206.

Morgan, G. (1986). *Images of organization.* Beverly Hills, CA: Sage.

Newcomb, T. (1953). An approach to the study of communicative acts. *Psychological Review, 60,* 393-404.

Okada, K.-i., Maeda, F., Ichikawa, Y., & Matsushita, Y. (1994, October). *Multiparty video-conferencing at virtual social distance: MAJIC design.* Paper presented at the ACM conference on Computer Supported Cooperative Work, Chapel Hill, NC.

Orlikowski, W. J. (1988a). Computer technology in organizations: Some critical notes. In D. Knights & H. Wilmott (Eds.), *New technology and the labour process* (pp. 20-49). New York: Macmillan.

Orlikowski, W. J. (1988b). *Information technology and post-industrial organizations: An examination of the computer-mediation of production work.* New York: New York University Press.

Orlikowski, W. J. (1991). Integrated information environment or matrix of control? The contradictory implications of information technology. *Accounting, Management and Information Technologies, 1*(1), 9-42.

Orlikowski, W. J. (1992). The duality of technology: Rethinking the concept of technology in organizations. *Organization Science, 3,* 398-427.

Orlikowski, W. J. (1996, March). Improvising organizational transformation over time: A situated change perspective. *Information Systems Research, 7,* 63-92.

Orlikowski, W. J., & Baroudi, J. J. (1991). Studying information technology in organizations: Research approaches and assumptions. *Information Systems Research, 2*(1), 1-28.

Orlikowski, W. J., & Gash, D. C. (1994). Technological frames: Making sense of information technology in organizations. *ACM Transactions on Information Systems, 12*(2), 174-207.

Orlikowski, W. J., & Robey, D. (1991). Information technology and the structuring of organizations. *Information Systems Research, 2*(2), 143-169.

Orlikowski, W. J., Yates, J., Okamura, K., & Fujimoto, M. (1994, October). *Helping CSCW applications succeed: The role of mediators in the context of use.* Paper presented at the ACM conference on Computer Supported Cooperative Work, Chapel Hill, NC.

Pearson, J. (1993). *Business process management.* Unpublished lecture notes, Pearson Associates, Old Shire Lane, Chorley Wood, Hertfordshire, England.

Pickering, A. (1995). *The mangle of practice.* Chicago: University of Chicago Press.

Poole, M. S., & DeSanctis, G. (1990). Understanding the use of group decision support systems. In J. Fulk & C. Steinfeld (Eds.), *Organizations and communication technology* (pp. 172-193). Newbury Park, CA: Sage.

Poole, M. S., & DeSanctis, G. (1992). Microlevel structuration in computer-supported decision-making. *Human Communication Research, 91*(1), 5-49.

Poole, M. S., Holmes, M., & DeSanctis, G. (1991). Conflict management in a computer-supported meeting environment. *Management Science, 37,* 926-953.

Poole, M. S., & McPhee, R. D. (1983). A structurational theory of organizational climate. In L. L. Putnam & M. Pacanowsky (Eds.), *Organizational communication: An interpretive approach* (pp. 195-219). Beverly Hills, CA: Sage.

Poole, M. S., Seibold, D., & McPhee, R. (1985). Group decision-making as a structurational process. *Quarterly Journal of Speech, 71,* 74-102.

Randall, D., Bentley, R., & Twidale, M. (1994, October). *Ethnography and collaborative systems development II: Practical application in a commercial context* [tutorial notes]. Paper presented at the biennial conference of Computer Supported Cooperative Work, Chapel Hill, NC.

Raymond, D., & Giroux, L. (1998). L'évaluation d'une nouvelle technologie en milieu hospitalier: Une rencontre des définitions entre concepteurs, gestionnaires et usagers [The evaluation of a new technology in a hospital setting: At the interface of designers', managers' and users' definitions]. Unpublished manuscript, Communication Department, University of Montreal.

Riley, P. (1983). A structurationist account of political culture. *Administrative Science Quarterly, 28,* 414-437.

Sachs, P. (1995). Transforming work: Collaboration, learning, and design. *Communications of the ACM, 38*(9), 36-44.

Schank, R. C., & Abelson, R. A. (1977). *Scripts, plans, goals and understanding.* Hillsdale, NJ: Lawrence Erlbaum.

Searle, J. R. (1969). *Speech acts.* New York: Cambridge University Press.

Shore, J. (1985). *The sachertorte algorithm and other antidotes to computer anxiety.* New York: Viking.

Silverstone, R., Hirsch, E., & Morley, D. (1992). Information and communication technologies and the moral economy of the household. In R. Silverstone & E. Hirsch (Eds.), *Consuming technologies: Media and information in domestic spaces* (pp. 15-31). Boston: Routledge & Kegan Paul.

Star, S. L. (1991). Power, technology and the phenomenology of conventions: On being allergic to onions. In J. Law (Ed.), *A sociology of monsters* (pp. 26-56). Boston: Routledge & Kegan Paul.

Star, S. L. (1996). Working together: Symbolic interactionism, activity theory, and information systems. In Y. Engeström & D. Middleton (Eds.), *Cognition and communication at work* (pp. 296-318). Cambridge, UK: Cambridge University Press.

Star, S. L., & Griesemer, J. (1989). Institutional ecology, "translations" and coherence: Amateurs and professionals in Berkeley's Museum of Vertebrate Zoology, 1907-1939. *Social Studies of Science, 19,* 387-420.

Star, S. L., & Ruhleder, K. (1996). Steps toward an ecology of infrastructure: Design and access for large information spaces. *Information Systems Research, 7*(1), 111-134.

Star, S. L., & Strauss, A. (1999). Layers of silence, arenas of voice: The ecology of visible and invisible work. *Computer-Supported Cooperative Work: An International Journal, 8*(1-2), 9-30.

Steuten, A. (1998). *A contribution to the linguistic analysis of business conversations with the language/action perspective.* Unpublished doctoral dissertation, Technical University of Delft, Delft, The Netherlands.

Stinchcombe, A. (1990). Milieu and structure updated: A critique of the theory of structuration. In J. Clark, C. Modgil, & S. Modgil (Eds.), *Anthony Giddens: Consensus and controversy* (pp. 47-56). London: Falmer.

Strauss, A., Fagerhaugh, S., Suczek, B., & Weiner, C. (1985). *Social organization of medical work.* Chicago: University of Chicago Press.

Suchman, L. (1987). *Plans and situated actions: The problem of human-machine communication.* New York: Cambridge University Press.

Suchman, L. (1994). Do categories have politics? The language/action perspective reconsidered. *Computer Supported Cooperative Work, 2,* 177-190.

Suchman, L. (1995). Making work visible. *Communications of the ACM, 39*(9), 56-68.

Suchman, L. (1996). Constituting shared workspaces. In Y. Engeström & D. Middleton (Eds.), *Cognition and communication at work* (pp. 35-60). Cambridge, UK: Cambridge University Press.

Suchman, L., & Trigg, R. H. (1991). Understanding practice: Video as a medium for reflection and design. In J. Greenbaum & M. Kyng (Eds.), *Design at work* (pp. 65-90). Hillsdale, NJ: Lawrence Erlbaum.

Taylor, J. R. (1993). *Rethinking the theory of organizational communication: How to read an organization.* Norwood, NJ: Ablex.

Taylor, J. R. (1995). Shifting from a heteronomous to an autonomous worldview of organizational communication: Communication theory on the cusp. *Communication Theory, 15*(3), 1-35.

Taylor, J. R., Cooren, F., Giroux, N., & Robichaud, D. (1996). The communicational basis of organization: Between the conversation and text. *Communication Theory, 6*(1), 1-39.

Taylor, J. R., & Van Every, E. J. (1993). *The vulnerable fortress: Bureaucratic management and organization in the information age.* Toronto, Canada: University of Toronto Press.

Taylor, J. R., & Van Every, E. J. (2000). *The emergent organization: Communication as its site and surface.* Mahwah, NJ: Lawrence Erlbaum.

Thompson, J. B. (1989). The theory of structuration. In D. Held & J. B. Thompson (Eds.), *Social theory of modern societies: Anthony Giddens and his critics* (pp. 56-76). Cambridge, UK: Cambridge University Press.

Toulmin, S. E. (1988). *The uses of argument* (9th ed.). Cambridge, UK: Cambridge University Press.

van Eemeren, F. H., Grootendorst, R., & Henkemans, F. S. (1996). *Fundamentals of argumentation theory: A handbook of historical backgrounds and contemporary developments.* Mahwah, NJ: Lawrence Erlbaum.

Van Maanen, J. (1988). *Tales of the field: On writing ethnography.* Chicago: University of Chicago Press.

van Reijswoud, V. E. (1996) *The structure of business communication: Theory, model and application.* Unpublished doctoral dissertation, Delft University of Technology, Delft, The Netherlands.

Warnecke, H.-J. (1993). *The fractal company: A revolution in corporate culture* (M. Claypole, Trans.). New York/Berlin: Springer-Verlag.

Weick, K. (1979). *The social psychology of organizing.* Reading, MA: Addison-Wesley.

Weick, K. (1995). *Sensemaking in organizations.* Thousand Oaks, CA: Sage.

Werth, P. (1993). Accommodation and the myth of presupposition: The view from discourse. *Lingua, 89,* 39-95.

Westrup, C. (1996). Transforming organizations through systems analysis: Deploying new techniques for organizational analysis in IS development. In W. J. Orlikowski, G. Walsham, M. R. Jones, & J. I. DeGross (Eds.), *Information technology changes in organizational work* (pp. 157-176). London: Chapman & Hall.

Willmott, H., & Wray-Bliss, E. (1995, December). *Process reengineering, information technology and the transformation of accountability: The remaindering of the human resource?* Paper presented at the International Federation for Information Processing Working Conference on Information Technology and Changes in Organizational Work, University of Cambridge, Cambridge, UK.

Winograd, T. (1994). Categories, disciplines and social coordination. *Computer Supported Cooperative Work, 2,* 191-197.

Winograd, T., & Flores, F. (1986). *Understanding computers and cognition: A new foundation for design.* Norwood, NJ: Ablex.

Woolgar, S. (1991). The turn to technology in social studies of science. *Science, Technology and Human Values, 16*(20), 20-50.

Yourdon, E. (1989). *Modern structured analysis.* Englewood Cliffs, NJ: Yourdon/Prentice Hall.

Zuboff, S. (1988). *In the age of the smart machine.* New York: Basic Books.

Zuboff, S. (1996). The emperor's new information economy. In W. J. Orlikowski, G. Walsham, M. R. Jones, & J. I. DeGross (Eds.), *Information technology changes in organizational work* (pp. 13-17). London: Chapman & Hall.

Author Index

Subject Index

About the Authors

James R. Taylor is Professor Emeritus of Communication at the University of Montreal in a department that he founded in 1971. Over the years, he has divided his time between his academic pursuits and a practical career as advisor to industry and to the Canadian government. His interest in technology and its relation to organization dates back to the beginning of his academic career and increasingly has focused on computerization over the past quarter century. He has published widely on organizational theory and the role of technology and communication in organizational structuring. His books include *The Vulnerable Fortress: Bureaucratic Organization and Management in the Information Age* (1993, in collaboration with E. Van Every), *Rethinking the Theory of Organizational Communication: How to Read and Organization* (1993), and *The Emergent Organization: Communication as its Site and Surface* (2000, in collaboration with E. Van Every).

Carole Groleau is Assistant Professor in the Department of Communication at the University of Montreal. She obtained her Ph.D. from Concordia University. Her research examines the structural and communicational dimensions of technology within organizations. More specifically, her research has focused on the evolution of work practices associated with the implementation of new technology in different work contexts. Her publications include articles discussing the application of distributed cognition, situated action, and structuration to computerization in organizational settings.

Lorna Heaton is Lecturer in the Department of Communication at the University of Montreal. She holds a Ph.D. in Communication from the University of Montreal. Her research centers on the social aspects of the design of computer systems and how design and use phases might be brought closer together. Other research interests include the social implications of new media at work and in the home and how international trends and technologies take on a local flavor as they encounter particular institutional and social characteristics in various situations. She also is preparing *Culture in Design,* a monograph based on her doctoral dissertation.

Elizabeth Van Every is a sociologist and writer. She taught at Concordia University in Montreal and was a research associate at the University of Montreal.